T0369810

Robert Beavers

Rebekah Rutkoff (Ed.)

Österreichisches Filmmuseum
SYNEMA – Gesellschaft für Film und Medien

A book by SYNEMA ☰ Publikationen
Robert Beavers
Volume 30 of FilmmuseumSynemaPublikationen

SYNEMA – Gesellschaft für Film und Medien
Neubaugasse 36/1/1/1, A-1070 Wien

Design and layout: Gabi Adébisi-Schuster, Wien
Copy editors: Alexander Horwath, Regina Schlagnitweit
Cover photo: © Robert Beavers
Printed by: REMAprint
Printed and published in Vienna, Austria.
Printed on paper certified in accordance with the rules of the Forest Stewardship Council.

ISBN 978-3-901644-69-6

The publication of this book was supported by Thomas Bechtler (Zurich).

Österreichisches Filmmuseum (Austrian Film Museum) and SYNEMA – Gesellschaft für Film & Medien
are supported by Bundeskanzleramt Österreich / Kunst und Kultur – Abt. (II/3) Film and by Kulturabteilung der Stadt Wien.

BUNDESKANZLERAMT ▪ ÖSTERREICH

Table of Contents

Rebekah Rutkoff

Preface

The writers who published the first critical responses to the films of the young American Robert Beavers would have encountered just the smallest sliver of the work for which he is best known today: *My Hand Outstretched to the Winged Distance and Sightless Measure,* an 18-film cycle of completed films made since 1967 (many shortened and re-edited over the course of a decade, starting in the 1990s). It is all the more striking, then, that these first essays, composed between 1967 and 1973 by Gregory Markopoulos, Jonas Mekas, Tom Chomont and René Micha, and collected in the first of this volume's three sections, share an urgency: the drive to announce the discovery of not only an as-yet unknown artist but an altogether new cinematic language. This newness is such that it inspires another quality shared by these early texts: an anxiety about doing Beavers's work justice. How to speak back to films of such poetic complexity and visual sumptuousness, to capture their unfamiliar angle of address to spectators, to report to others about their fused mystery and lucidity and their subtle spiritual priorities?

The largely unseen status of Beavers's work for almost three decades heightened this dilemma. Screenings in the late 1960s and early 1970s – including at EXPRMNTL, the experimental film festival in Knokke-le-Zoute, Belgium, and at the Austrian Film Museum – were followed by a period of isolation for Beavers, who had moved to Europe with his partner, the American filmmaker Markopoulos, in 1967. Frustrated by dissatisfactory screening conditions, they halted distribution of their films (they stopped showing their work in the U.S. altogether in 1974, and screened it only sporadically in Europe) and devoted their energies to making films instead. These priorities were also spurred by Markopoulos's deepening commitment to developing the Temenos, a site for the exclusive screening of his and Beavers's films in remote Greece. Starting in 1980, Beavers and Markopoulos presented their works to small audiences at annual Temenos screenings in the Peloponnese.

It was not until Markopoulos's death in 1992 that Beavers began to distribute his films regularly again. His Whitney Museum of American Art retrospective in 2005 inaugurated a new phase of visibility and was followed by similar events at the Tate Modern, Austrian Film Museum, and Pacific Film Archive. At the time of the Whitney screenings – a "revelatory retrospective, and stunning solo debut" – *New York Times* art critic Roberta Smith celebrated Beavers's "astounding achievement," saying,

"Mr. Beavers has spent his career being precociously ahead of schedule and also somewhat outside his time."[1]

Paradoxically, while Beavers has been ceaselessly producing work for five decades, a combination of his films' intrinsic qualities and the historical trajectory of their circulation seems to render his art persistently new. It is especially fitting that this first monographic study of Beavers's work should find its home in the FilmmuseumSynemaPublikationen series: In 1969, directors Peter Kubelka and Peter Konlechner showed four of his films – *Winged Dialogue, On the Everyday Use of the Eyes of Death, Plan of Brussels*, and *The Count of Days* – in Vienna, and the Film Museum has been collecting, preserving and screening Beavers's work ever since.

In keeping with the multiple realms of art and aesthetics with which Beavers's films establish dialogue and intertextual relation – literature, architecture, painting, ancient art, and craftwork – the range of contributors to this volume includes practitioners from a wide spectrum of disciplines. The second section of the book is comprised of texts by filmmakers Luke Fowler and Ute Aurand, architect James Macgillivray, composer Erik Ulman, dance critic Don Daniels and film critics and programmers Susan Oxtoby, Ricardo Matos Cabo, P. Adams Sitney, Kristin M. Jones, and Haden Guest. Each establishes a fresh zone of interpretive interface and an original constellation of references.

Even at their most scholarly, however, these essays are undeniably laced with threads of felt gratitude for Beavers's work. Indeed, intimacy is not only part of Beavers's very subject matter (from the ecstatic celebration of his relationship with Markopoulos in *Winged Dialogue* to his post-cycle portraits of familial and romantic love) but encoded in his films' metabolic being. He has spoken of the "opening" or "door" his films summon their spectators to pass through – one is beckoned by beauty, invited to adjust to a particular poetic respiration, and granted space to discover her own imaginative response. Beavers is genuinely curious to know what his viewers find after crossing the threshold of poetic acclimation, and this book is in part a gathering of some diverse accounts of that intimate encounter. The texts will doubtlessly resonate differently before or after having seen the films under discussion; I hope that they will catalyze new opportunities to screen and share Beavers's work.

The third section of this volume is comprised of texts by Beavers himself. Writing is central to his filmmaking practice; daily note-making generates new ideas and accompanies and informs every stage of film production. Writing also belongs to the many varieties of handwork that Beavers finds fascinating and features in his films (filmmaking itself among them). The texts collected here were composed to accompany his completed films; many were printed originally in Temenos brochures. As in his filmmaking, Beavers often edits and revises his own writings over time. They occupy a special posi-

1 Roberta Smith, "Avant-Garde Films 'Repatriated' at Last," *The New York Times*, October 21, 2005.

tion between philosophy and poetry and give vital voice to Beavers's understanding of his vocation in many dimensions; they resonate with care for the ethical, psychic, material, and embodied aspects of creating and watching films.[2]

On the eve of his departure from the Film Museum, I am most grateful to Alexander Horwath. He not only wholeheartedly supported the idea for this project from the start but hosted the 2010 retrospective of Beavers's work that allowed me to move more substan-tially into a study of his films. I am exception-ally grateful to Gabi Adébisi-Schuster for her beautiful book design. Thank you to Mitsos Triantopoulos, Tommaso Isabella and Ellie Suttmeier for assistance. The work in the book is built on important labors that preceded it, es-pecially the 1998 *Millennium Film Journal* issue dedicated to Beavers and Markopoulos and P. Adams Sitney's multiple chapters on Beavers in *Eyes Upside Down: Visionary Filmmakers and the Heritage of Emerson* (2008).

I am above all grateful to Robert Beavers.

2 The texts written by Beavers that are included in this volume appear in their most current versions. However, writers in this volume sometimes quote from earlier versions of Beavers's texts; please consult footnotes for details.

Robert Beavers in *Early Monthly Segments* (1968–70/2002)

Gregory J. Markopoulos

10th of July, 1967

1967

Recognition. How does one recognize one filmmaker from another filmmaker? I pose this question to myself amid the din of the small craft named *Aegina*, which at the moment is speeding towards the island of Aegina, the first stop on its way to the island of Hydra. The laughter and spray of the sea is conducive to this afternoon's extravagant gesture. Especially, when left behind is Athens in the oppressive heat like that of any other American city.

There are several reasons why I am considering this balmy afternoon the question of distinguishing one filmmaker from another filmmaker. The most important reason being that for the past more than several weeks – a little longer a little less – I have observed a young American filmmaker preparing his second film.[1] Interestingly enough I note that he has never once referred to his film in any other way save "my film." I lay emphasis on this point because so often one is near filmmakers who think in terms of the "avant-garde," "experimental," "New American Cinema" or "commercial" during the actual filming. Too, I entertain this narrative in the midst of the serene, sparkling Aegean because of a heartfelt letter from another filmmaker and friend from Chicago, who also has attempted (though with temporary defeat) to prepare his first project.[2]

In the beginning is always the filmmaker, just as in the beginning there was Light, the visible murmur of the wind, the invisible Word, and the Image of the inevitable inventor. Each waved to one another though weightlessly through aeons of light years to today which is the moment of the American Filmmaker. And this filmmaker in the tradition of Aeschylus (though he is not totally aware of the similarity of both situations) has left country and home in order to brush from his myopic eyes the smog of the cities he is familiar with, and the heavy mist (now become poisonous) that drifts across the daily actions of those he calls family, friends and acquaintances. This in order to charm the

1 Initial projects were portrait studies of Mrs. Bernice Hodges, Gail Beavers (the filmmaker's sister) and Gregory J. Markopoulos. The completed film was *Spiracle*.

2 "Then as if we were not blessed with troubles enough the weather turned very bad. This area had tornado warning nearly everyday and fierce almost tropical rainstorms as often. And after some rather elaborate planning and preparations my actors and myself were rained on almost continuously during one weekend's outdoor shooting until we finally gave up, were then caught in a impossible highway traffic jam caused by flooding and our car almost turned over in our efforts to get out ..." *Letter to GJM from BSW; Chicago,* 23rd *of June* 1967. (Editor's note: Barry Warren [BSW] was a friend of Markopoulos in Chicago.)

souls of the beasts who claim that his country is without Song.

He has proceeded with his task no differently than the peasant who fashioned those distant terraces, some of earth, some of stone, by which I am passing at this precise moment. The moment, which will be no less precise when this is read. That the filmmaker did not know exactly where to begin (he had only his notes which were accumulated slowly, perhaps painfully from instant to instant, day to day, week to week, month to month) was his first breath of Being. Then breathing a second, a third, a fourth and fifth time he urged the Sleeping Eros within his own nature to awaken. The tripod taken, extended like Eros's arms stretching from his long sleep brought him Joy and Pleasure. Later this selfsame act (in reverse – the putting away of the tripod at the end of a day's shooting session) would leave him in an exhilarated mood.

But merely beginning is no safeguard or guarantee that one will be able to continue. This second act of continuing, the desire to continue, can often be as hazy as a distant shore, which is imagined covered with sand and is in reality covered heavily with light and heavy rocks. Whoever as filmmaker has ever voyaged toward such shores at the beginning of his career and is able to still remember the hazards of

each approach (second to hour, day to month) will readily applaud with smiling fingertips the very recollection. And observing the young American filmmaker's certainty in handling camera, tripod and exposure meter his way, he may well wonder once more at the mysteries of the human creative act. Indeed, consider what the human creative act is, where it comes from, and what it contributes to a society totally unconscious of its greater life giving force.

The filmmaker of whom I am writing has been working on the island of Hydra, which is about four hours from Athens. Quite early in his career he surmised the possibilities of the film as film. Slowly with the grace, diligence and demonical, critical frenzy of a Paul Valéry he became acquainted with his medium. This, more so, during his first encounter with Greece: the sea, the laughter, and the braying of donkeys.

To describe what he has been accomplishing, even before he himself has seen privately his film rushes, is unthinkable. I, as a filmmaker, observing Venus's latest born, can only suggest and suggest, I am certain, inaccurately. A filmmaker can never understand during the filming, especially, what another filmmaker is doing. The reason for this being simply put that the filmmaker observing the film being made, at every turn and twist that the head, elbows,

Pages 11–13:
Gregory J. Markopoulos to the Austrian Film Museum, September 12, 1967, followed by an enlargement of the film strip pasted to the second page of the letter.

12th of September, 1967
Roma

Mr. Peter Konlechner, Director
Oesterreiches Filmmuseum
Augustrinerstrasse 1,
1010 Wein
Austria

Dear Mr. Konlechner:
This after our conversation by
phone. Enclosed the authorization to have MING GREEN
printed at cost, and for your permanent collection;
from which no copies, etc., may be made without my
permission.

The BLISS film I shall bring with
me. BLISS was shot in August 1967 on the island of
Hydra. It was filmed in the Churhc of St. John The
Baptists. Two rolls were shot. All the editing is
done in the camera. I used a Bolex camera and two
lenses: 10mm., and two inch. The bit of sound was
added in Roma, as was the print/made there. BLISS is
dedicated to Alice Burkhardt of Chicago, Illinois.
Your showing will be its premier.

Enclosed is a cut of myself which
I thought you might have enlarged for any publicite.
It was taken by R.B. in the Piazza Navona, August 1967,
Roma.

Any publicite' or articles I would
appreciate your sending me at your convenience for
my files.

I have never been to Vienna and I
look forward to visiting; perhaps, it would be possible
to speak in an exchange with film students or enthusiasts;
is a lecture fee ever available for this sort of thing?
Maybe other parts of Europe? (In Roma it is impossible.
Filmmaking here is on a very low and commercial level.)
Warmest regards,

Sincerely yours,

Gregor J. Markopoulos
c/o American Express
Roma, Italia

P.S. I am applying for a
Guggenheim Grant in a few
weeks, might I be able to
use your name as a recomm-
endation?

NOTE: ENCLOSED A DIFFERENT CLIP THAN THE ONE
MENTIONED IN MY LETTER - THE CUT IS FROM
THE MAJOR WORK OF THE YOUNG FILMMAKER,
ROBERT BEAVERS. THE WORK HAS NO NAME, BUT
I AM THE PROTAGONIST OF IT. IT WAS SHOT IN
GREECE BY MR. BEAVERS THIS PAST SUMMER.

BIOGRAPHICAL: MR. BEAVERS IS ONE OF THE
YOUNGEST FILMMAKERS OF THE NEW CINEMA. HE
IS EIGHTEEN YEARS OLD. LAST YEAR WHEN HE WAS
SEVENTEEN HE SHOT HIS FIRST FILM IN COLOUR,
ENTITLED: SPIRACLE. THERE IS A PRINT AVAILABLE,
I BELIEVE IN NEW YORK IN COLOUR, SILENT.

A PRINT WITH SOUND WOULD COST $$200. I AM
CERTAIN MR. BEAVERS WOULD BE VERY HAPPY IF
YOU WISHED TO BUY A PRINT AT COST: THIS FOR
YOUR COLLECTION. HE MAY BE REACHED CARE OF:
AMERICAN EXPRESS, ROMA, ITALIA.

THE EXTRAORDINARY THING ABOUT MR. BEAVERS IS
THAT HE HAS HAD NO OTHER FORMAL FILM TRAINING
OTHER THAN PICKING UP A BLOEX REFLEX CAMERA
AND SETTING TO WORK. ALL HIS WORK IS DONE IN
THE CAMERA. AND THOUGH VERY YOUNG HE SHOWS A
KIND OF PERFECTION AND NOBILITY SELDOMER SEEN
IN THE NEW CINEMA: OR IN ANY OTHER CINEMA FOR
THAT MATTER.

PRESENTLY HE IS WORKING NOT ONLY ON THE EDITING
OF HIS NEW WORK, BUT ALSO, ON THE USE OF GEVART COLOUR:
FILMING ALONG THE TIBER RIVER, AND ALSO, THE TREES
OF THE VILLA BORGHESE.

MARKOPOULOS
ROMA, 13th of September, 1967

P.S. He has never been shown, to this date, by
anyone!

shoulders and legs of the filmmaker at work make, knows he would do it differently; desires to do it differently; almost urges the filmmaker at work to do it differently. The state of the filmmaker observing the filmmaker at work is no different in its temptations than those of Orpheus leading Eurydice out of Hades. That the fade-out device in his hand becomes as light as the play of dolphins; that his use of the very limited Bolex filter slot[3] is put to such extraordinary use that another filmmaker, observing, feels certain he doesn't know what he is doing; that his instructions and use of an individual is as unknown as unchartered waters; that the certainties and uncertainties of the dialogue he has made on Hydra will hopefully be as daring as the leaps of young men across the backs of charging bulls seen on Mycenean Warrior Vases; that his use of superimpositions will hopefully defy the brilliance of the Greek atmosphere; that the use of black background, his own private celestial manner with its drops of water will create certain crystallizations upon his handsome head akin to the athlete's olive branch.

Any film account if it does not completely satisfy the curiosity of the reader or expectant film spectator, should at least offer one specific detail. In this case let it be the name of the filmmaker: Robert Beavers.

Originally published in
Cinema, No. 53–54, Spring 1968.

3 The filmmaker wanted very much to use a matte box, which was not available in Athens; though he even made inquiries at USIS, where he was also informed that they did not have 16mm equipment available.

Tom S. Chomont

A Note on *The Count of Days,* a Film by Robert Beavers

1970

The film is seen as though upon and through the structure of its spiritual partitions. One might say that there are three elements or levels to the images: narrative, descriptive or analytic, and abstract. But this statement is one of convenient separation to approach a description, and I add that in the film these levels are wholly interdependent, complexly so since the frame is broken and played against in rapidly changing relations. Black is drawn aside like a curtain or opened like a door to reveal a landscape or the stout man with thinning hair. Images of the blonde girl waiting for a tram occur on the left half of the screen while a spectrum of colors pass in counterpoint and fold in upon the other half (both the spectrum and images being filtered through the colors at moments). The young boy's face is suddenly a black rectangle which goes out of focus to become a circle framed by his head, and then, later, in the black rectangle which replaces the man's face, the boy's face and shoulders appear.

By no means is this simply an exercise in geometrics. The film-maker, Robert Beavers, demonstrates full comprehension of the degree to which any image is and may be an abstraction both of the form and idea represented. For example, the shots of the shoes and the discarded clothes convey narrative and connotative meanings, but they appear, as though on the white of the illumined screen itself, with the impact of their form isolated as is the idea of shoes of this design or pants and shorts laying in a heap conveyed in a written description.

In fact, the film is not unlike a short novel in three parts or chapters, each dealing primarily with one of the novel's three characters and all touching upon aspects of the city (Zurich) and references or incidents involving one or both of the other characters. This resemblance does not seem accidental since the man appears to be a writer or publisher (I am told he is, in fact, the Swiss author Stefan Sadkowski). In one sequence (in the later part of the film) he is on a red couch reading aloud while images of the dissection of a white rat are interpolated. Then the images of the dissected rat are framed by the pages of the book as though to explain that his writing is a dissection (analysis) just as the film is an analysis (of him). Thus, to some extent the film may be a representation of the author's concept or treatment of himself and the other two. But if so, it is a *correspondence* realized by completely visual means. (The abstractions are of color of movement of planes and division [dissection] of frame.)

Furthermore, this is only one aspect of the form. There are, in some of the images of the

15

boy and girl, references to contemporary (popular) cinema, of which the language might be equally, if not more, familiar for them than that of the literary form for the (older) writer. For example, the candid gesture of the boy turning to shrug at the camera or panning across the activity of the street in which the girl is standing suggest the "cinéma-vérité" touches which appear in films such as Godard's *(Masculin-Féminin* or *Une Femme Mariée)*. Again, these moments do not occur apart from the complex activity of the frames, the reflective connections of the interfolding images.

An accurate description of my impressions is difficult, because within the whole the details of narrative and relation do not become exact but lucid... clearly *seen*. The boy and girl are related in separate shots, on each half of the screen, which nevertheless imply a meeting. The boy is framed by the writer. And there is the intimacy of the underwear (but whose?) evoking what may only be the possibility of a romantic triangle, perhaps only the emotions which approach this connection of the characters. A conflict is manifested in the sequence of the girl talking to the writer, during which her profile undergoes a visual play from vertical to horizontal, and in the scene of the writer humiliated by the boy in the train station.

The Count of Days is not an account so much as an accounting of the essence of the days in which three separate persons are related at points...a penetration through the masks and habits of these days to reveal the nature of the charade and the arena in which it is enacted.

The sight required for this film is demonstrated by the sequence showing an image of a landscape which occupies the left half of the screen and another of landscape which occupies the right half; when the two images are repeated in sequence and then together, one sees that they are two halves, a whole. It is the same with the complex planes of *The Count of Days*.

Originally published in Film Culture,
No. 48–49, Winter-Spring 1970.

The Count of Days (1969/2001)

Jonas Mekas

Introduction to the Work of Robert Beavers

1971

It is a privilege to write this small introduction to a book on one of the youngest, but one of the very few truly original artists working in cinema today. Let this small introduction be In Praise of a Film-Maker as a Young Artist. I'll be open, elated, and generous.

It is a paradox, that you are holding in your hands this book, and not watching the film on which this book is based. But such is the fate of all true artists: they have to master the art of waiting, too. The truth is, that not only you, but practically all of the Public of the world, hasn't seen Robert Beavers's work. But this same Public has seen all the bad works of all the bad film-makers that many thousands of cameras keep grinding out all around the world. Even those who create cinema, the film artists – only a very small handful of them have seen Beavers's work. But the final paradox, which, perhaps, is more a miracle than a paradox, is this: despite this total neglect by both the public and the artists themselves, Robert Beavers has continued, and is continuing working and creating new works, and he has done so and is doing so with an unwavering passion, with a total and unwavering concentration, with an insistence and urgency that comes closer to the natural forces of nature than anything human. Such is the miracle that we call an Artist: that

he is cast here by gods to do his work, he comes charged with certain energies, certain secrets, certain knowledge that he has to give to humanity, and he gives it through his works and nothing can stop him. No matter how deep is the darkness around him, how loud is the turmoil and bustle; no matter whether the people praise him or ignore him: he accomplishes his Mission Impossible. It's the politicians and the social workers, all the so-called socially concerned citizens who are asking for "justice": they are still practicing the law of "an eye for an eye." The artist is the only one who practices the politics of gods and gives it all without asking anything in return.

So here is Robert Beavers, a Film-Maker as a Young Artist, giving us work after work after work, and this work is not like anything any other film artist has given us. Because, really, what he's giving us is a new film language, or the beginnings of a new film language. When we look really close, no matter what the artist is saying, if he is a true artist – what he's giving us is a totally new language. I don't really know any real example, in cinema or any other art, where the originality of an artist can be separated from his language, from the newness and originality of his language. D. W. Griffith, Eisenstein, Dziga Vertov, Brakhage, Marko-

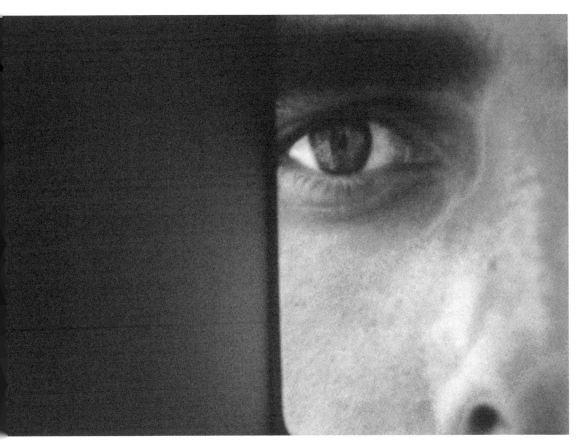

Still Light (1970/2001)

Still Light

poulos, Warhol – it has always to do with a new film language. Later, of course, others come, and they use the found languages in their own way, make them into "techniques." And soon there will be those who will use Beavers's language as a "technique," the same way as there are already many who are using Markopoulos's and Warhol's and Brakhage's languages as "techniques": soon Robert Beavers, a Film-Maker as a Young Artist, will become a Film-Maker as an Old Master. But no matter how many will use Beavers's "technique," it will be only in Robert Beavers's work that it will remain totally, inseparably and miraculously fused with the content of the film, and it will

be difficult, impossible to say which is the language and which is the content.

It is impossible for me to attempt here to describe to you what are the specifics of Beavers's language, how he differs from the other film-makers: to do that I'd need another book of the size of this book. Because, really, to see Beavers's language you have to see his films. His language, his tongue is his art, is his films. Still, Gregory Markopoulos has described Beavers's film language most accurately, I think, when he called it "the language of diamonds" in a recent essay in *Film Culture* magazine. Robert Beavers's film language is curiously close to the crystalline qualities of stones and minerals – in shapes, in tones, in feeling, in quality. Beavers's film language is a unique merging of the actual, living reality, with the abstract, geometric realities, and the Light. I could say, perhaps, that Robert Beavers is a scientist who, by means of the alchemy of art, is transforming the known realities in order to gain a deeper insight into them and create new realities that transcend them. I could also say that Robert Beavers is a philosopher, meditating on reality by means of juxtapositions and transformations of the Real, the Geometry, and the Light. By means of his films, that is, by means of his meditations, he presents us with a completely new philosophy of life and reality.

Whichever way I look at it – and the more I look at it the wider the gates begin to open, with more and more mysterious and different knowledge pouring out (because a new artist is a new language, and a new language is a new knowledge) – so that I, who is writing this brief introduction, on this early Sunday morning, with a pale New World light pouring over New York that is still half asleep – all I can do is but express my humble capitulation in face of the mysteries of Art, and close my own part here. Let the book itself speak, let the work of Robert Beavers speak.

"Brothers, sisters, take me and read me,
*   And reading, consider this:*
Your fathers fervently desired to have this doctrine
*   But were not able to obtain it in any way.*
They wanted to see it with their eyes
*   And also to hear it with their ears.*
Now what your fathers never saw
*   Now all this has come to you.*
All men, look and pay attention." *

Thus I honor and sing, through Robert Beavers, all the Film-Makers as Young Artists today – wherever they may be.

Originally published in Robert Beavers,
Still Light: Film Notes & Plates,
Florence: Il Torchio, 1971.

---

* From "The Old Lithuanian Catechism of Martynas Mazuydas," 1547.

René Micha

Robert Beavers or Absolute Film

1973

Robert Beavers writes in *From the Notebook of…* (which is a film): "Film is not the illusion of movement; it *is* movement." This can be understood in many ways. A digression begins here, a long parentheses that we will have to traverse.

MOTION

At the origin of cinema, the things and people that move across the screen of Louis Lumière's *The Arrival of the Train at the Station* represent motion at its simplest. We see the train arriving from a distance, it comes closer, and finally occupies the foreground. In this way, the spectator finds, or believes to find, the habitual conditions of vision. Space is figured in the same way that Western painting has done it from the Quattrocento to Cézanne: according to the rules of triangulation, the constriction of vanishing points, the separation of picture planes and the shrinking of figures as they move further away. In short, it follows the structures set forth by Alberti. Curiously, there is another sort of motion in the film, or more precisely, an interval amidst the motion. Hardly has the engine exited the screen, when the camera shows

Madame Lumière and her children heading toward a wagon, the doors opening, travelers scurrying across the platform – and this sudden contraction of time creates an encounter between two types of spaces, and between two types of depth. A little later, Georges Méliès will exploit these scene changes to great effect, superimposing scenes shot at different times: we see a man throw off his head, for example, or we see a hot-air balloon rising majestically through the stars. Still, Méliès's images, always keeping the same distance from the spectator, remain strictly in their frames, prisoners of the theatrical cube. Calmettes and Le Bargy, in *The Assassination of the Duke of Guise,* make use of a similar process, but add rhythm and repetition. One sees the Duke traverse, from left to right, the chambers of the king, a small study, and the guardsroom, where he stops; after [he is stabbed] he makes the same trajectory in reverse, thus, from right to left. The time it takes to move through a given space varies from one shot to another, which, joined with the game of the swordsman, emphasizes the dramatic effect.

With Griffith, things take a decisive turn. He discovers two types of motion that his successors, and particularly the Soviet filmmakers, will bring to perfection. Since Griffith, the camera advances and retracts, moves from above the scene to below it, or offers a long, sweeping look from one side to the other. In this way, the camera angle and the spectrum of the shot change. Now, we are no longer fixed to our seat in the orchestra. The film calls forth its characters, then abandons them, then takes them back; it considers them from constantly changing perspectives; it magnifies them and shrinks them; cuts them in half, isolates a face or a hand. André Malraux speaks of an "aesthetic revolution" and Jean Mitry of a "brilliant intuition." The author of *The Aesthetics and Psychology of the Cinema* writes: "The birth of the cinema as a means of expression (as opposed to reproduction) can be said to date from the breakdown of the *limited space*, from the period when the scriptwriter conceived his narrative in terms of separate shots, when he began to think not of photographing a play but of recording a succession of moments."[1] Nonetheless, the multiplicity of viewpoints and the mobility of space, as important as they are, do not completely break with the power that luck

and reverie maintain over us. If, for example, I watch and listen to Prokofiev's *Romeo and Juliet* in the open-air theater of San Giorgio in Venice, I can, if I like, move from one part of the garden to another, and I will see the ballet differently depending on where I am. I can focus my lorgnette on the detail of the décor, or on the face of the heroine. Even the magic lantern, if we disorient it, as did Proust, gives birth to strange, marvelous beings: Golo and Geneviève de Brabant moving across the curtains, swelling across the pleats, swimming over the surface of a doorknob, accommodating the obstacle as if it were an astral body.

In truth, the singular language of the cinema does not proceed just from out of the comings and goings of the camera. It is born from out of the movement that links images together and gives them meaning; the movement, which, building up from each image, traverses them all and brings into being a unique image, a work in the process of being made. But this image-in-process becomes, in a certain sense, the work itself. We can think of this movement as *movement-meaning*, or, as Maurice Merleau-Ponty puts it, the movement of the representation (as opposed to the representation of movement).[2] Each image can be seen in itself, but only in the blink of an eye, because the next one takes its

1 Translator's note: In fact, Mitry is quoting André Malraux from *Psychologie du cinéma*. Jean Mitry, *The Aesthetics and Psychology of the Cinema*, trans. Christopher King, Bloomington: Indiana University Press, 1997, p. 67.
2 Trans. note: In this paragraph, I translate *mouvement* as "movement" though elsewhere I translate it as "motion."

place, puts the previous one in question, imposes itself in turn – as it already announces the one that follows. Each image is a day in the creation of the world, and is its creation. The montage exists precisely to organize this perpetual becoming, to enumerate the signs, and to link them into one sign; to delineate space in terms of time, but also time in terms of space: to create an open form.

And so, the cinema seems a cluster of different types of motion: that of the very materiality of the film itself, that of the objects which are filmed, that which occurs in the act of filming and recording, and that which brings them all together.

NARRATIVITY

It is remarkable that this creative process aims, without fail, for narrative. Film, writes Eisenstein, is "a particular kind of painting which, through the montage, achieves the rhythm of the change of real intervals, and the sensory succession of things that repeat in time; all elements that, in their pure state, are specifically musical." And again, "It is a type of 'postpainting' passing into a distinctive type of 'premusic.'" In other words, film belongs to both space and time: it is both picture and story. The two are obviously inseparable. Nevertheless, I would remark that, with a few exceptions, the cinema has for some time now aspired, more than anything else, to narrative. It is working hard to catch up to the novel, which, after two centuries of relative stability, now is taking up new strategies and forms, *grosso modo* those of Proust, Joyce, and Kafka at the time of

World War I; those of the *Nouveau Roman* after World War II; and those of the *Nouveau Nouveau Roman* today (though it turns out that, paradoxically, this last movement distances itself from fiction so as to no longer remain in the space-time of speech). I can call up in this regard the great filmmakers of this epoch: Luis Buñuel, Orson Welles, Ingmar Bergman, Federico Fellini, Robert Bresson, Alain Resnais, Walerian Borowczyk, Bernardo Bertolucci, Nagisa Oshima: that is to say those who have benefited well from commercial cinema. But one would object that the cinema is by definition inevitably in the servitude of psychological portraits, allegories and social dramas. I prefer to approach the issue through a discussion of experimental film, which is at the heart of my subject. The work of Gregory Markopoulos – which initially influenced Beavers – is, in this case, exemplary. While there would be plenty to say about it from a variety of aspects, and most of it commendatory, let us, without diminishing the scope of it, observe that his work tends mainly toward finding a visual equivalent of the stream of consciousness of Joyce, Virginia Woolf, Faulkner, and Italo Svevo. To do this, Markopoulos makes use of images (as well as noises and scraps of music) that, in the space of a flash, traverse the sequence of the story and, far from stopping or even suspending it, give it new meaning – not just an elucidation of the story, but a transverberation into a sister-substance, as a new level of interpretation arises. These take nothing away from the beauty of the film: they are those suddenly immobile arrows of light that pierce the perfect body of Saint Sebastian (for example as portrayed by Mantegna in Vienna). I would add that *Twice a Man* and *The Illiac Passion* owe their effectiveness in part to Markopoulos's modern, post-Freudian take on a mythology which has always been natural and familiar to him. Experimentation of this sort is invaluable to the extent that even those authors aiming for a larger public – such as Richard Lester, in *Petulia* – can draw on it.

ROBERT BEAVERS

But Robert Beavers offers still a different approach. It is one that is deliberately formal (it will be necessary to return to this ambiguous word), and one closer to the act of creation than of the thing created, engrossed in its rigorous and ascetic search. In addition to all the types of cinematic representation of motion which I have discussed, Beavers invents – or reclaims – others.

Though an American, he has only made one film in the United States: *Spiracle*. The film is closely linked to the kind of seductive but fragile game that dominated (in 1966) the NAC (New American Cinema). His core values derive from Markopoulos's teachings, which he assimilates without the slightest hesitation.

When he was not yet 20, Beavers left for Europe, where he remained (except for one brief stay in New York). He would go on to direct 11 short and medium-length films, works that, while making use of different materials, nonetheless are quite similar. His films share

the quality of being very inexpensively made (not one cost more than two thousand dollars) and of attracting no attention to their author. When his films are shown, which is more and more rare, it is in film clubs and in museums of cinema during series devoted to showcasing "underground film." Beavers sells copies of his films to cinematheques, or receives the occasional grant (he received one from the John S. Guggenheim Memorial Foundation). While this naturally makes for a difficult existence, nonetheless, Beavers singularly pursues his life's project with whatever limited means are available.

PLACE

If one could characterize Robert Beavers's films in one word, one would think first of the places in which they were shot: Brussels (*Plan of Brussels*), Zurich (*The Count of Days*), Berlin (*Diminished Frame*), Greece (*Still Light*), Florence (*From the Notebook of…*). But Beavers is indifferent to these places. Or rather, they are for him what the water lilies were to Monet, a guitar or a newspaper for Gris, or a pool table and *gueridon* for Braque: things among other things, things that become, by chance, part of his vision. Even though we only see a tiny piece – a street, a roof, a façade, a passerby – of these cities, nonetheless, Beavers offers us a *new vision*. In the instant that we recognize the place, it seems to us that we also seize upon something essential to their being, yet up until now missing from our perception. Now, we can no longer imagine Florence without the painted window of the Via Maggio rising up before us, or the shadow cast by the Dufour-Berte palace on the house across from it, or the birds flitting around the Bargello. The shadows, in particular, are fascinating: of an infinite diversity and of a secret light. There is a sense of frustration each time the image changes (never lasting more than a few seconds): either it yields its place to another scene, or, more commonly, it is obscured, or fragmented, or obliterated, struck by one of those innumerable geometric figures that appear throughout his films. Confronted with the loss of the image, it is as if we possessed, for a moment, a fragment of the puzzle, but it was suddenly taken from us along with all that surrounded it. We may let our gaze wander through an open window: but then, a flag suddenly obscures the view. Yet at the same time, a kind of repose is born – a certainty. Here we are, delivered over to the view. Truth outweighs chance, a grid is imposed upon the world.

APPARATUS

But why does Robert Beavers make use of elements that are external (or apparently external) to the ordinary image – filters, diaphragms, frames, transparencies, and other accessories – which other filmmakers use only rarely, if at all? Why does he show us when he is using them – up to the extreme limit where they stop being seen in order to become themselves the gaze?

The answer, I think, is twofold.

First, we can say that the evolution of cinema over the past 75 years has rarely deviated from its trajectory toward an increasingly narrow – though certainly very subtle – imitation of the Real. Understood in this way, the passage from muteness to speech, from black and white to color, not to mention 3D, is without doubt striking. Who knows but that one day *The Invention of Morel* will become a reality and those empty forms that Adolfo Bioy Casares describes, dressed and painted and invested with speech, will move among us? Nonetheless, I hold the kind of motion that film has already given us, and which I have briefly described, to be even more remarkable. This mimetic tendency in film results in a constant reconfiguration of means and materials whose end (God forbid it ever arrive!) would signify the coincidence of life and its reflection. Robert Beavers rises up against the fatal consequences of such a trajectory. Returning back to the sources of cinema, or of pre-cinema, he re-introduces in his work those elements which the medium has progressively thrown off from its repertoire out of fear that it will take away from film's credibility. For example, he resurrects the thaumatrope and the phenakistoscope, cardboard disks that, when twirled rapidly, produce animation in the entanglement of the quickly-moving images that are printed on either side. We see, for example, a bird, in the act of leaving its cage; a glass of wine being brought to a pair of lips; a voyeur, spying on a woman dressing, and receiving a kick to his backside. It is motion, perceived as such, as the spring for action. Beavers, evidently, greatly enjoys this kind of excess which has left its mark on the cinema in the same way that Siena and Florence, early on, have done for painting. The paintings of Sassetta or of Domenico Veneziano do not appeal to our eye – to the conventional way of seeing that has formed itself patiently over five centuries of art – but I would declare that, stripped of their sharp edges, and their white fractures, the mountains neighboring Monte Oliveto are exactly those which they painted: theater machines, absolute truth.

MATERIAL

Secondly, and following the example of the primitives and the modern innovators, Robert Beavers holds to the tenet that the tools and the materials one employs are just as important as the work itself, or, more precisely, that they are part of it. Nonetheless, the color-grinding of the painter does not work in the same way as the transformation scenes in the Elizabethan theater, or the intervention of black-robed figures in Kabuki who obstruct the audience from seeing the play of masks, or an edition of poetry that offers variants on a text. These mechanisms serve to destroy a part of the illusion only in order to allow another to rise up before us. For Beavers, for whom the act of creation – or better, the fabrication – of the film is of the highest order, this goes further. If I speak of his formalism, it is because he constantly makes use of a process of stripping-bare. Linguists have found models for this same process in Cervantes's Exemplary Novels, Sterne's Tristram Shandy, and in the futuristic poems of Khlebnikov and Mayakovsky, all of which exemplify the Mallarméan disjunction between form and reality. If experience, once (or a thousand times) validated, turns into language, nonetheless, consciousness can still overtake it.

Let us look clearly at how this works.

The shot is linked to the position of the object, to the form the light makes, to the angle that is selected; but also to the process itself, to the time it takes to film, to the space it reveals, to its hesitations and regrets. It is possible to draw a figure all in one line (Dürer), or to make the figure appear from out of a jumble of many lines (Giacometti), or to generate the figure through a series of overlays (Francis Bacon), or to disarticulate it (Jiří Kolář). The shutter of a camera, writes Beavers, is like the wings of an insect: their motion is inscribed both in space and in the eye. But still, Beavers adds something to them: masks cut out of black cardboard are placed between the lens and the visual field to obstruct the image. He calls this a matte. In French, the word evokes a kind of tight mass – suggesting sometimes a wire mesh, sometimes a clump of grass underwater. I would like to add another connotation: in music, the matte as the "key" of a composition. It is in this way, for example, that Beavers comes to film one by one the objects that he finds in a bedroom and to impose a strict frame upon them, then to bring the images together and to enclose them in a unique frame, as one thing; then, to break the frame apart, and to reconstitute it ex nihilo. Beavers attributes the same importance to the montage as Eisenstein – and, I imagine that he sees in it, as did Eisenstein, a "metrical, rhythmic, tonal and harmonic" process. Yet he accords an almost equal importance to what I would call the pre-montage: the montage inside the shot. The center of gravity – the "shock" as Eisenstein preferred to call it – is not only be-

27

René Micha

tween the images, it is in the image. The image has its own structure. If the tonality of the light is changed, or if its construction or articulation is changed, the entire structure is modified. At the same time, I do not think that Beavers ever wanted to isolate the image by freezing the motion. Others have been tempted to do so: Roland Barthes, for example, founds his "theory of the photogram" on just this notion.

LIGHT

I turn, now, to color, which has a capital role in Beavers's films.

In Beavers's eyes, color could only be a discipline of light: the infinite decomposition and recomposition of the spectrum. Either he plays with its degrees, such as he would do with sound, in music (Feustel, we know, studied these types of correspondences), or he photographs light as he would a shape, or he photographs the filters themselves. The colors moving across a mobile screen; or the colors that are born from out of the filter echoing the screen, shining further and further out until they almost take over the screen; or the colors which finally settle into an image with the rhythm of the shot – all this is precisely what Boccioni, beginning with the first exhibition of Futurist sculpture in 1913, called "force-forms." Paul Valéry, in one of the five unpublished fragments of *Monsieur Teste*, inverts the terms, and in doing so, superbly affirms them: "I want to borrow from the visible world only the force – not the forms – but what we need to make the forms." It is thus that light reigns over space and time.

The shadows are no less subtle than the light. The more the object approaches them, the more they take on significance; the more the object retreats, the more they become light again. The continuum asserts itself when several shots are filmed showing only shadows without their objects, but shadows so soft that they are almost immaterial; then, the object advances into the shadow, and gives it new force. The quality of the shadow naturally changes depending on whether the light source dominates the object or just accompanies it.

AN EXAMPLE

Finally, passing to the other side of the divide, I would like to try to describe the work of Robert Beavers as it is presented to the spectator. I would like to do it as simply as possible, taking my examples from *Diminished Frame*.[3]

Diminished Frame is 20 minutes long. It takes place in Berlin. It is comprised in part of city views in black and white, and in part by views of the camera and its many accessories – mattes, transparencies, filters – that show the film in the process of being made. These last views are in color (sometimes just one color, sometimes many).

The first image that we see is a quay, and a tree which almost completely blocks it from view. Following this comes the movement of a green light, guided by the matte. Now we see the branches of the tree, dividing the sky as they do in the half-fauve, half-cubist paintings of

3 Editor's note: Micha is writing about the first version of *Diminished Frame* (1970).

28

Diminished Frame
(1970/2001)

Diminished Frame

Mondrian; also, there are birds. Then again the matte with filters, the feeling of the river close by, the tree. The frame expands and contracts; a black square appears over the image – imagine a pillow over an eye. But then a hand imposes itself, and we find the tree again. A new obliteration, a new image. A [wrought iron] rosette, and quite a beautiful one, appears and dominates a corridor. A man opens a door – to a scintillating red. The rosette will appear several times, becoming a sort of leitmotif, but finally gives way to a rectangular courtyard with garbage cans strewn throughout, surrounded by high walls on all sides, a kind of caravanserai, full of a grey light. The cameraman intervenes here and there: we observe him as he moves to his position behind the camera, and then we understand that it is his fingers that move across the screen, or if not the fingers, one of those sticks that he borrows from the days when Méliès performed his magic at the Cabinet Fantastique. Now the images are those of mostly empty streets: cars pass from time to time, women approach the screen, and then suddenly, as if an important sign had come from far away to seal this memorable reel of film, a Maltese cross arises which, while already half-erased, takes up all the space. An elevated metro station, a bit of the Spree, and a rather dark building, all behind a cluster of trees, alternates with the face – two thirds of which is hidden – of the cameraman, or of the shadow of his hand, along with vertical and horizontal bands of white, yellow, red and green, that swell and flutter, and that turn together around a standard (dominating the scene – it could be

Altdorfer's *The Battle of Alexander*).[4] We see, in the style of the magic lantern, a train passing through a green frame; some women at a crossroads who stop and then continue on their way; a building that seems to be the Reichstag, whose cracked ornaments surprise us; some cyclists who have put their feet on the ground and then continue on (one wears a cap like those of runners, the two others wear wool hats ornamented with flowers); a sphere on top of a column; huge puddles of water on the pavement; an empty restaurant, and, from out of its window, a suddenly lively street. We seem to recognize a house on the Kurfürstendamm, the Zoo train station, and suddenly, one of the three cyclists – he is almost a child. The rosette traverses the entire film, extending its glassy demon-flowers.

There are also noises, but so imperceptible, so unexpected, so far away, so little recognizable – the sounds of steps, or of wheels on a metal bridge, or of the pounding of tools? – that we are not sure whether they come from outside the film. Or from the accessories themselves. In their own way, they create a sense of distance.

My recollection of the film is notable in its failure to identify a particular theme: it could be, for example, the melancholic quality of an extensive but almost empty city, which the

4 Trans. note: Micha is using the word 'standard' (*étandard*) in its meaning as 'flag' or 'banner,' likely referring to the small metal filter holders that Beavers shows on a table before placing one in the camera filter slot. These little frames of filters remind him of the banner in a painting by Altdorfer.

miracle of wrought iron further accentuates. But Beavers cares nothing about theme, or symbol. If he films a grand Secession gateway, it is, unlike in the work of Joseph Losey, not a matter of an aesthetic choice. This is a medium that was chosen because it perfectly reflects and divides the light, because it is the center of gravity for thousands of colored particles.

If he does it right, his filmic description of Berlin has every chance of being just (in the same way that Warhol's *Trash* offers a just description of New York). If it is beautiful, it is an added grace.

The black matte or the filter cache that goes back and forth across the lens resembles a razor blade at times, and at others, the little flags of children's play-battles. They are just as important, if not more important, than the images of the city. The same goes for the avenues of color that are those of Morris Louis, of American highways at night. Together, they are the source of light – as our eyes are, according to Plato.

A NEW LANGUAGE

We are dealing with absolute film: with creation, reflection, and re-creation; here is a prodigious power over material, or more exactly, over language. In its narrow domain, Beavers's work is not without resonance of the will of the spirit and the exacting quality that appears in Leonardo's *Notebooks*, in their treatment of vision, shadows, color. *Still Light, From the Notebook of…, Diminished Frame* do not speak of motion. They are motion. They do not speak of light. They are light. They are

nothing but themselves. Maybe we could call them "anti-films." Do they destroy the image of the cinema as we know it?

The Theater Houdin and the image play of Méliès come from a Douanier Rousseau. It was time for a no less admirable art to arise, one closer to Klee, to his labyrinths, to his magic squares, to his hesitant angels.

Originally published as "Robert Beavers ou le cinéma absolu," in Art International, *Vol. 17, Issue 6, Summer 1973.*

Translated from the French by Noam Scheindlin.

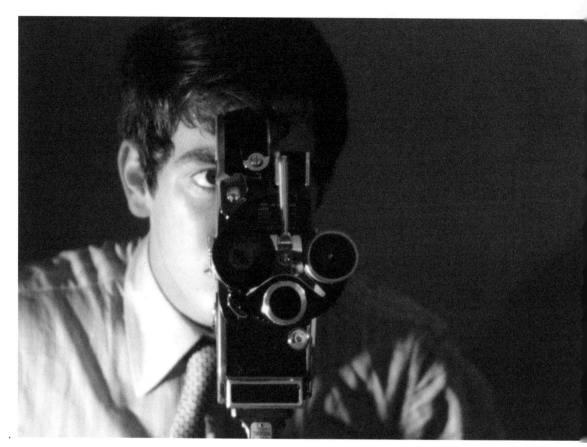

Early Monthly Segments

Rebekah Rutkoff

He Made this Screen

Toward Robert Beavers's Poetry

Born in Brookline, Massachusetts, in 1949, Robert Beavers watched as many as four movies a week as a child. He took in films like Sirk's *Imitation of Life* (1959), Robert Pirosh's Eastmancolor adventure *Valley of the Kings* (1954) and DeMille's *The Ten Commandments* (1956) at a cinema in Weymouth. At 14 his cinematic education widened: at the Brattle Theatre in Cambridge, dedicated to foreign repertory programming, he encountered work by Bergman and Fellini. Guided by the wish to establish a film club at Deerfield Academy, a boys' boarding school in western Massachusetts, Beavers traveled to New York City during the summer after his junior year in order to conduct research and gather films. He visited the film library at the Museum of Modern Art and Jonas Mekas's Film-Makers' Cinematheque, collecting suggestions and perusing catalogues filled with a curious new category of films: those made by individual artists. After weeks of labor, he sent a proposed inaugural program to his Deerfield faculty sponsor, who swiftly cancelled the initiative; mentions of nudity and homosexuality in the description of *Scorpio Rising* – Kenneth Angers's short 1963 film –

were sufficient to dash Beavers's pursuit. But the weeks in New York City had given him a more important gift: the idea that he could possibly make a film. He had learned of the New American Cinema, and watched the experimental films of Carl Linder and Gregory Markopoulos. Until that summer of 1965, Beavers had only imagined films as "big," dependent on enormous budgets and collaborations.

Beavers dropped out of Deerfield Academy just a few months later. After a short stint working in Boston, he moved into a small loft on the Bowery in Manhattan. He had met Markopoulos (1928–1992), a key figure in the burgeoning New American Cinema scene, the previous summer; they were now a couple, and the relationship endured until Markopoulos's death. Beavers was 17 when he accompanied Markopoulos on some of the shoots for *Galaxie* (1966), his feature-length compilation of 33 in-camera-edited portraits of New York artists and writers. Beavers held a tungsten light on W. H. Auden and listened to him speak. "The poets were outstanding," he recalls. In contrast to the painters whose vanity burned brightly, the poets "saw the person opposite them, tried to say something – it was a gift, astonishing."[1]

It was only a year later, in 1967, that Markopoulos and Beavers decided to leave

---

1 Robert Beavers interview with the author, November 13, 2016.

New York City. They had grown deeply disenchanted by U.S. film culture and screening conditions and spent the next decades living in various European locations in self-imposed exile. The narrative of their leave-taking is a dramatic and remarkable one: the filmmakers' seclusion and the removal of their films from distribution climaxed in the establishment of the Temenos (the site in the remote Peloponnese that Markopoulos identified as the exclusive location for the screening of his and Beavers's films) and the creation of *Eniaios* (Markopoulos's 80 hour film designed for screening in this location). In the years following his partner's death, Beavers has taken on the enormous task of restoring the unprinted *Eniaios*. He has personally organized and hosted *Eniaios* screenings in Greece every four years since 2004, devoting significant time and energies to overseeing the complex fund-raising and film repair work that make the Temenos events possible.

In accounting for Beavers's achievements, it would be a mistake to deny the profoundly generative impact of his partnership with Markopoulos; the latter played a crucial role in offering a model of uncommon dedication to a creative vision and by providing Beavers with protective encouragement to pursue his vocation no matter the material costs (which were severe: the two men often lived on the brink of poverty). But the compelling story of the filmmakers' partnership, leave-taking and sequestration can overwhelm attention to the quieter register of drama that resides in the nuances of the singular film poetry Beavers has developed over the course of 50 years. This book is a step

in that direction, toward a fuller attention to the particularities of Beavers's cinematic imagination as it has unfurled since 1967. The filmmaker reported to a film audience in 2013 about "becoming alert" upon discovering the American poet Marianne Moore's assertion that "I see no reason for calling my work poetry except that there is no other category in which to put it."[2] Beavers's poetry prods his spectators into states of perceptual and psychic wakefulness as well. He calls it "direct seeing."

~

It may come as a surprise that it was Beavers who eloped to Europe first. In 1967 the 18-year-old traveled to Brussels (at the Cinémathèque Royale, he met Jacques Ledoux, who would become a life-long supporter, and submitted a project proposal that enabled him to receive free rolls of film) and Athens before arriving on the Saronic island of Hydra where Markopoulos later joined him. The resulting *Winged Dialogue* (1967 / 2000), multi-layered with mattes and superimpositions, is the earliest of Beavers's works that we know today; he withdrew *Spiracle* (1966) from circulation and destroyed *On the Everyday Use of the Eyes of Death* (1966). A briskly cut celebration of hybrid creative and erotic bliss, it features the nude Beavers and Markopoulos bathing under Aegean light and the sign of Apollo, god of the visual world. The film unwittingly reveals how essentially nourishing Greece will become for

2 Robert Beavers speaking at Princeton University, October 22, 2013.

Winged Dialogue (1967/2000)

Beavers's cinematic imagination: the sea's saturated turquoises and the rainbow array of colored light Beavers finds in the encounter between sunlight and a glass pitcher of water appear as prototypes for his subsequent use of colored filters. Markopoulos writes with wonder about witnessing this moment of early mastery on Hydra: "Slowly with the grace, diligence and demonical, critical frenzy of a Paul Valéry he became acquainted with his medium. This, more so, during his first encounter with Greece: the sea, the laughter, and the braying of donkeys."[3]

Winged Dialogue has two identities; it is a stand-alone film and also one of Beavers's *Early Monthly Segments* (1968–70/2002), a chronological series of formal sketches and trials he undertook on a monthly basis between the ages of 18 and 20 as he pursued increasing intimacy with his apparatus. The *Segments* allow various parts and potentials of Beavers's camera to articulate themselves; they showcase his experiments with both a compendium (an accordion-like structure for holding shaped mattes that Beavers attached to the front of his Bolex) and the placement of colored filters in the space between aperture and lens. He made five longer works during the same period – *Plan of Brussels* (1968/2000), *The Count of Days* (1969/2001), *Palinode* (1970/2001), *Diminished Frame* (1970/ 2001), and *Still Light* (1970/2001) – and the *Segments* are interspersed with footage shot expressly for these films. Over the two-year course of making *Early Monthly Segments*, Beavers transitioned from character-oriented psychodrama (*Plan of Brussels, The Count of*

Days) into an exclusive focus on non-narrative work.

Beavers looked closely at Stan Brakhage and Markopoulos's films in the late 1960s; he attributes the speed, rhythm and layering that drive the *Segments* to an editing model he encountered in the New American Cinema. But in contrast to Markopoulos, whose preoccupation with the single film frame as material and perceptual unit led him to a radical grammar of pictorial flashing and isolation (no two images in *Eniaios* touch, for example), Beavers established an orientation to the frame as compositionally multi-registered and spacious, temporally fluid instead of fragmentary. In his 1973 ode to Beavers's emergent cinema, René Micha calls this "the pre-montage: the montage inside the shot." He continues:

"The center of gravity – the 'shock' as Eisenstein preferred to call it – is not only between the images, it is in the image. The image has its own structure. If the tonality of the light is changed, or if its construction or articulation is changed, the entire structure is modified. At the same time, I do not think that Beavers ever wanted to isolate the image by freezing the motion. Others have been tempted to do so: Roland Barthes, for example, founds his 'theory of the photogram' on just this notion."[4]

3 Gregory Markopoulos, "10th of July, 1967," *Cinema*, No. 53–54, Spring 1968. See also p. 9 in this volume.
4 René Micha, "Robert Beavers ou le cinéma absolu," *Art International*, Vol. 17, Issue 6, Summer 1973. Translated from the French by Noam Scheindlin; see p. 22 in this volume.

Plan of Brussels (1968/2000)

Still Light

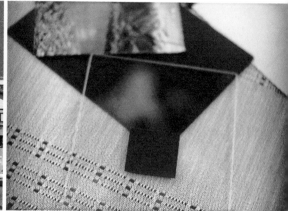

Early Monthly Segments

Micha theorizes that Beavers's very particular contribution to the art of cinema revolves around the filmmaker's "use of *a process of stripping-bare*" where the priorities of illusionism are exchanged for a performance of a film's very "fabrication," one in which "the tools and the materials one employs are just as important as the work itself, or, more precisely…are part of it."[5] In *Early Monthly Segments* we see the first and purest example of this primary orientation. In one late sequence, the representation of deep space is interrupted by a square matte, and Beavers walks us through his composition. He sits at an outdoor table in Locarno and slides a glass-mounted matte into the compendium, presenting the real-time collaboration of hand and camera in the production of an image. There is a democracy surrounding Beavers's performative auto-didacticism: the filmmaker errs on the side of sharing the means of his work's making rather than hiding, wizard-like, behind scenes of structural spectacle or impossible beauty.

The *Segments* present Beavers's new grammar and formal language fluently at the very moment he is learning to speak it. They debut what will become a signature move – the turning of his lens turret while filming. This produces a swift exit of an image into black and a built-in transitional moment that Beavers later exploits in editing. The *Segments* also introduce his mode of integrating self-portraiture and autobiography; the many scenes of Beavers and Markopoulos in temporary domestic spaces in Switzerland, Germany, and Greece offer an emotional context for the palpable energy of discovery at the *Segments'* core. We witness Markopoulos, whose fame was at a high point during these years, typing and addressing envelopes, soliciting funds from

5 Ibid.

40

individuals, companies, and cinematheques so that Beavers's explorations could go on without interruption.

~

Beavers fully edited his *Early Monthly Segments* at the time of their making, but he left them unprinted. In the 1990s, he decided to integrate all of his work into a single cycle, *My Hand Outstretched to the Winged Distance and Sightless Measure* (1967–2002), which consists of three parts and 18 individual works. The process involved an arduous reconsideration of the films he had made since 1967; nearly every one was shortened and re-edited, and Beavers sometimes returned to original shooting locations in order to re-record sound. When he revisited the unprinted *Segments,* he found them too complicated, too heavily layered. The films we see today are about half their original length and have been stripped of many of their original superimpositions. "I wonder if I wasn't secure enough to rely on the image as composed," Beavers reflects.[6] *Winged Dialogue* is the most radically condensed of all of Beavers's films – once 17 minutes, it is now three.

Beavers assigned the *Segments* an unusual double role. Together, headed by *Winged Dialogue*, they function as a silent prelude to the entire *My Hand Outstretched* cycle, but they subsequently reappear with sound, side-by-side and in dialogue with the five films made concurrently. The *Segments* embody Beavers's orientation to the vitality of his medium: in the multiple lives he grants his films, he betrays both his capacity to tolerate an immensely complex material and psychic process – the syncing up of older work with a present-tense consciousness – and a certainty about the value of those earlier creations. "There is a whole family of artists who believe in the *non-finito*," he told a Princeton University film audience in 2013, identifying himself as a member.[7] In this work with such long swaths of time (to which he asks his viewers to adapt by presenting them with the cycle), Beavers offers a portrait of creative mind as much as of medium. But we glimpse signs of this capacious mind in individual images too. In the *Segments*, we encounter the filmmaker at an editing table blanketed with coils of separated shots. Rather than relying on repeated Steenbeck viewings, Beavers edits by memorizing his material and internally composing it. His reliance on the mind's eye extends to shooting as well; he rarely looks into the camera while filming.

Aware of Beavers's appreciation of Marianne Moore, I think of *Early Monthly Segments* alongside her short poem "He Made this Screen." In Moore's imagistic vision of creation itself – greater than the sum of its representational and figurative parts (the very oceanic, floral, vegetative and physiognomic ones Beavers incorporates so often in these monthly experiments) but dependent on them for value – the poet

6 Robert Beavers phone conversation with the author, January 3, 2017.
7 Robert Beavers speaking at Princeton University, October 22, 2013. Beavers was referring not to artists known for their intentionally "unfinished" creations but to those who return to heretofore completed works for reconsideration and revision, including Henry James, Wordsworth and Degas.

Early Monthly Segments

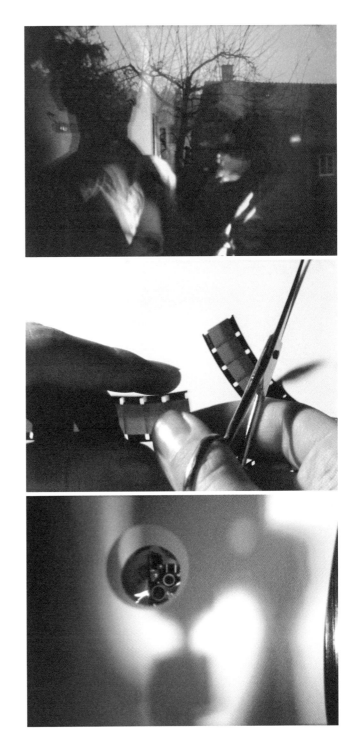

prematurely announces Beavers, whose own *Early Monthly Segments* announces the arrival of a major American poet.

He Made this Screen

not of silver nor of coral,
but of weatherbeaten laurel.

Here, he introduced a sea
uniform like tapestry;

here, a fig-tree; there, a face;
there, a dragon circling space—

designating here, a bower;
there, a pointed passion-flower.[8]

But if *Early Monthly Segments* contains all the components of Beavers's new film language, we would miss many of them if we focused solely on representational ones – those that reside *on* the screen. As he guides us through the steps of his process and the insides of his device, Beavers nurtures a fresh awareness in the spectator of her own embodied role: she is not only an agent in the unfolding chain of associations the filmmaker sets in motion but participant in a network of lines connecting her to maker, camera, screen, projector and world. A latent and expansive constellation lights up as Beavers draws attention to the poetics of the very scene of cinema itself.

In Beavers's hands and mind, the cinematic apparatus is a material, mechanical fact with a metaphysical shadow. "Projection is not only through the frame to the screen," he writes in *Acnode*; it is also "a highlight [that] passes from one edited frame into the same part of the next image." But "projection" pertains as well to an encounter between parts of a self (within an individual filmmaker, actor or spectator – or among them) that can occur under the auspices of cinema: "The soul projects movements in the body, and other movements are projected from the body into the soul."[9] The declaration "He Made this Screen" conjures Beavers's variety of poetry: one in which each of the elemental givens of the cinema – spectator, screen, projector – is imagined and resonates anew.

8 Marianne Moore, "He Made this Screen," *Poems*, London: The Egoist Press, 1921, p. 9.
9 Robert Beavers, "Acnode," *Robert Beavers: Die ausgestreckte Hand*, Vienna: Austrian Film Museum, 2010. See also p. 167 in this volume.

Film strips from
the first segment
of Early Monthly
Segments showing
"edited phrases"

Early Monthly Segments film strips

Luke Fowler

In the Shadow of a Sound

Sonic Montage in the Works of Robert Beavers

FROM THE NOTEBOOK OF...

When I filmed From the Notebook of... *in 1971, I had already developed the use of mattes with colored filters as a structural and expressive means. My earliest films, made between 1967 and 1970, presented various erotic and spiritual themes in the context of the places where I had been living. I began to see the film frame as a many faceted whole that could unite a quantity of diverse visual elements in the same composition. I superimposed images, editing on several bands of film, each with its own rhythm, and brought these layers together in printing the film. I also tried to edit directly the optical sound track, using the same measures as in the image. The result was a dominance of the image's rhythm and a grotesquely aggressive sound accompaniment, but I nonetheless developed the patterning and positioning of image fragments within the film frame that led to* From the Notebook of... *(Robert Beavers)[1]*

Robert Beavers's *From the Notebook of...* (1971/1998) begins with the roving eye of the camera, searching the streets of Florence: a shot of caged doves is followed by a shot of their release. These views are formally dissected by a matte that slides half way across the screen, like a gliding portal; by the time a handwritten note reads "film convention is time flowing forward in the mind of the viewer," this convention has already been refused by the repetition of certain shots and the resulting discontinuity in time and space. Further confronted with image masking and superimposition within the film's 4:3 frame, the spectator experiences a simultaneity of distinct perspectives unfolding. The film then cuts to a shadowed Florentine apartment where we see a man (the filmmaker) opening the shutters and flooding the room with sunlight. These images, a mix of violent spasms and more controlled pans and tilts, are edited with a highly musical and poetic sensibility.

Accompanying these images is a soundtrack – though perhaps it would be more accurate to call it a sound montage – that caused something of an epiphany when I first encountered it. It brims with detailed close-ups: flapping birds' wings, clacking horse hooves, ringing bells, waves flowing on the Arno River, writing on and turning notebook pages, stone chiseling, the whirring of the camera's spring wound motor, shutters creaking, and various sounds of

1 Robert Beavers, "From the Notebook of...," *Cinéma exposé / Exhibited Cinema: Exhibiting artists' films, video art and moving image,* ed. François Bovier and Adeena Mey, Lausanne: ECAL/Les presses du réel, 2015, p. 96. See also p. 178 in this volume.

From the Notebook of... (1971/1998)

*From the
Notebook of…*

external, public life. It is the highly distinctive, subjective and intelligent approach to sound and image construction which Beavers has cultivated in *Notebook* and other films that has kept me returning to his work and which I want to take the time to examine here in all its fullness. By providing some historical background and concepts, from both the birth of sound film and the world of electro-acoustic composition, I hope to open up a wider context for appreciating Beavers's work.

The filmmaker's position with respect to sound and montage is born out of a regard for the distinctness of acoustic space and its reflexive and associative qualities in relation to the image. I would argue that Beavers is one of the few practitioners in the experimental canon to fully realize the notion, first raised by the Soviet pioneers, and later developed by film theorists including Béla Balázs, Siegfried Kracauer and Rick Altman, of a *sound montage*. My analysis draws not only on published writing (by Beavers and others) but on interviews with the filmmaker and his unpublished notes in an effort to shed light on this rarely discussed aspect of his work.

SOUND SCALE

27.3.69 Sound in relation to the distance of camera to subject; in relation to the light and shade of the frame. (Robert Beavers)[2]

In his finely argued essay "Sound Space," Altman traces the history of Hollywood microphone placement since the advent of the "talkies."[3] He describes the warning that J. P. Maxfield, acoustics specialist and technician for Electrical Research Products Incorporated, issued to sound engineers in 1930: the mismatch between sound and image scale in the nascent sound film could have deleterious consequences; instead, "the eyes and ears of a person viewing a real scene in real life must maintain a 'fixed relationship' to one another."[4] To achieve the necessary illusion of naturalism, Maxfield argued, a sound recordist should aim for a balance between the focal length of the camera and the distance of the microphone. But with the advent of new technology, this goal would become ever harder to achieve.

In a break with the paradigm that forced an actor to keep in close proximity to a single sound recording device, the first microphone mixers in the early 1930s allowed for the simultaneous installation of several microphones on a film set. The mixing of multiple microphones (carefully concealed in foliage and other props) created a heightened sense of clarity but had a major drawback: the spectator encountered a completely constructed and sanitized point of audition; no longer did an actor's voice exist within a specific and unique acoustic space. A second invention which Maxfield may have

2 Robert Beavers, *From the Notebook of...* (1971/1998).
3 Rick Altman, "Sound Space," *Sound Theory, Sound Practice*, ed. Rick Altman, London: Routledge, 1992, p. 49.
4 Ibid., p. 49–55.

Luke Fowler

balked at was the "boom mic," a portable microphone attached to a long pole (or "boom").[5]
Also known as a "gun mic," it was a break-
through for sound recordists because it kept
the apparatus out of shot while also allowing
the stalking of a moving actor/actress. Today,
Hollywood's insistence on manicuring microphone perspective via sophisticated technology
has been normalized to such a degree that Maxfield's arguments are regarded as merely a foot-
note in film history. Prioritizing intelligibility
and narrative comprehension over a more naturalistic sound (one that embraces the 'signature' of the acoustic – the echoes, reflections and
reverberations that color sound in space) has
meant that industrially-produced cinema either
discards or fakes this dimension of sound.[6]

My point, however, is not to place Beavers's
films within the canon of structural materialist
film concerned with revealing the illusionistic
nature of the medium. This political aim is not
Beavers's project. Instead, his approach is that
of a self-described "collagist," and his orientation to the metaphoric sonic image dovetails
with a concern for the "contours" of acoustic
space and the use of the artist's body to activate
it.[7] This can be observed in his films shot in
Greece (including *The Ground* [1993–2001] and
The Stoas [1991–97]) which feature the reverber-
ation of a chisel across a hillside or the distant
sound of monks in a glen. Indirect sound pre-
vails also in *Pitcher of Colored Light* (2007); its
soundtrack is comprised largely of unintelligible, off-axis speech spoken by the filmmaker's
elderly mother. Here speech takes on an unusual quality of "acoustic smearing" where the

vocal utterances become almost inseparable
from the room's acoustic. It is only in close listening that we can distinguish odd words and
phrases.

Sound designer Walter Murch describes his
"general predisposition to always think about
the air that surrounds [a sound]" when recording. "[I]t's incredibly emotional…it's sort of a
perfume of sound," he says.[8] Murch's "perfume" – an affective aura that cannot be located
in sonic information – can also help us understand "anamnesis," a term coined at the Centre
for Research on Sonic Space and Urban Environment (CRESSON) in Paris, to describe "[a]n
effect…in which a past situation or atmosphere
is brought back to the listener's consciousness,
provoked by a particular signal or sonic context…the often involuntary revival of memory
caused by listening and the evocative power of
sounds."[9] In Beavers's lengthy personal notes
on the sound design of *Pitcher,* he articulates a
wish to create sound with just such an evocative
quality; he states that neither naturalism nor

5 Ibid., p. 53.
6 In his essay "The Material Heterogeneity of Recorded
Sound," Altman states that no microphone can ever be
completely faithful to the human perception of sounds
due to the technical limitations of recording devices;
recorded sound will always carry the imprint of the
recording apparatus. *Sound Theory,* ed. Altman, p. 26.
7 Public remarks by Robert Beavers, February 2007, on the
occasion of the film exhibition *To the Winged Distance:
Films by Robert Beavers,* Tate Modern, London.
8 Vincent LoBrutto, "Walter Murch," *Sound-on-Film: Interviews with Creators of Film Sound,* Westport: Praeger
Publishers, 1994, p. 88.
9 *Sonic Experience: A Guide to Everyday Sounds,* ed. Jean-
François Augoyard and Henry Torgue, Montreal: McGill-
Queen's University Press, 2005, p. 21.

50

ambience are the aim but that the sound should possess a "voice-like clarity."[10]

SYNCHRONY, ASYNCHRONY AND NEUTRALIZING THE IMAGE

Beavers's films often query the means by which we apprehend a subjective meaning or relationship to place. In his frequent use of disjunctive or asynchronous montage, he examines how we associate the memory of place with a multitude of perspectives and sensations rather than a single image. Beginning with *Early Monthly Segments* (1968–70/2002), Beavers has cultivated this multiplicity via a number of techniques, including rhythmic editing, the use of hand-made mattes and colored filters, the turning of the lens turret (on his 16mm wind-up Bolex) and the insertion of his own body into his films beyond an implied behind-the-camera presence. In tandem with these visual strategies, he has developed his own language in the field of sound, paying close attention to the acoustic space as well as to the percussive qualities of sound to reinforce and augment the effect of a cut. His imaginative use of associative and metaphoric sounds opens up the montage beyond natural illusionism or mere musical accompaniment.

At the same time that Maxfield was arguing

for the cinematic integration of sound and space through recording techniques, a more theoretical debate about the aesthetic role of sound in cinema was taking place among Soviet pioneers Eisenstein, Alexandrov and Pudovkin. In 1928 they issued "A Statement on Sound" in which they identified naturalistic sound – the illusionistic kind in "talking films" – as a threat to the primacy of montage.[11] They believed sound's first role should be not support for the image but rather counterpoint. Asynchronous or non-synchronous sound could advance the complexity of montage in order to, as Pudovkin said in 1934, "augment the potential expressiveness of the film's content."[12] This would help seal sound's role as an essential component within the cinematic art form.

In a March 2013 interview with Beavers in Switzerland, we discussed the role of sound in his early works and the development of his sound montage into a more nuanced realm of metaphorical sound:

Tell me about your approach to using sound in your early films. What equipment were you using?

We had a friend in a TV station in Locarno; I used a Nagra loaned from this TV station. The sounds were recorded after the filming. In the beginning of all those early films, the sound was always secondary … Going back to those early films made here in Zurich, there was recorded reading and singing on both of them – I cut the sound mimicking how I was cutting the image…

How did you do that in those days?

By numbers! If the image was 10 or 12 frames

10 Robert Beavers, *Pitcher of Colored Light* filming notes, Temenos Archive.
11 S. M. Eisenstein, V. I. Pudovkin, and G. V. Alexandrov, "A Statement," *Film Sound: Theory and Practice*, ed. Elisabeth Weis and John Belton, New York: Columbia University Press, 1985, p. 83–85.
12 V. I. Pudovkin, "Asynchronism as a Principle of Sound Film," *Film Technique and Film Acting*, New York: Grove Press, 1960, p. 86.

long I would make a hard cut in sync with the image. In any case the development of my sound, which led to *From the Notebook of...* and came from *Diminished Frame,* began with a very definite and simple idea: that sounds should be suggestive of crowds. I was looking at Berlin in the early seventies and it was my impression that it was still heavily connected to Nazi Germany. I had read in the work of Elias Canetti how crowds move in certain forms – how they are swarm-like, so I used the sound of bees, the traffic, droning sounds, the beginning of the page sounds and the flame – because fire moves in an uncontrolled way like crowds. So that was a very different way of using sound than, say, having a singer and just using his voice.

The means were much more limited but I was trying to suggest something. Then, when I came to *Notebook,* I was ready for my first successful metaphoric editing of sound.

The motivation behind Beavers's metaphoric technique is elucidated in his uncharacteristically polemical essay "La Terra Nuova" in which he criticizes a literal or illustrative relationship to sound in film: "Synchronization is the point at which the image and sound touch. The value of each point depends upon its appropriate placement in the film's perspective, where it must reveal part of an acoustic equal to the composition of the image. The spoken word and musical accompaniment are no more than a distraction in the film if they fail to participate in the basic image-sound unit. Neither the word nor the image should be used to devalue the other, yet the misuse of the word, ei-

ther as commentary or melodrama, endangers the film most frequently by neutralizing or abbreviating the image."[13]

These remarks echo Robert Bresson's sentiments in *Notes on Cinematography*:

"When a sound can replace an image, cut the image or neutralize it. The ear goes more towards the within, the eye towards the outer.

If a sound is the obligatory complement of an image, give preponderance either to the sound, or to the image. If equal, they damage or kill each other, as we say of colors.

Image and sound must not support each other, but must work each in turn through *a sort of relay.*"[14]

Although Bresson uses sounds in a considered and reduced manner, they are still bound in the service of narrative. Beavers's use of sound, on the other hand, becomes part of a far larger schema that is "neither to be observed by the spectator nor even completely seen by the filmmaker."[15] That is to say, space and time are continually dislodged; fresh associations and metonyms are conceived in a war against the well-worn metaphor or montage.

SOUND METAPHORS AND SYMBOLISM

Sound symbolism rarely has been emphasized in film discourse. As discussed, the normative function of sound is to reinforce the illusion of

13 Robert Beavers, "La Terra Nuova" [early version], *Millennium Film Journal*, No. 32/33, Fall 1998, p. 41–42.
14 Robert Bresson, *Notes on Cinematography*, trans. Jonathan Griffin, New York: Urizen Books, 1977, p. 28.
15 Robert Beavers, "La Terra Nuova," *The Searching Measure*, Berkeley: UC Berkeley Art Museum and Pacific Film Archive, 2004. See also p. 193 in this volume.

reality, but in the 1950s, Kracauer urged film-makers to go beyond the realist use of sound, to evoke ideas and states not bound to the natural. Sound symbolism can be used as a counterpoint to or substitute for traditional montage; however, Kracauer warns against sliding into a merely arbitrary, formal language: "Sound used contrapuntally must relate to the synchronized images in an understandable way to signify something comprehensible."[16]

The disembodied, non-diegetic sound in film has been usefully related to the notion of the "acousmatic," a term first used in the mid-1950s by the now legendary *musique concrète* pioneer Pierre Schaeffer.[17] He came to define it as "a sound that one hears without seeing the causes behind it."[18] Schaeffer was influenced by French phenomenology and struggled to establish a performer-less music at the Groupe de Recherches Musicales (GRM) in Paris which embraced "sound for itself" as one of its guiding principles.

Several composers and writers have challenged this now highly institutionalized notion, most notably next-generation GRM composer

Luc Ferrari, whose fascinating works employ fragments of environmental field recording ("shreds of reality") that he called "anecdotal music."[19] In contrast to the French, the English electroacoustic scene was at once more concrete and playful in employing this new musical language. Composer and theorist Trevor Wishart (active since the early 1970s), for instance, developed a practice of engaging with symbolic sound in the creation of sonic landscapes that resonate with Beavers's approach.[20] Wishart argues that there has always been a survival instinct connected to close listening: the ability to pinpoint a sound to a source and location is a primitive human reaction. His implied critique of Schaeffer is that limiting sound to a purely sensual dimension denies the sonic component of our multi-sensory faculties; removing either the visual or sonic referent is disorientating and undermines our ability to decode sensory information as intelligible and meaningful.[21]

Wishart's method of overcoming the ambiguities of vague symbolism was to draw on an almost universal grammar of sound-images. This enabled him to use sounds so familiar that they take on a nearly mythic dimension. Although Beavers works in a different field, his embrace of recognizable sound betrays a comparable sensibility. Both artists also take a lyrical approach to editing; this allows their respective compositions to develop complex networks of metaphors.

Leaving aside these historical arguments and correlations, let us return to Beavers's use of aural metaphors in *Notebook*. Of central significance is the kinship set up between the percus-

16 Siegfried Kracauer, "Dialogue and Sound," *Film Sound: Theory and Practice*, ed. Elisabeth Weis and John Belton, New York: Columbia University Press, 1985, p. 140.

17 Pierre Schaeffer, "Acousmatics," *Audio Culture: Readings in Modern Music*, ed. Christoph Cox and Daniel Warner, New York: Continuum Books, 2006, p. 76.

18 Pierre Schaeffer, *Traité des objets musicaux*, Paris: Le Seuil, 1966, p. 91.

19 Simon Emmerson, *Living Electronic Music*, Hampshire: Ashgate, 2007, p. 7.

20 Trevor Wishart, "Sound-Image as Metaphor: Myth and Music," *On Sonic Art*, ed. Simon Emmerson, Amsterdam: Harwood, 1996, p. 163–176.

21 Trevor Wishart, "Sound Landscape," *On Sonic Art*, ed. Emmerson, p. 129–161.

sive, repetitive sound of the camera's shutter and the fluttering page-turning sound of the notebook as it is thumbed through. This metaphor draws into relation the production and mechanics of filming with that of Beavers's other discipline: writing in his notebook. (Beavers later returns to this metaphor in *Ruskin* [1975 / 1997].)

A particularly compelling sequence in *Notebook* features a self-portrait of the artist: Beavers's head and neck are shot in the reflection of a mirror and he rocks playfully back and forward so that the narrow strip of sunlight, created by a crack of light in the shutters, illuminates his features. As in the previous metaphor with the camera shutter / book pages, Beavers draws our attention to parts of the film-making process which ordinarily remains hidden. In this particular case he is manipulating the blinds to "expose" selected areas of his own profile. The crack in the shutters evokes the filmmaker's process of creating images by exposing light on a film strip.

Notebook sounds fade in and out, displacing synchronization and often foretelling the images to come. Associations between different acoustic and visual perspectives are often evoked (the following examples might refer to an image, a sound, or both):

the striking of horses hooves / the rhythm of chisel against anvil / the flapping wings of the dove / the opening and closing of camera shutter / the turning of book pages / the motion of waves / the act of writing.

When Beavers does use musical sounds in his films, they are usually minimal; the single organ note in *Ruskin* and the few bowed notes of a viola in *Notebook* are as close to conventional musical accompaniment as the filmmaker gets.

During my visit to the Temenos Archive in 2013, Beavers shared some of his extensive notes on the sound editing of *Notebook*. They were written at a moment in the 1990s when he was re-making the soundtracks of many of his films. His notes reveal both the adversity he faced and the inventiveness he harnessed in this act of revision.

4.12.97 Work on sound for *the Notebook* has started and it seems as if it will be endless because the image is so complex. [...]

23.12.97 Attention not sustained today. I arrived late, made only one or two changes, went to lunch and almost decided not to return in the afternoon, but I did. Again one or two additions. One of these gave me pleasure; it was my intention to place the sound of the bird's wings in the camera aperture. [...]

4.1.98 First reel is nearly complete. Has it already become too cluttered, too heavy? The only moment of delight is when the bird's wings are heard with the view of the camera shutter in action.

8.1.98 More hopeful. I placed the sound of the chisel with the single frame of the aperture, and this also works. [...]

Sound representing invisible things.

2.4.97 Analogy of waves of water, light and sound.

1. Place the river sound, or other wave sound, in the shadow which I create on my desk and in the camera.

2. Create a pattern; first the sound is heard with the location, then with a note, or in camera or in matte. […]

Sound of water rippling in the curls of hair […] 26.11.97 Use a 'bass-tone' where single color predominates ex: the reds in sweater, in matte, in camera…[22]

RETURNING TO PLACE

Notebook was shot in 1971, astonishingly when Beavers was merely 22 years old. When he decided to re-edit his films, one of his intentions was to shorten the duration of individual films and to sequence them within a cycle: *My Hand Outstretched to the Winged Distance and Sightless Measure.* During this process he realized that the gulf between the image and sound track was simply too wide and required serious attention. Beavers recalls this awareness:

"I have a basic wish that the sound and image will retain a living quality… what's so difficult is to retain the initial energy, the life that you put into it. When I re-edited it was so clear that there was now [as opposed to the perception at the time of original editing] an even bigger gap than before between the image and sound. It has less life, I want to breathe life back into it."[23]

Thus he pursued the enormous task of returning to the original locations with his microphone and DAT recorder to capture sounds afresh. He must have faced substantial obstacles in faithfully retracing his steps, especially since the sonic landscape had radically transformed over the course of the ensuing decades as manufacturing moved east and Northern Europe shifted toward a service and finance economy.

Indeed, an interesting dynamic emerges in the process of re-recording; it severs the temporal link between the film and the sound track. Beavers acknowledges that in some locations the absence of "old sounds" (those he recorded originally) was problematic. It is surprising that he invokes Venice (the setting for *Ruskin*) as an example since it must be one of the few cities in the world devoid of cars. Intriguingly, this temporal rupture between image and sound collection is not especially apparent when watching the final work, underlining, perhaps, just how careful and considered Beavers is in both drawing certain objects toward his gaze and rejecting others.

SOUND SHADOWS

One of the central points of inspiration for me was Leonardo's observation of shadows. I used the surface of my notebook and desk to translate some of his observations into film and also discovered the shadow as a place for sound. Both the matte and shadow are vehicles that join together diverse details of image and sound. (Robert Beavers)[24]

In his 1949 *Theory of the Film*, Balázs notes some of the marked differences between the image and sound in film. He observes that "sounds throw no shadow," "have no sides" and therefore "cannot be isolated" as can a visual detail.[25]

---

22 Robert Beavers, filming notes for the re-editing of *From the Notebook of…*, Temenos Archive.
23 Robert Beavers interview with the author, March 2013.
24 Beavers, *Cinéma exposé*, p. 97.
25 Béla Balázs, "Theory of the Film: Sound," *Film Sound: Theory and Practice*, ed. Weis and Belton, p. 123.

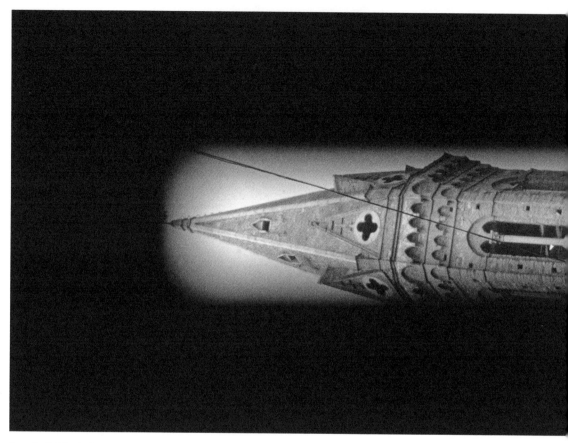

From the Notebook of...

In *Wasted Words,* Michel Chion also invokes the figurative language of light, here discussing the notion of eminent speech, wherein the voice is present but rendered largely unintelligible and indistinct (either because the microphone is off-axis or at too great a distance from the subject). He describes this rarely observed phenomenon as "verbal chiaroscuro."[26]

The incorporation of visual metaphors into explanations of the behavior of sound can lead us astray since sound (and the practice of its recording) has an entirely different grammar than that of light and optics. But in Beavers's films, we find an opportunity to consider this terminology anew; refuting Balázs's certainty to the contrary, we might say that both acoustic sides and sonic shadows are in fact found in abundance in Beavers's sonic montage. As

stated in the above quote, Beavers is drawn to visually shadowed and contoured spaces as a means of providing a place for the image and sound to breathe. In fact he cultivates a method of manufacturing negative space by turning the turret or closing down the camera's shutter. These partially obscured views often provide sound with its own space within the fused film / sound unit.

In his remark that "sound has a space coloring," Balázs infers that each space has its own unique acoustic character.[27] He goes on to discuss how the "space-quality" of a given sound (related to where it was originally recorded) stays with a sound and is integral to the transport of a film spectator to a particular place. Beavers takes this one step further by suggesting that sound and light – the two key components of film – are spatially and phenomenally linked and engaged in mutual impact. He wonders, for instance, about "[s]ound contained in certain materials and brought out of these materials by *light?*"[28] When I asked him to provide an example of this idea, he described the mental image he once had of a wind instrument bathing in a pool of light; he had the feeling that the light itself, rather than human manipulation, could produce sound from the instrument.[29]

MUSICAL NOTES AND NOISE

In this essay, I have attempted to stress the importance of Beavers's contribution to sound montage and in doing so have outlined a historic context for his work through a set of loose, associative reference points.[30] I stress that I write all of this from the position of an artist / film-

26 Michel Chion, "Wasted Words," *Sound Theory, Sound Practice*, ed. Altman, p. 106.
27 Balázs, "Theory," p. 124.
28 Robert Beavers, "Acnode," *Robert Beavers: Die ausgestreckte Hand,* Vienna: Austrian Film Museum, 2010. See also p. 167 in this volume.
29 Beavers states in hindsight that "this idea is really 'far-fetched' because I have never really managed to capture such a quality in a film. The idea is still vital with the hope that one day I may find a way." Robert Beavers e-mail correspondence with the author, September 19, 2016.
30 I am, of course, not the first to remark on this. Markopoulos in his 1971 essay "In Other Words It Is His Tongue" (*Film as Film: The Collected Writings of Gregory J. Markopoulos*, ed. Mark Webber, London: The Visible Press, 2014, p. 304–310) uses the opportunity to herald Beavers as the first filmmaker to realize the true potential for sound in creating a "psychological distance between sound and image." He goes on to note that "Beavers sensed what was needed: sound must stand to image in perfect accord and discord [...] He is a master because he will not use all the sounds that are available to him. It is more than being selective."

maker who has a deep affection for the concerns of Beavers's work and for the sonic in general.

Prior to 2012, Beavers's work was almost completely devoid of conventional uses of sound; instead, as I have argued, he worked in a quietly radical manner with symbolic noises and associative montage. I was surprised, then, to encounter in *Listening to the Space in My Room* (2013) a soundtrack that featured Beavers's own legible voice: he ponders the meaning of a German phrase that has occurred in a dream, for instance – *"ich bin eine andere Person geworden"* (I have become another person) – and repeatedly asks "Who are you?" as we see images of the filmmaker Ute Aurand (Beavers's partner) looking into the camera lens and a nasturtium leaf. The soundtrack features not only this voiceover but solo cello music; diegetic scales are performed by Beavers's elderly neighbor and landlord Dieter Staehelin, who is filmed at home practicing Bach sonatas. The swooshing sound of Staehelin's bow as he limbers up is a vivid reminder of the wings of the released doves in the opening scene of *Notebook* – underlining a recurring motif in Beavers's oeuvre.

In his essay "EM·BLEM," Beavers notes that the "image…is as different from a natural view as a musical note is from noise."[31] As I read it,

this statement implies a clear value judgment, and his apparent dismissal of "noise" seems to stand counter to his practice as a whole. But *Listening*, I think, with its rare featuring of music, offers a chance to reconcile the opposition between "music" and "noise." The film's sound montage constantly vacillates between the acoustic space of the small wooden house and the sound of Staehelin's cello playing. Resisting the inclusion of a finished musical performance to accompany his images, Beavers instead highlights the daily practice of the musician: the sounds of tuning up, the whips of the bow. Contrary to the opposition implied by his statement about the stark "difference" between "musical note" and "noise," the sound montage here suggests instead that they are equivalents – or, as Bresson so presciently observed, "[t]he noises must become music."[32]

At about midpoint in the film we hear the sound of rain – first introduced with black leader and then accompanying a pan as the rain falls on the garden and elephant leaves. This rich and complex soundscape breathes with life and exudes a quality which opens the soundtrack to the outside – to that which is traditionally outside of music (noise) and to the world beyond the visual space of film.

31 Robert Beavers, "EM·BLEM," *The Searching Measure*. See also p. 195 in this volume.
32 Bresson, *Notes*, p. 10.

*Listening to the
Space in My Room*
(2013)

2·1·72 Twenty objects/scenes - Europe
each ten minutes
 The parts controlled by the color
of each object/scene, removed and
modulated by the filters (which
will not be self-apparent as
when used earlier.)
 Remember the filming of the
wheat (?) field on Cos. yellow-blue.

15·3·72 Ice/ outre-tombe / the frozen frame
different images in the mirror
as the camera moves closer

16·3·72 Filmed six hundred feet. Fifty shots.

21·3·72 The object and surrounding space;
the relations are infinite and
in a film one may ~~progress~~ change
for another in the manner that
a single piece of music may be
in more than one key.

8·4·72 Via dei Serragli - the blood crêpes
in October (25·10·72)

12·4·72 Alternate indoor with outdoor

27·4·72 No main title, just the word of
each object before it. Or is this
necessary?

1·5·72 Tentative title: Work Done

1·6·72 Scene/view from Scuol
Add and subtract quantities of blue,
white, and green : sky, snow, trees
Use wratten no. 85 to naturalize the
unfiltered part of frame

1·6·72 10 objects. 10 scenes

List
Ice , river
Blood
Trees, grass
Book, blue flame
Arm
Stones — mountain

1·12·72
200 F ice
300 S river
500 F book
200 S tree
300 F arm
  S mountain
300 F stones
300 F blood (all)
 2 hour
 sixty.

28·5·72 Freeze the last
frame surrounded
by black.
Superimpose the
beginning of next
object/scene?

To reveal the
sense of time in
the making of
the object; and
the sense of when
in the time of the
film, it was made.

Pages from
Beavers's *Work
Done* notebook

15.8.72 The objects are made from elements.

ice   object
river / hill   2 elements
trees, cut   act-object
(book) →
              next: simple act (indoors)
              then first spoken statement (?)

Each part of the film being object, element, or act; or a mixture of these.

20.8.72 The tree is cut : the film is cut
the ice is frozen : the frame is frozen
Each object has its film essence

4.9.72 Filmed 200 ft. of grass location above Bad Ragaz

11.9.72 Each spoken statement starting during the indoor objects and related to the order of Element, Act, Object. Two or three sentences with each having the same word order.

Statements beginning over image(s) of an unopened book

17.9.72 Object : not of value or age.⌉ The book interrupted this intension. (a Latin text)

30.9.72 Vertical pans with camera on the same level as the book, very close. (To be filmed at Bruscoli's)
         (23.10.72 Filmed five hundred feet at Bruscoli's)

9.10.72 The chest, side and arm of a man while he is speaking; the sound will be his words. (see 15.8.72, last part)

25.10.72 Filmed three hundred feet of the blood pancakes.

29.10.72 ~~Reorder~~ Re-order the footage to form the object on the screen

                element (act) object (statement)
        to equal the form of film making (20.8.72)
              filming editing printing projection
                           frendily

Work Done (1972/1999)

Ricardo Matos Cabo

A Single Image

Two Versions of Work Done *(1972, 1999)*

How was the strength found to gather the images? From within a solitude of being, enduring/accepting the moment when a single color is the only sign of feeling in an environment of which all else is opposition... (Robert Beavers)[1]

Robert Beavers completed *Work Done* in 1972 and re-edited it in 1999 for inclusion in his cycle *My Hand Outstretched to the Winged Distance and Sightless Measure*. Most of the films included in this encompassing series were first finished in the 1970s and 80s and many were shortened and re-composed for the cycle. *Work Done* has always struck me as not only one of the strongest of Beavers's films but one that marks a shift in the way the filmmaker practiced his craft. It follows a first period in Beavers's filmmaking – one that includes *Diminished Frame* (1970) and *From the Notebook of...* (1971) – that is distinguished by the primacy of biographical details (including those of his life in Europe with Gregory Markopoulos) and a distinct and single driving subjectivity. While true to the structural and compositional principles that guided Beavers's earlier practice (including the embrace of mattes and filters), *Work Done* displays

not only a newly found economy of elements (it is composed of fewer images and sounds than earlier films) but a trust in the nature of encounters among the filmmaker, his camera and the locations, people and objects he films; the film relies more on improvisation than on predetermined rules.

Work Done was shot in a variety of locations in Florence and the Alps. The film is composed of images of both interior spaces – a *bottega* where a block of ice sits inside a vault, a book binding workshop, a room in which a man's naked torso is subject to shifts in light and focus, a small restaurant kitchen in which a fried blood delicacy is prepared – and exterior ones: an alpine landscape with a river running through it, a dark forest where trees are felled, an imposing mountain, a city street with some type of construction going on. But when I returned to the original version of *Work Done*, I was surprised by its stark difference from the 1999 film. In the first version, each of the above locations is self-contained and kept separate from the others: there is a *bottega* sequence, a book binding one, etc. The only break in this pattern occurs at the end of the film where there is a single integrated sequence that combines shots from all the previous clusters except that of the initial ice block. The final version of

1 Robert Beavers, "Editing and the Unseen," *Millennium Film Journal*, No. 32/33, Fall 1998, p. 39. For a later version of this text, see p. 198 in this volume.

Work Done

Work Done, however, sees Beavers revisiting the images and sounds he had made in 1972, subjecting them to a structuring principle of fragmentation and filtering them through a more explicit theme of memory.

Beavers expresses his thoughts about the structure of the first version of *Work Done* by describing an in-the-moment response to the dominant objects and acts in each of his locations as he shot them: "[H]ow the filming could itself suggest the form of the object that I was filming – to film more carefully and to reach the clearest composition and length for each image. It wasn't edited in the camera, but I tried to have every action realized in relation to the object during the filming." He goes on to articulate the achievement of "unity" among these various objects and locations: "I began with an image of a block of ice, then went to the transformation of the solid element in the next image, which was a river. Then I filmed the cutting of trees, followed by the binding of a book.

Each object was seen in itself and the unity was implied. In the first version, I did not intercut any of the scenes until the last element, the blood, is introduced and then I intercut with all of the earlier elements except the ice. It was as if I were saying that it needed all of these images to represent the ice in the film. This is one way of seeing it."[2]

The relation between the filmed objects and actions and the film image creates a tension that works through the entirety of *Work Done*. Beavers's focus on the to-be-filmed object facilitates a process of discovery whereby the immediate, material qualities of things are put in relation with the actual filmmaking tools available in the moment of shooting. His processes of composition-making are made plainly articulate, inseparable from the objects and spaces represented: camera movements (via tripod or

2 Tony Pipolo, "An interview with Robert Beavers," *Millennium Film Journal*, No. 32/33, Fall 1998, p. 11.

hand), the scale and length of shots, the distance between the camera and the filmed object, the effects of naturally changing light, the use of filters and mattes. In each segment, Beavers chooses a particular grammar of apparatus-use as a direct response to the subject matter or the object he is trying to describe. The prominent element or action (ice block, bookbinding) determines the very *way* the images are composed.

In the initial sequence, for instance, the space of the *bottega* is described with the block of ice in mind; everything is filmed as a set of distances from and relationships to it. The filmmaker approaches the ice block and then moves back to show different details of the space where he found it: posters, signs written in Italian, a metal hook in the ceiling, a door knob. The ice is bright as if lit from some exterior light source (or, conversely, as if it had a light of its own). When the camera gets closer, we can see the ice beginning to melt; as it fills

the frame, the ice also becomes an abstraction, a source of composition for later shots in the same segment, including the joining arches of the vaulted ceiling and the shot of a door framing a black rectangle (a negative mirror image of the ice).

In the next group of images, the filmmaker seems to be playing with the conventions of classical landscape representation; the camera surveys the place with fast shots panning up and down, left and right movements creating chromatic fields of green and blue. The river running through a mountainous valley is shown both from afar and very close, becoming surface and color. In another sequence, a distorted, out-of-focus tableau slowly clarifies to reveal a dark forest where trees are being felled. Later, we see an antique book being bound; its pages are shot in extreme close-up and act as a focal plane, allowing the filmmaker to reveal, in selected focus, various aspects of the printed text. In the following sequence, we see the isolated and naked torso of a man who appears to be standing, in tension. The body in this intimate section is defined by its silhouette as the man is shown against shifting light that originates from a window behind him. As the camera gets very close to the body, we can see the texture of skin, perceive the rhythm of breathing. Our gaze is drawn into the hollowed space between the man's arm and body, a dark gap that changes slightly with each movement and is transformed by the light that passes through it.

The way Beavers conceives of the material and sensual encounter with a given location and object is best described in a text he wrote about *Efpsychi* (1983/1996), a film I see as linked to *Work Done* in its representation of ordinary objects: "Parallel to the face is the space of the wholesale stores and workshops below street level. These spaces possess shadows that rise and descend like waves; a space built for escaping the destructive forces of heat and light, the fire of light that slowly dissolves everything. Heat, weight and light interact to create the sense of movement in still objects. I see how an object, resting its weight and pressing down on the ground, possesses a movement; this invisible gravity is equivalent to quiet desire. It gains serenity through the light, heat and silence in these spaces."[3] Beavers's films are records of encounters, and every image, in its rendering of a face, place or an object, is an expression of memory and fleeting desire.

There is a sense of revelation pervading the images and sounds in *Work Done* that seems to emanate from the things themselves. The reasons *why* a shot was made in a particular way are not always evident – but the objects in the film appear with both a striking clarity and a mystery that doesn't vanish after several viewings. I mention mystery, but there is nothing *obscure* about this film (or about Beavers's work).

~

In the 1999 version, the filmmaker revisits the same images and sounds he had edited more than 20 years earlier, subjecting them to a new paradigm of temporality and sequencing. Every scene is now composed of fewer, and shorter, shots than in the first version (the entire film is also shorter – now 22 rather than 34 minutes). But paradoxically, the scenes simultaneously expand as they are intercut by images of other scenes; instead of assembling his sequences as a series of self-contained units of time and space, Beavers mingles images from one location with those of another in a play of ongoing intercuts. The sewing frame used to hold the book together in the third scene could be seen as a model for the film's structure: the five cords tensely hold the loose pages that are bound together by an interweaving thread. As the sequences and the objects in them (things, places, bodies, gestures) interpenetrate each other, a new *sense of movement* emerges from a play of differences: between the represented elements themselves, their qualities (solidity and liquidity, weight and lightness) and via an ongoing narrative of transformation.

3 Robert Beavers, "Efpsychi." A slightly different version of this text was published in *My Hand Outstretched: Films by Robert Beavers*, New York: Whitney Museum, 2005, p. 6–7.

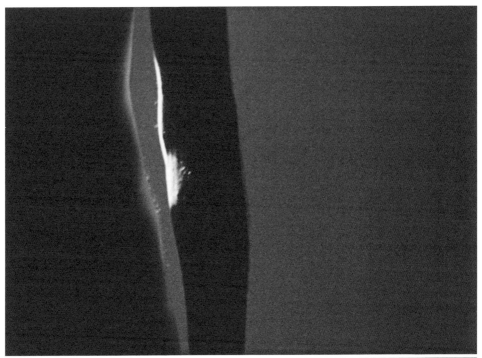

Work Done

The first version of *Work Done* is mostly silent, punctuated occasionally by seemingly non-diegetic sounds. In the 1999 version, however, sound becomes an organizing, structuring principle and a vital component of the energy that facilitates the ongoing interpenetration of images. Not only are there many more diegetic sound events in the second version (Beavers recorded new sound during the re-edit), but the passage from one image to another is facilitated via associative sound work.

For instance, the sound of moving water (which will later emerge in concert with its apparent source image, the rushing river) is first associated with the slowly melting block of ice in the initial sequence; it also bridges the cut between the final *bottega* shot and the first mountain/river one. Similarly, the sound of a gas stove hiss precedes a brief image of the associated flames (part of the bookbinding apparatus) further forward in the film. The use of sound in the re-edited version both heightens the sense of location (both in association with and opposition to given images) and suggests a human presence off-screen through the slightly indistinct voices, steps, clanking doors.

As mentioned, the first ice block sequence remains a single unit of time and space in the second version. But the landscape shots in the second sequence are intercut with images from the following bookbinding sequence. This pattern continues, with each sequence containing fragments of and announcing the one that will come next, until the final scene, which brings together images of all the previous scenes – except, importantly, that of the ice block. It is a missing image, evoked *in absentia*. This final sequence is like a wheel of memory, reactivating a selection of images: the landscape and running water, the book being bound, a tree falling in the forest, the naked torso – a kaleidoscope of changing gestures, locations, textures, colors and materials thus united through montage. As Beavers constructs the film as a series of incisions in time, *Work Done*'s singular beauty lies in this balance between physical absence and the presence-generating work of memory. Interruption and gaps in continuity play an important role in many of Beavers's films; fragmentation in his cinema is, however, not a form of incompleteness, but a way to recompose the world in its unity. Interrupted actions are always completed in the end: a book is bound, a tree is felled, the blood is cooked, the filmmaker's work is done.

Objects and actions in *Work Done* are put together through a play of associations that suggest changes in state – melting ice turns into running water, chopped wood and splinters into paper, skin and pavement stones into blood. In the kitchen sequence (the final one before the integrated last sequence), images from the preparation of blood pancakes (bright red liquid, dollops of lard, the black disk of fried blood) trigger a series of associations, equivalences and oppositions that reach back into previous scenes in the film, importing images both intact and fragmented in a play of memory and recognition. More important than a scientific analysis of each associative act is an understanding of the way objects, words and gazes spread themselves imperceptibly. This, I think,

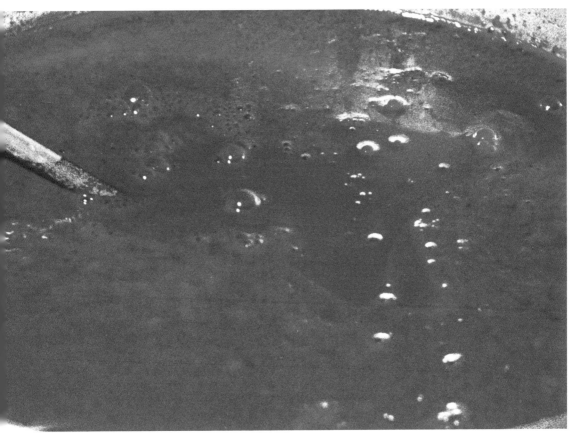

Work Done

is a productive way to approach how composition and editing work in *Work Done*.

~

When I think about Beavers's films, I often remember them via single images (a hand touching a leaf, a pair of scissors cutting through cloth, a turning page of a notebook, a naked male body diving into the water) and sounds (the fluttering of wings, the cracking open of a window, a word repeated [*teleftea,* Greek for "the last one"]) – sometimes fleeting, but always precise and haunting. I also recall poetic procedures, especially the use of interruption-as-meaning and fracture-as-form. I have come to see Beavers as inviting the spectator to engage self-consciously with the work of memory. He has written about the "delays with which certain images reveal their worth," something that *Work Done* exemplifies beautifully.[4] As with some poetry, these images become stronger as acts of remembrance; they are obstinate, they resurface again and again as singular, sensual and powerful events.

I also remember images of suspended gestures in Beavers's films – especially that of the cellist prepared to play his instrument in *Listening to the Space in My Room* (2013). His hand holds the bow in tension before hitting the strings, a performance that will not occur until later in the film. Such a gesture seems to contain the potential of everything that is to come:

not only the music, but all the elements of the film we are about to watch. There are many of these moments in Beavers's work, image fragments that anticipate the revelation of a full event or location, gestures and actions on the cusp of conclusion: two hands about to clap, a hand touching something or someone, the open blades of a pair of scissors before cutting cloth, lips about to pronounce a word.

These thoughts on the isolated and suspended image lead me to query just how the filmmaker brings his images and sounds together in *Work Done*. I return to Beavers's earlier-quoted remark that, in *Work Done*, "[i]t was as if I were saying that [I] needed all of these images to represent the ice in the film." In order to maximally describe and conjure the ice and to produce a unified film form, the filmmaker turned to association among the other elements in the film.

I have come to think of the *single image* not only in terms of my own memory of images from Beavers's films but with respect to his reflection on the "[implied] unity" of *Work Done* and the ultimate condensation, in the single image of the block of ice, of every other sound and image in the film. Each object offers a challenge to the filmmaker; he must find the correct means to show it and express its presence. To concentrate in a single image is a mode of attention, a quality that is at the heart of the poetics of Beavers's cinema.

4 Robert Beavers, "EM·BLEM," *The Searching Measure,* Berkeley: UC Berkeley Art Museum and Pacific Film Archive, 2004. See also p. 195 in this volume.

P. Adams Sitney

Masked Rhythm in *Ruskin*

Robert Beavers's masterpiece *Ruskin* (1975/ 1997) presents views and details of Venice in exquisite cinematic rhythms, occasionally cutting away to images from the streets of London or the Swiss Alps, in an homage to John Ruskin, the great critic and essayist. In the best study of the film yet printed, Tony Pipolo wrote of its aesthetic majesty in these terms: "[my essay] can only hint at its great beauty and richness…Perhaps the most remarkable achievement of the film is its extraordinary balance between the value given to individual images and the film's formative impulse…Cuts seem preternaturally timed and charged with the pulse of the filmmaker's attentions…"[1]

In *Eyes Upside Down*, I wrote of the film in the context of its place in *My Hand Outstretched to the Winged Distance and Sightless Measure,* Beavers's three-part cycle of films, and in relation to its wide range of literary and artistic references.[2] Here I would prefer to pick up on the direction where Pipolo pointed, by concentrating on its rhythmic and visual qualities, for they are extraordinary and unique. Anyone familiar

with Beavers's other films would recognize his style immediately. The description of the parameters of that style is the task of this essay. I shall concentrate on the opening six minutes of the film, which is composed of approximately 60 shots ranging in length from less than one to 20 seconds.

The film begins in the Venetian lagoon, isolates the campanile of Torcello, examines the landscape of islands in the lagoon and moves briefly to a busy street in London (Portland Place) before concentrating on details of the façades of buildings on Venetian canals. Before four minutes have elapsed, the filmmaker introduces shots of a mountainous terrain in the Val Bregaglia of Switzerland, and subsequently gives us several shots of Campo San Beneto, a small Venetian piazza with pigeons. Throughout the opening six minutes, the image of a black book (one of three volumes of John Ruskin's *The Stones of Venice*) appears; it is lying flat on a table or a hand lifts it up or places it down, moving the volume with the palm flat on its cover. By the end of the film we will glimpse the Victorian critic's *Unto This Last* as if it were the very book we first saw on the table.

The first six minutes of *Ruskin* are typical of the whole film. Later there are a few brief shots

1 Tony Pipolo, "*Ruskin*: A Film by Robert Beavers," *Millennium Film Journal*, No. 32/33, Fall 1998, p. 61–69.

2 P. Adams Sitney, *Eyes Upside Down: Visionary Filmmakers and the Heritage of Emerson*, New York: Oxford University Press, 2008, p. 164–169.

of familiar monuments in Venice: the Gothic Ducal Palace seen across the Grand Canal from San Giorgio and the Romanesque Duomo of Murano; there are also several returns to Portland Place in London, and glimpses of gorgeous Swiss landscapes and a mountain village. At the end of the film, Beavers whirls through pages of *Unto this Last*, too fast to read the sentences, but one can make out words and phrases.

From the outset Beavers presents us with a place or places that are at once concretely real and utterly imaginary, geographical sites and mere images. That is not a new strategy in his cinema. From early on he used hand-made masks and filters to delimit, circumscribe, and divide his cinematic images. Not only does he use the masks to reshape what he films; he films the masks themselves, sometimes in motion, sometimes statically. In calling attention to the masks he simultaneously, but inversely, directs attention to the "natural" framing of the camera when no masks are employed. Or rather, to the fact that motion picture cameras have always used a rectangular mask behind the circle of the lens to shape the filmic image into a space bounded by right angles, no matter what the aspect ratio at which it is projected.

Inventive masking played a significant role in the films Beavers made between *Plan of Brussels* (1968/2000) and *From the Notebook of...* (1971/1998), culminating in the complex page-turning form of the latter. In *Ruskin,* the first mask, a black oval centered in a white field, appears in the seventh shot. It initiates a brief sequence of nine shots, lasting a little over half a minute.[3] Only two of them do not utilize the oval mask. In the first, the filmmaker makes the mask slowly enlarge by progressively lowering the exposure; then with the next shot, after a few seconds of blackness in which we hear the falling of water, we see a lagoon landscape within the oval shape created by the mask, with blackness surrounding it: the virtual negative of the previous masking. The next shot brackets the landscape image by a reversal of the exposure shift (now brightening) on the mask itself to return it to its original size.

Subsequently, the landscape first seen within the oval returns, now filling the rectangle of the conventional frame. This is the first of two shots in the series of nine without a mask. The next two are very rapid: the full mask lying on a black background, then an even quicker vertical flutter, which the filmmaker executed by twisting the lens with the matte box in place; in effect, one lens rapidly replaces another. The vertical move is followed by an image of a small lagoon island masked by the oval frame; and, after another exposure shift on the mask to enlarge it, the same island appears full frame (the ninth shot in this series).

Let us call for convenience the sequences so far a stanza, even though the film rigorously eschews the segmentation that stanzas give to poems. The alternation of isolated masks with masked and unmasked views of the Venetian lagoon gives eloquent rhythmic expression to the reality of the location, to its solemn beauty,

3 Due to the nature of Beavers's shooting techniques and editing, shot beginnings and endings are sometimes ambiguous.

Ruskin (1975/1997)

Ruskin

and at the same time to the apperception of the filmmaker catching himself in the act of fashioning images, weighing and testing them. As he follows one shot by another, he manages to overlap evidence of his judgment of both the cinematic illusion and the palpable actuality of the water, land masses, vegetation, and architecture. If this had previously been the distinctive feature of Beavers's cinema, it attains its fullest articulation in *Ruskin*.

This opening 'stanza' sets up that double consciousness by implementing a new cinematic strategy from the start. Very frequently throughout *Ruskin*, Beavers rotates the lens turret while the film is running in the camera, making the whole screen image float up off to the right or sink below the frame on the left, depending on which way he twists the turret. He had experimented with this technique earlier, as we can see in *Early Monthly Segments* (1968–1970/2002), but in *Ruskin* he employs it extensively and with a formative valence. Sometimes he does not twist the turret completely but dislocates the lens so that it registers a partial image under or above a black arc on the frame where the turret mechanism blocks off the light. He offers the very first image of the film this way, with an arch of blackness over the lagoon inlets; it produces a dome of grey sky touching the horizon line at the right and left. Although we can hear the movement of waves, the water we see is still. But the next shot, a full-frame view of a different lagoon spot, captures

the breaking of a small wave in the far distance, simulating synchronous sound. We next see the same location, a little further back, until the image quickly lifts offscreen. Whereas the previous shot remained for 10 seconds, this one rose and disappeared into blackness after four. Just as it left, a corresponding downward movement of the turret brought the campanile down from above the frame line for not quite three seconds. Since the shot ends as soon as the turret movement ceases, it resembles a downward pan. The full-frame shot of the same campanile from a distance seems long at 13 seconds. The sudden silence terminating the sea sounds, audible thus far, emphasizes that duration. The filmmaker completes the sequence by twisting the turret in the opposite direction from a reflection of the tower in the water, up its height for four seconds.

At different times Tony Pipolo and I have asked Beavers what the twisting lens turret meant to him. He responded:

"This turning of the lens becomes a means for catching the double movement of sight. In a number of films, I have balanced this lens movement or a camera movement with the movement of the figure or object coming into the frame.[4] I believe that it [the previously invoked 'double movement' of sight] has something to do with being aware of the edges of our field of vision. I could also mention that much later I was impressed by William James's statement that consciousness of self could be represented by looking in a mirror and describing the tilts of the head and neck. Basically this means that when I turn the lens on the turret upwards,

4 Tony Pipolo, "Interview with Robert Beavers," *Millennium Film Journal*, No. 32/33, p. 15.

what we see is a movement like a small pan upwards & at the same time we see the curve of the lens moving downwards. I have for a long time thought that this is like both seeing something come into view by moving your eyes and seeing at the same time the movement of the eyes [themselves]."[5]

However, as I intimated earlier, the stanzaic division is potentially misleading. The soundtrack belies it: The silence of the previous two campanile shots (the fifth and sixth of the film) carries over for a few seconds into the image of the black oval mask, but as the exposure changes to enlarge the oval, the sea sound returns. It is silenced by the oval-framed landscape only to repeat with the reversing of the size of the mask both times we see it. Until the book appears, the only other sound we hear is the flapping of bird wings or the fluttering of book pages. But without any suggestion of synchronism, that sound appears over the brief lens and matte effect I previously called a "vertical flutter."

The second stanza might be said to begin with the thud of its hitting the table that accompanies the image of the book (even though that action is not shown as it is at other times). A single note from an organ follows the thud. The play of synchronous and asynchronous sound within that shot reflects the shifts between the illusions of auditory realism and the confessions of authorial manipulation that occur throughout the film. Beavers achieves this most frequently by the simple alternation of one shot (with apparently ambient sound) with another shot of the same location (in si-

lence). Thus he places a shot of Portland Place with traffic sounds in London before one with silence; likewise, in Venice, we hear workers whistling on the sidewalks of a canal or water lapping against the buildings one time, and another time the same places appear in silence. At times the flapping of bird wings accompanies a Swiss landscape where there are no birds, but on another occasion the same sound is heard as pigeons fly onto a Venetian piazza.

The organ sounds 10 times during the film. Three of those notes occur in rapid succession 30 minutes into the film. (It does not recur in the final eight.) If we allow those organ notes to mark what I have been calling stanzaic breaks, then the units are irregular. The first four instances accompany some of the images of the book (at 1:50, 3:30, 7:13, and 9:32 minutes). But the fifth covers the transition from a Swiss landscape to an oval mask at 18 minutes. The next one can be heard as we see a young man swagger down a London street (22:06). Then, just before another image of the book appears, the organ sounds over a foggy cityscape of Venice, filmed through the lens halfway turned on the turret, causing the image to appear below a black arc on the screen. Typically the filmmaker first builds up the expectation that the organ sounds belong with the book, and that they will recur at increasingly longer intervals, only to change the pace later as the rhythmic and image materials grow more complex. Similarly, his extensive use of the twisting turret,

5 Robert Beavers e-mail correspondence with the author, November 2, 2015.

and perhaps some panning up-and-down movements, lures us into the assurance that any camera movement will be on a vertical axis. There is even a shot of a façade taken apparently from a gondola or an anchored raft where the rising and falling of waves in the canal gives the camera an up-and-down movement. This vertical consistency lends a striking emphasis to a series of horizontal pans made in a busy Venetian piazza some 25 minutes into the film.

It would not be until what we might cautiously call the second stanza, by allowing the book and organ synchronism to mark the stanza breaks, that the locale shifts from Venice and its watery environs to London. In this same grouping of images, shots of Venetian buildings on a canal shift between black and white and color, with alternations of sound and silence. The flickering reflections of light on the water and on the stone walls extend a counter-rhythm across the musical pacing of the shot changes. Not every shot in this section records the vibrations of the light on Venetian surfaces, but enough do to make it a dominant organizing principle. In just this way, the third and even longer 'stanza' would be marked by triangular shapes within the rectangle of the frame. Many of them are created by diagonal masks blocking – usually – the upper part of the screen. But they rhyme with beautiful patches of light falling like isosceles and scalene triangles on the pavement of a piazza or on the water of a canal. Even the image of the book, with the filmmaker's hand on it, which I take to conclude the first section of this stanza, is interrupted by a diagonal mask bisecting the screen into two triangles with the lower right in black.

What Beavers does in the opening minutes of *Ruskin* he does throughout the film. In this he differs from his master, Gregory Markopoulos, who always asserts his authorial hand with an insistent montage rhythm imposed upon images packed with sensuality. Nor is Beavers's testing of the reality of the world before him like that of Stan Brakhage, who projects his colossal subjectivity through shifts of focus, fast swishes of the camera, and subtle movements within and at the borders of the frame. Curiously, he shares with Ernie Gehr, the other preeminent filmmaker of his generation, an implicit faith in the need to find an apposite rhythm for each new film. The closest work I know to the achievement and ambition of *Ruskin* would be Gehr's *Side/Walk/Shuttle* (1992). In that film Gehr shoots the San Francisco skyscape from the outside elevator of a high-rise hotel. Running takes upside down, backwards, and with different sounds, he examines, declares, and tests the substantiality of the city, more dramatically than Beavers does, but like him he foregrounds cinematic rhythm as the basis of meaning.

In *Ruskin* Beavers demonstrated his precocious genius, his astonishing originality, while at the same time acknowledging a stronger and more personal affiliation to the European cultural tradition than any creator of the American avant-garde cinema.

Amor (1980)

James Macgillivray

Tectonics and Space

Architectural Thought in the Films of Robert Beavers

TECTONICS

Il me faut dire quelque part que des monuments
comme le Parthénon, ou la Maison Carrée, ou
n'importe quel monument comportant un péristyle
à colonnes, évoque le plus adéquatement, dans
l'ordre de l'architecture, un instrument à cordes.
Car il y a, sur le devant, les colonnes tendues
commes les cordes de la lyre (par exemple), et
derrière, le temple ou la maison elle-même, c'est-
à-dire la caisse de résonance. (Francis Ponge)[1]

The room in the title of Robert Beavers's *Lis-*
tening to the Space in My Room (2013) is on the
ground floor of a house that the filmmaker
shared with an elderly cellist, Dieter Staehelin,
and his wife, Cécile. Before it was occupied by
the Staehelins, the structure was used for agri-

cultural purposes, and before that it housed a
small textile manufacture. The Swiss architect
Oskar Burri had initially intended to establish
an artists' community in the small neighborhood in Zumikon, a town on the outskirts of
Zurich, but was only able to build four houses
there, including the Staehelins' renovation in
1962. Burri's work on the building was extensive; it mostly involved converting the industrial space for habitation, but also adding
columns to the first and third floors where the
structure of the slabs was not sufficient due to
differential settlement in the foundation.[2] Early
in the film, Beavers is heard to say "each column made of a tree trunk" as the dark knotted
wood of one of the columns fills the center of
the screen. It is one of the tree trunk columns of
Burri's renovation.

For Burri, a column made from a tree must
have been a stark contrast from the white *pilo-*
tis he would have been exposed to in his ap-
prenticeship at Le Corbusier's office. It's likely
that the trunk presented the simplest and most
economical option but also a satisfying resolution of the factory building and its natural setting. The straightforward transformation from
living tree to architectural column provides an
interesting counterpoint to other themes of
making in Beavers's work. In *Work Done*

1 "I must say that monuments like the Parthenon, or the
Maison Carrée, or any monument consisting of a peri-
style with columns evokes most appropriately, in the
realm of architecture, a stringed instrument. For there
are, on the front, tight columns like the strings of the
lyre (for example), and behind, the temple or the house
itself, which is to say the resonance chamber." Francis
Ponge, *Pour Un Malherbe*, Paris: Gallimard, 1965,
p. 188–189. Author's translation in consultation with
P. Alan Meadows, *Francis Ponge and the Nature of*
Things: From Ancient Atomism to a Modern Poetics,
Lewisburg: Bucknell University Press, 1997, p. 61.

2 Robert Beavers interview with the author, October 22,
2015.

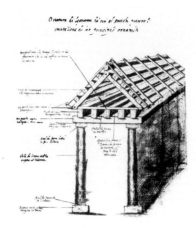
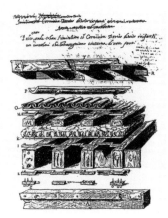

Fig. 1   Fig. 2

(1972/1999), for example, the filmmaker contemplates the processes that turn the turbulent waters of a river into a block of ice, mountain rock into the cobble stones of an urban street and a stand of green trees into the stacked and bound pages of a book. Burri's column is not subject to any such transformative process; it is still the trunk of a tree and also, now, something which we call a column. Yet the tree trunk column is not only of interest for the labor of construction that it represents but also as a reference to the origins of Hellenic architectural form and ornament, origins that carry through the Roman, Renaissance and Baroque architectures that figure so prominently in Beavers's films. Films like *Amor* (1980), *Ruskin* (1975/1997), *From the Notebook of...* (1971/1998) and *The Hedge Theater* (1986–90/2002) not only depict the material and space of canonical Western architec-

ture (descended of Greek origins), but they do so with an unparalleled sensitivity and awareness of the architectural thought that went into those forms and spaces, one which I hope to clarify in the following pages. When these architectural forms relate to their archetype, the classical Greek orders, they do so in ways that innovate and sometimes contradict their origins. At the same time, the Greek orders themselves are a stone translation of what was originally a wood-based construction. The tree trunk column in *Listening* short circuits the centuries of formal allusion in Western architecture by presenting an unadorned version of the earliest Greek column, the trunk of a tree.

De architectura (c. 15 BC), the first recorded architectural treatise by the Roman Vitruvius, establishes the origins of architecture in the rudimentary wood structure that came to be known as the primitive hut. He describes a pre-architectural building culture where early humans "erected forked uprights, and weaving twigs in between they covered the whole with mud."[3] But Vitruvius does not go on to explain the development of the masonry form of ancient Greek architecture from this primitive model. Indeed, when the Greeks translated the details of their own wood construction into the sculpted forms of stone, they severed ties with the strictly mechanical nature of the joinery.[4] As a result, there is an abiding anxiety in architectural theory derived from the archetype of Hellenic form; we have the built form of the Greek temple, and from Vitruvius, the notion of a wooden origin, but the precise correlation between the two becomes a hermeneutic dilemma for architects starting in the Renaissance. Attempts to articulate lines of connection from the primitive to the classical vary: For example, in 1568, Gherardo Spini published a

treatise containing several plates that attribute all elements of the orders (the cornice, dentils, frieze, architrave, triglyph, etc.) to distinct wood forms resulting from a comprehensive but still theoretical structural system (Fig. 1).[5] In 1755, Marc-Antoine Laugier's *Essai sur l'Architecture* elaborated on Vitruvius's "forked uprights" with the addition of a pediment-shaped roof and foliage at the joint between column and roof suggestive of the acanthus leaves in the capital of a Corinthian column (Fig. 2).

TECTONICS: KARL BÖTTICHER
AND *THE HEDGE THEATER*

The primitive hut figures very strongly in Beavers's film *The Hedge Theater*. The film weaves between architectural settings (two of Francesco Borromini's masterpieces, San Carlo alle Quattro Fontane and Sant'Ivo in Rome) and images of man-made structures in nature, one a *roccolo* outside Brescia and the other an outdoor theater in the Mirabell Gardens in Salzburg. Early in the film, the camera lingers on the composite column capitals of the exterior pilasters at San Carlo and intercuts these shots with images of the tree canopy of a *roccolo*, a netted circular enclosure of trees for catching birds. As in Laugier's famous print, the leaves in the canopy of the grove of trees point to the natural and ancient origins of the sculpted acanthus leaves at the top of Borromini's columns. The light of the sky coming through the canopy of the *roccolo* looks similar to the coffering of Borromini's dome (Fig. 3). Later the double columns in the courtyard of the church are compared to the doubled trunk

3 Vitruvius Pollio, *Vitruvius: Ten Books on Architecture*, ed. and trans. Ingrid D. Rowland, New York: Cambridge University Press, 1999, p. 34.

4 This is readily seen in the shaft of the column: In wood construction, the shaft would have been a single piece – the trunk of a tree. At the capital, timbers came together in complex joints of three or more pieces. In the translation to masonry construction, the shaft is made up of short cylindrical sections whose size is a function of their weight. The capital, where the column joined to the beam and roof, is often rendered from a single piece of stone, obscuring the joint while transcribing its outward appearance in a kind of three-dimensional silhouette. This adherence to outward appearance without inward consistency introduced an ambiguous relationship between structure, construction and ornament.

5 Hanno-Walter Kruft, *A History of Architectural Theory from Vitruvius to the Present*, London: Zwemmer, 1994, p. 96.

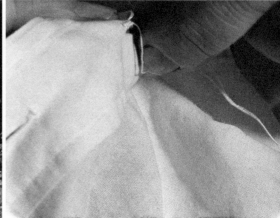

Fig. 3, 4

of a tree set apart from the others. These analogies to primitive enclosures in *The Hedge Theater* substantiate a direct lineage from pre-architectural origins, the simple but persuasive myth of the primitive hut. However, other analogies in the film are far more sophisticated and take advantage of the ambiguity of architectural form.

Within the discourse of architecture, attempts to clarify the intersection between structure, construction and ornament are referred to under the rubric of *tectonics*. In the 19th century, with the beginnings of modern archaeology and the opening of Greece following independence, German theorists sought to make more systematic claims on Greek ornament but also more broadly on tectonics as a distinct part of architectural thought. The archaeologist Karl Bötticher delineated the relationship between structure and ornament. In his major work *Tektonik der Hellenen* (1844), he theorized the Greek formal orders as having *Kernform* and *Kunstform*,

that is a *core-form*, pertaining to the mechanical or structural purpose, and an *art-form*, a decorative symbol which often references the origins of wood construction.[6] One of Bötticher's more famous examples is that of the cyma, a moulding course that joins together the different strata in the Doric entablature. Bötticher noted that when it occurs higher up in the entablature (with less weight above it), the cyma is still a steeper and more vertical profile; when it occurs lower, its profile is shallower and more horizontal, as if it had been compressed by the greater weight of the elements above it.[7] The forces inside the stone of the

6 Wolfgang Herrmann, *Gottfried Semper: In Search of Architecture*, Cambridge: MIT Press, 1984, p. 143. Original text in German: Karl Bötticher, *Die Tektonik der Hellenen*, Vol. 1, Potsdam: Riegel, 1844, p. XV.
7 Gottfried Semper, *Style in the Technical and Tectonic Arts, or, Practical Aesthetics*, trans. Harry F. Mallgrave and Michael Robinson, Los Angeles: Getty Research Institute, 2004, p. 40.

cyma, which transfer gravity loads from a wider portion to a more narrow one, bring forth a core-form which fulfills this structural function. At the same time, through the plastic medium of stone, the art-form of the cyma translates this purpose into a symbolic expression of its function. The symbol enlivens the stone by analogy, making it appear to behave like a material other than stone which reacts to larger gravity loads by splaying out. Thus in Greek tectonics, "the intention is not to characterize the stone as dead stone but, on the contrary, to let the dead substance of the stone fade away... As soon as the stone is covered by a form analogous to its idea [i.e., an art-form], the concept of the stone has disappeared and that of the analogue takes its place."[8]

All this is to say that when Beavers trains his camera on the Renaissance, Baroque and Rococo architectural objects of Rome, he is framing subject matter that is uniquely suited and already subject to several layers of analogy. In *The Hedge Theater*, for example, among the shots of San Carlo and the *roccolo*, Beavers introduces the image of a buttonhole being sewn

in a white shirt (Fig. 4). With respect to analogy between the bird trap and church forms, P. Adams Sitney reads a shared trajectory toward the sky and ceiling as suggestive of the possibility "that the church might be a cage to catch the Holy Ghost or, conversely, the Holy Ghost's snare for human souls."[9] However, there is a complimentary gravitational movement in the film toward the ground, embodied in the form of the button. Once we have seen the sewing of the buttonhole several times, the tectonic aspects of the church take on a new tactile quality and clarity. When the camera's view moves down a column and comes to rest at the base, the analogy to the buttonhole has imbued the image and the stopping of downward movement with the structural performance of the spread base of the column; the circular column might be pushed into the soft ground by the vertical loads of the building above it were it not for its wider button-like base. In another shot of the *roccolo*, Beavers again compares the base of the column to the primitive hut, showing the bottom of the rudimentary structure of sticks sunken in the ground. Just as Bötticher described the different profiles of the cymae reacting to the varying gravitational loads they took from the entablature, Beavers amplifies the symbolic aspects of the column's art-form while making palpable the core-form of its structural performance in equilibrium. Inherent in this analogy is an identification with objects based on the axis of gravitational forces. It is through our upright stature and experience of gravity that we feel the forces going through the column, as if we were a caryatid in its place.[10]

8 Herrmann, *Gottfried Semper*, p. 143. Original text in German: Bötticher, Vol. 2, p. 29.

9 P. Adams Sitney, *Eyes Upside Down: Visionary Film-makers and the Heritage of Emerson*, New York: Oxford University Press, 2008, p. 364.

10 Inherent in this analogy is an empathy for objects that approaches the poetry of Francis Ponge, one of Beavers's favorite poets. It could just as easily be compared to the architectural sensibility of someone like Louis Kahn; his famous query of brick ("What do you want, Brick?") was the beginning of a reinvention of tectonics and ornament in modern masonry construction.

James Macgillivray

Moreover, in the modern house of *Listening to the Space in My Room*, with its reframing of the tree column, we can see even more expression of structural loads and gravitational forces; Beavers's camera pans down the wooden columns with the same movement used in *The Hedge Theater*, but the forces inside the tree trunk columns are far less stable than those in San Carlo. While Beavers was living at the Staehelins' house, he noted that the hillside it was built into was constantly in the motion of settlement. In other words, the movements in the soil that made the columns necessary in the first place are still at work, leading to an imbalance in the vertical and horizontal axes of the house. This instability is especially present in the diagonal camera movements looking at the windows where the shots appear equally unmoored from the vertical of the jamb and the horizontal of the sill.

TECTONICS: GOTTFRIED SEMPER,
WORK DONE AND AMOR

Contemporary with Bötticher, the architect Gottfried Semper also developed a theory of tectonics, although it was not limited to the Greek orders but applied more broadly to the influence of primitive material culture in architecture. In his most radical work, *Der Stil in den technischen und tektonischen Künsten oder Praktische Ästhetik* (1863), instead of relating every aspect of ornament to a primitive origin, Semper put forward four elements of architecture which were developed through four different materials and techniques. These were the hearth, roof, enclosure and substructure

(Fig. 5). Semper's quasi-materialist table, showing the origin of architectural elements from matter and as transformed through craft practice, is strikingly similar to the various material processes that Beavers implies in the images of *Work Done,* where water is frozen into ice, a mountain is quarried for stone, trees are made into paper, and pig's blood is fried into pancakes. While Semper's crafts come together in the idea of a building, the various materials in *Work Done* are in a sense a reconstructed genealogy of a poetic image.

Elsewhere I have argued that Beavers and Gregory Markopoulos developed unique editing practices based on their materials (16mm reversal film) and their sensitivity to technique (A&B roll printing).[11] For Markopoulos, this culminates in the form of his final film *Eniaios* (1948–c.1990), with its long stretches of black leader akin to the dark ground of a mosaic.[12] For Beavers, committing his footage to memory allows him to edit for A&B printing without dependence on repeated viewings. This imbues the connections between shots with the inward quality of memory, a quality that has its mirror opposite in the viewer:

"The spectator must discover why an image was chosen to be represented; the silence of such a discovery becomes a moment of release. It is not the filmmaker's work to tell you: his

11 James Macgillivray, "Film Grows Unseen: Gregory Markopoulos, Robert Beavers and the Tectonics of Film Editing," *The Journal of Modern Craft*, Vol. 5, Issue 2, July 2012, p. 179–201.
12 Robert Beavers, *Eniaios* panel discussion, Museum of the Moving Image, New York, February 19, 2011.

work is to make the film and to protect what he does, in the serenity of a thought without words, without the quality in words which would destroy what he intends to represent."[13]

The inward moment of revelation, what he calls "release," makes use of memory in the same way that the filmmaker's editing does; the spectator brings together the images of different shots by comparing the memory of one with the present-tense experience of another. These moments of unspoken contact between filmmaker and spectator constitute the joint, the tectonic assembly of Beavers's films, much as the cement splice holds strips of film together.

For Semper, the origin of the technical arts, and in turn architecture, is the knot: "The knot is perhaps the oldest technical symbol and…the expression for the earliest cosmogonic ideas that arose among nations…The weaver's knot is the strongest and most useful of all knots, perhaps also the oldest or at least the first that figured in the technical arts."[14] Perhaps due to his own intimate experience with hand splicing film, Beavers expresses a similar feeling for the primacy of the knot in several of his films. I have mentioned the stitching of the buttonhole in *The Hedge Theater*, but there are also the knots in the bird-catching nets of the *roccolo* and

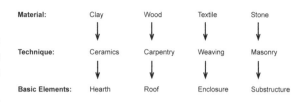

Material:	Clay	Wood	Textile	Stone
	↓	↓	↓	↓
Technique:	Ceramics	Carpentry	Weaving	Masonry
	↓	↓	↓	↓
Basic Elements:	Hearth	Roof	Enclosure	Substructure

Fig. 5

the stitching of the book binding in *Work Done* as well as the sewing of a bespoke suit in *Amor*. These references to knots and textiles not only acknowledge similarities among the diverse subject matter in the films but also point outwards to the craft of his own editing practice and the work of joining objects together through analogy and visual similarity. As such, many of Beavers's films possess a self-similar symmetry; the analogical knots of his editing join together depictions of craft traditions with still more knots, joints and handmade assemblies of material.

In *Der Stil*, beginning from the knot, Semper elaborates the textile arts in all their aspects, eventually attributing the invention of architectural enclosure and the origin of the wall to the hanging of fabrics and carpets by early humans. This he further illustrates by the common root of the early German words *Wand* (wall) and *Gewand* (garment).[15] In *Amor*, the correspondence between architecture and textiles comes closest to Semper's conflation of wall and garment. Early in the film, Beavers introduces this theme through a repeated juxtaposition of the tailoring of a bespoke suit with images of debris netting on a building undergoing restoration. As the fabric of the suit twitches

13 Robert Beavers, "EM·BLEM," Temenos screening brochure, 1984. For a later version of this text, see p. 195 in this volume.
14 Gottfried Semper, *The Four Elements of Architecture and Other Writings*, Cambridge: Cambridge University Press, 1989, p. 217.
15 Ibid., p. 55.

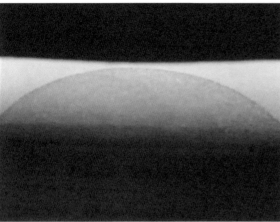

Fig. 6

Fig. 7

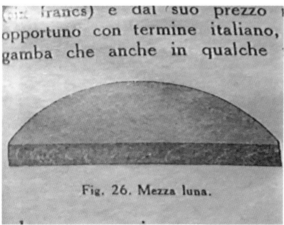

Fig. 8

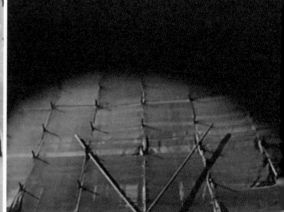

Fig. 9

and sways under the unseen hand of the tailor, so too does the diaphanous fabric on the scaffolding billow in the wind. The thin steel poles of the scaffolding emerging from the shadows behind the fabric look very similar to the white tacking stitches used by the tailor to keep fabric in place while the suit is constructed. Among these shots of the suit and scaffolding, Beavers also includes a static shot from an Italian book of tailoring showing an illustration of a tool called a "mezzaluna," a block of wood shaped by a shallow arc with a straight edge on one side (Fig. 6). Beavers's reaction to this shape in sequence goes back to a shot of the scaffolding (Fig. 7), but shows it in a broad sweeping pan, as if mimicking the arc of the half moon. After two shots of hands clapping, the shot of the mezzaluna repeats (Fig. 8) and then we see the scaffolding again; this time, however, instead of mimicking the curved shape with the moving arc of a pan, he shows the fabric of the scaffolding framed, its image cut off, by the arc shape of the top of the lens rotated on the turret of his Bolex camera (Fig. 9).

These early mimetic exercises seem to be a preamble for a more lengthy consideration of the Piazza Sant'Ignazio in Rome later in the film. Designed by Filippo Raguzzini in 1728, the piazza is the space in front of a group of Rococo buildings gathered around a series of ellipses in plan (Fig. 10). The panning shots of the piazza recall the earlier pan in response to the arc of the mezzaluna, but this time the camera follows the shape of the piazza's plan. Unlike the pan of the scaffolding which shows the building receding in the diagonals of perspective at its

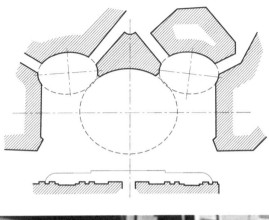

Fig. 10, 11

beginning and end, the pan of the piazza is in a sense followed at a constant radius by the curved form of the building. The pan follows the taut horizontal string course of the Rococo façade and, influenced by the earlier images of the suit, it looks more like the bas-relief of fabric piping (Fig. 11). That the two spaces, inside the suit and within the street-walls of the piazza, rely on a secret geometry – an architectural plan and a sewing tool – is an extraordinary corroboration of Semper's equivalence of wall and garment.[16]

TECTONICS: RUSKIN AND THE TECTONIC OF CRAFT

Ruskin is Beavers's second long-form film with a historical subject matter. It is an oblique portrait of the 19th-century theorist and art critic John Ruskin and looks at its subject by retracing the locations of his major work *The Stones of Venice*. As Beavers films the various architectural objects and landscapes from the book (primarily in Venice, but also the Swiss Alps and London), his camera is in a sense interrogating Ruskin's character by trying to recreate his gaze. As in the book, the result is the delineation of a very specific aesthetic taste, yet, in contrast, Beavers's film has no recourse to words or text as a means of legitimizing his taste in aesthetic theory (Beavers later edited out voiceover passages from *The Stones of Venice* that he had included in the first version of the film). The feeling of watching the film is one of constantly questioning the images for a personal taste behind the lens, a sensibility that would collect the images under the rubric of beauty.

Beavers's *Ruskin* is exceptional in its ability to elucidate his subject's theory of architectural ornament by simply filming the places and things that Ruskin used to illustrate it. As Semper did, Ruskin also theorized a "wall veil" as the primary tectonic element and used this image to further Alberti's derivation of column from wall in *De re aedificatoria*.[17] He is conscious of the vertical axis of gravitational forces acting through columns; however, he maintains that columns are gathered together from the material of the wall veil.[18] As such, the forces in Ruskin's walls don't only act vertically but also in accretion along an axis going in and out of the wall. In *Ruskin*, Beavers's camera is especially attentive to the accumulation of texture and detail in surfaces. The encrustation of ornament and patina, the build-up of mortar nearly engulfing a sculpted angel's wings, the iron anchor plates that keep the masonry walls from buckling outwards: all of these details suggest a tectonic system measured by the growth of detail in a surface of deep relief.

16 Although Beavers has not read Bötticher or Semper's work on tectonics, they are part of a longer history of philhellenism in German culture of the 18th and 19th centuries that both he and Markopoulos would have been exposed to when they lived in Munich for seven years. Munich itself is site to many public works built at the behest of the greatest German philhellenist, Ludwig I. Bötticher's work on tectonics was made possible through the greater access to antiquities after Greek independence, a war partially funded by Ludwig I. Ludwig II commissioned Semper to build an opera house in Munich. The design of that unbuilt work was used whole cloth, without the architect's knowledge, for Wagner's *Festivalhaus* in Bayreuth. Markopoulos in turn was deeply inspired by Bayreuth as a model for the Temenos. Harry F. Mallgrave, *Gottfried Semper: Architect of the Nineteenth Century*, New Haven: Yale University Press, 1996, p. 266–267. Robert Beavers interview with the author, May 19, 2011.

17 Semper discusses woven fabrics as the first (prehistoric) wall. Ruskin uses the term "wall veil" and proposes that columns could be interpreted as a gathering together or bunching of the veil, as when curtains are drawn and make columnar-looking shapes of cloth on either side of a window.

18 John Ruskin, *The Stones of Venice*, ed. J. G. Links, New York: Da Capo Press, 1985, p. 64.

Ruskin

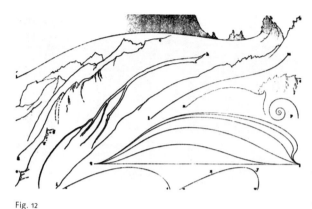

Fig. 12

This aspect of the wall veil becomes strikingly apparent when Beavers films a grassy hillside in the Grison Alps from above. For a moment, the black and white image lacks a discernible trace of up or down, but reinforces the axis going in and out of the picture plane. It looks very similar to another image in the film of a decaying wall whose variegated texture is accentuated by raking sunlight and because it is filmed in black and white, the image of the grass surface of the hill sustains its scalar and directional ambiguity up until the wind causes the grass and branches of small bushes to move. It also expresses Ruskin's immense appetite for visual aesthetics, almost to the point of entirely eliminating the context of objects in order to better appreciate their qualities. In the section of *Stones* titled "Abstract Lines," Ruskin compares the scale-less lines of a willow leaf, a glacier, the branch of a fir tree, a mountain range above Lake Geneva, and a paper Nautilus shell among other things (Fig. 12).

Although they were roughly contemporary, Ruskin's tectonic thought is vastly different from that of Bötticher or Semper. To begin with, he abhorred the architecture of neoclassicism, perceiving architecture's fall from grace in the derivative copying of Roman and Greek form during the Renaissance, copying that reduced the craftsperson to an automaton. Ruskin's tectonics doesn't refer to a symbolic language imposed upon structural necessities, but rather is scaled to the labor of the individual artisan in a medieval economic structure which he called the Gothic. The individual craftsperson works within the parameters of a portion of a building's ornamentation and is given a latitude of self-expression on that piece of the ornament. When taken as a whole, the individuality of the different pieces, an expression of different hands, leads to a variety of form which Ruskin calls "changefulness." The well-being of the workman is expressed in the beauty but also the lack of perfection in the ornament:

"The degree in which the workman has been degraded may be thus known at a glance, by observing whether the several parts of a building are similar or not... if, as in Gothic work, there is perpetual change both in design and execution, the workman must have been altogether set free."[19]

Moreover, the craftsperson's work is to transmute the natural and abstract forms of God's work into ornament. Ornament is distinct from sculpture because it fulfills an architectural function; unlike sculpture, the degree of detail and composition in ornament is fitted to its location on the building. The motif that

19 Ibid., p. 164–165.

Ruskin particularly commends is that of foliage. One example is in the "Vine Angle" at the Ducal Palace depicting the drunkenness of Noah with a dove perched among the leaves (Fig. 13, 14); Ruskin called this relief "faithful as a representation of vine, and yet so designed that every leaf serves an architectural purpose, and could not be spared from its place without harm."[20] Later he marvels at the depiction of wind: "…in several cases, the sculptor has shown the undersides of the leaves turned boldly to the light, and has literally *carved every rib and vein upon them in relief.*"[21] Another example is in the vaults of the porches of St. Mark's. Ruskin describes "sculpture, fantastic and involved, of palm leaves and lilies, and grapes and pomegranates, and birds clinging and fluttering among the branches, all twined together into an endless network of buds and plumes…"[22]

One sequence of shots in *Ruskin* features the Vine Angle prominently. Markopoulos describes the event of filming it in "The Threshold of the Frame" (1973): "Beavers has pointed to the birds, to the minute grapes, to the very beard of Noah himself; a beard beautifully entwined and, perhaps, the magic symbol of the man who created Noah."[23] In one of the most arresting shots in *Ruskin,* Beavers captures a liv-

Fig. 13, 14

ing pigeon in vine foliage. Again, Markopoulos relates that "…in a square a group of birds settled in the vines of the Church of St. Gregory. There Beavers filmed, and before the birds scattered, one kept fluttering in the air like the spirit of the place."[24] This shot is remarkable in its ability to recreate for the viewer a moment that Ruskin only theorized as having occurred in his Gothic workman: the moment of free inspiration and translation of animated natural phenomena into motionless stone ornament.

Ruskin saw vegetal form as the most intrinsically Gothic ornamentation, and he imagined workmen as having a particular fondness for the creation of plant detail. In the subject of foliage Ruskin conceives the natural predilection in the Gothic for tranquility and redemptive craft:

"In that careful distinction of species, and richness of delicate and undisturbed organiza-

20 John Ruskin, *The Stones of Venice*, 4th Edition, London: J. M. Dent & Sons, 1935, p. 184.
21 Ibid., p. 308. Emphasis added.
22 Ibid., p. 66.
23 Gregory Markopoulos, "The Threshold of the Frame," *Film as Film: The Collected Writings of Gregory J. Markopoulos*, ed. Mark Webber, London: The Visible Press, 2014, p. 314.
24 Ibid.

tion, which characterizes the Gothic design, there is the history of rural and thoughtful life, influenced by habitual tenderness, and devoted to subtle inquiry; and every discriminating and delicate touch of the chisel, as it rounds the petal or guides the branch, is a prophecy of the development of the entire body of the natural sciences, beginning with that of medicine, of the recovery of literature, and the establishment of the most necessary principles of domestic wisdom and national peace."[25]

The craft of carving was not unknown to Beavers before he made *Ruskin*. A large wooden tray in the shape of a leaf hangs on the wall of the living room in Beavers's mother's house in Falmouth. It was carved by Bernice Hodges, a neighbor of the Beavers family when they lived in Weymouth. Hodges had a workshop in her basement and worked on ornamental wood carvings for buildings in and around Boston, including Trinity Church. As a boy, Beavers spent time at her house and observed her at work. Later she taught him to carve wood as well. Although it is a different craft from masonry, perhaps it was this early exposure to wood carving that led him to search out and film the most famous carvings from Ruskin's book. Indeed it was Hodges who gave him a copy of the three volumes of *The Stones of Venice,* including all the plates and drawings, before he left for Europe with Markopoulos. In 1972, on a trip back to visit his family, Beavers found the book and read it, which ultimately inspired him to film *Ruskin* in Venice in 1973.[26]

SPACE

As much as Beavers's architectural films take part in a discussion of tectonics by virtue of their subject and also their analogical operations (so similar to those of architectural form), there is another aspect of architecture in the films, an ambition to give form to something which doesn't really exist in the two-dimensional image of film: space. Tectonics and space are of course hard to separate; the structural innovations of building materials and assemblies have for the most part been in the pursuit of the enclosure of space. At the same time, the proper architectural treatment of those structural elements has inflected and clarified the spaces that they enclose. Yet, in architectural discourse, the concept of space is relatively new.[27] Although Greek architecture lies at the origins of Western architectural theory, still its trabeated (post and lintel) structure did not so much create an interior space as it occupied the boundary between earth and sky. In his formative study *Strutture e Sequenze di Spazi* (1953), Italian architect Luigi Moretti traces the invention of space in architecture not to the Greeks but to the building culture of the Romans:

"The columns of the Greek temple enclosed rectangles with their blades of shadow, which seem to surround and form inviolable cells,

25 Ruskin, *The Stones of Venice,* ed. Links, p. 173.
26 Robert Beavers e-mail correspondence with the author, January 17, 2015.
27 Peter Collins notes that prior to the 18th century, there is no mention of the word in architectural theory. See his *Changing Ideals in Modern Architecture, 1750–1950,* 2nd ed., Montreal: McGill-Queens University Press, 1998, p. 285.

born of the bowels of the earth. Greek architecture was an algorithm of light and also of the shades of unknown forms where the gods hid. The high plane and the luminous vault of the heavens are the marvelous extraverted spaces which the colonnade pylon of the temple supports…The great spaces of architecture arise [instead] with Rome and are the magnificence of it. United with superhuman vaults, and with walls of incredible strength, instinctively breathing the indestructible military works that ruled them, they express the conscious power of a community…On the ruins of the walls indicating these volumes, from Brunelleschi to Michelangelo, Renaissance and Baroque space was born and with it the sense of the grandiose in the new polity of the west."[28]

The Greeks gave us the language of tectonics, but the Romans invented architectural space. Many of Beavers's films are implicitly concerned with space due to their subject matter and location: *Amor, Work Done, The Hedge Theater, From the Notebook of…* and *Ruskin* all prominently feature the architectural descendants of Roman space. Placing his camera within these architectures, Beavers pursues the representation of their space through several methods. One of these is camera movement. At

the Naturtheater (or hedge theater) in Salzburg, the Piazza Sant'Ignazio and the Churches of San Carlo and Sant'Ivo in Rome (in *Amor* and *The Hedge Theater*), the camera, placed some distance away from the curved surfaces of its architectural subject, rotates around the central point of the tripod describing an arc. This movement unrolls the curved or elliptical surface of the walls but also grasps at the elusive center of the space. In other words, when the panning motion of the camera doesn't elicit a change in the size of the objects it represents, the viewer can intuit a curved wall shape with the camera at its focal point.

In Renaissance architecture and even more so in Baroque and Rococo, the central point of space is a captivating but ultimately untenable place. The architectural historian Robin Evans has noted how elusive the center can be and indicates the example of nine potential centers in the eminently centralized circular layout of Raphael's Sant'Eligio in Rome.[29] When, in *The Hedge Theater*, we arrive at two of Borromini's churches, San Carlo and Sant'Ivo, we find the central point even further obscured: at Sant'Ivo by the compound geometry of the cornice line, at San Carlo by the extreme complexity of the oval shape. The architect Paolo Portoghesi has analyzed the form of San Carlo as a truncation of St. Peter's Basilica: the rectilinear pauses of the cruciform arms which delay contact between the central space and the apses have been removed and the entire plan (a cruciform of circles) has been, through an anamorphic process, transformed into elliptical and ovoid shapes.[30] In other words, what were once sepa-

28 Luigi Moretti, "Structures and Sequences of Spaces," *Oppositions: A Forum for Ideas and Criticism in Architecture*, Vol. 4, trans. Thomas Stevens, New York: Wittenborn Art, 1974, p. 124–126.

29 Robin Evans, *The Projective Cast: Architecture and its Three Geometries*, Cambridge: MIT Press, 1995, p. 9.

30 Paolo Portoghesi and Marisa Tabarrini, *Storia di San Carlino alle Quattro Fontane*, Rome: Newton & Compton, 2001, p. 73.

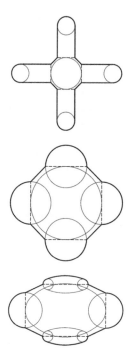

Fig. 15

rate spherical domes in St. Peter's with their own centers have been pushed together and overlapped in volumetric concatenation due to the distortion of anamorphosis (Fig. 15).

SPACE: ANAMORPHOSIS IN
THE HEDGE THEATER AND AMOR

Anamorphosis, the distortion of a form through projection (the most common of which is the foreshortening of perspective), shows up in Beavers's filming notebooks for *Ruskin*. Dated "14.9.73" and next to the words "Circle perspective:" is a sketch of an elliptical shape followed by "the lens and the third dimensional, horizontal circle in which the back becomes the bottom." (Fig. 16)[31] Beavers has attributed this note (which concerns the morphology of a re-

lationship between a form's front and back in three dimensions to one of top and bottom on the two-dimensional screen) to a trip he took to the Scuola San Rocco in Venice. Although the ceiling from the ellipse sketch is never seen in *Ruskin*, we do see an elliptical matte near the beginning of the film. The sketch of the ellipse refers to a series of rounded paintings by Tintoretto hung on the ceiling of the school. The most famous of these, *The Glory of San Rocco* (1564), shows the titular saint seen from below, surrounded by angels along the bottom edge of an elliptically shaped canvas. The illusion of San Rocco and the angels receding into the heavens is accentuated by the elliptical shape of the canvas, in effect portraying a circular opening in the ceiling as if it were seen in perspective. Beavers explains looking up at Tintoretto's paintings as part of a larger concern in the filming of *Ruskin*:

"My way of thinking & seeing while filming *Ruskin*…moved back and forth between the perspective of looking downwards to the ground or the desktop & volume of *The Stones of Venice*, upwards to the ceilings, to the façades or sky and straight ahead. I thought often about how to film and edit this looking downwards or upwards [for] the space on the screen which is always directly in front of the viewer…Looking up to the ceiling and seeing painted images within circular framed shapes, I thought how it would look when projected onto the screen instead of being above on the ceiling."[32]

31 Robert Beavers, *Ruskin* filming notes, Temenos Archive.
32 Robert Beavers e-mail correspondence with the author, December 30, 2015.

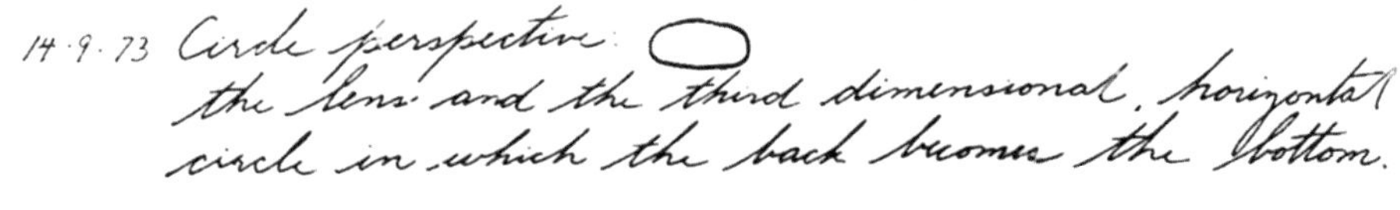

14·9·73 Circle perspective:
the lens and the third dimensional, horizontal
circle in which the back becomes the bottom.

Fig. 16

The mechanism of anamorphosis makes palpable the fact that the viewer is displaced from the center of a circle, a feeling that is heightened by the frontality of the film screen on which the image appears. More than a decade after the sketch, *The Hedge Theater* takes up the ambition of the note from *Ruskin* and explores the shape of the oval or ellipse to draw connections between the circular pool in the *roccolo* and the ovoid form of San Carlo's dome. Seen from a distance, the round pool reflects the tops of the trees and sky in the shape of an ellipse surrounded by grass and dirt. The dome would appear to be the inverse of the pool's ellipse, but in fact, since it is already an oval in plan, it cannot be reconstituted into a circle by the viewer's movement in space. *Listening to the Space in My Room* takes up the theme again in the elliptical shape of a circular mirror reflecting clouds and sky; with the shot focused and metered for the light of the sky, the rest of the image appears blurred and black as if it were a matte, a pure distillation of both above and below.

Could this exploration of anamorphosis entail an acknowledgement that the film image can only show a projection of space and not space itself? If one of Beavers's greatest ambitions in film is the depiction of space, the frustration of that desire by the flatness of the screen leads first of all to a celebration of its spatial ambivalence. In *Amor,* the equivalence of walls and garments elicits this ambivalence, as if space could be turned inside out like a piece of clothing. Salzburg's Naturtheater introduces one of the most powerful two-dimensional representations of space: the hedge wings of the theater get smaller and move toward the central axis of the stage as they recede in the composition of a "one-point" perspective (Fig. 17). This exaggerates the foreshortening of perspective by making the stage appear in the X-shaped composition where the center of the X is the vanishing point on the horizon and the tops and bottoms of the hedges make the diagonal lines of the X. Later this X shape is taken up again with two different objects. The first is the image of an envelope alternately backlit and frontlit. The leaves of the envelope are seen partially open, holding space, or closed and flat. Backlighting the open envelope allows Beavers to show the space either concave (like the theater) or convex, pushing toward the lens of the camera (Fig. 18).

The ambiguity of the X composition of the envelope is reinforced by the depiction in three different images of an architectural ornament known as "nailhead" or "diamond ashlar rustication:" a built example in Verona (Fig. 19),[33] a

33 Robert Beavers e-mail correspondence with the author, April 6, 2016.

Fig. 17

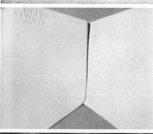

Fig. 18

Fig. 19   Fig. 20   Fig. 21

painted *trompe l'oeil* in a passage off the Piazza Dante Aligheri (also in Verona) (Fig. 20), and the façade of Gesù Nuovo in Naples as depicted on the 10,000 Lire banknote (Fig. 21). The X shape of the vertices of these diamonds rhymes with that of the envelope and the hedge theater but challenges the concave spatial reading of those images with a convex object (the carved "nailhead" ornament on the face of a building that appears like a stud or a spike) instead. The use of the backlit banknote and envelope would seem to suggest that the implied mirroring of the film's title (between *amor* and *Roma*) could equally apply to the two-dimensional depiction of space in film, which could be alternately concave, convex or flat. Space depicted by the cinema is thus somehow doomed to ambivalence. Beavers responds to this frustration of space with a playful inversion of the rules of perspective, both in *The Hedge Theater* and *Amor;* however, the films are not resigned to this flatness. While he does ironically acknowledge the limitations of the medium in one context, Beavers persists in his desire for the representation of space in others. He does this first and foremost with sound.

SPACE: SOUND AND RESONANCE

Beavers's films are intricately woven with sound which has resonated in the actual spaces where he filmed but was not recorded syn-

34 Michel Chion, *Audio-Vision: Sound on Screen*, ed. Claudia Gorbman, New York: Columbia University Press, 1994, p. 68.
35 Ibid.
36 Ibid., p. 79.

chronous with filming. Michel Chion has noted in *Audio-Vision* that just as an image in film is delimited and contained by the frame, "there is no auditory container for sounds, nothing analogous to the visual container of images that is the frame."[34] As such, when sounds are put together with the film image, "[t]hey dispose themselves in relation to the frame and its content. Some are embraced as synchronous and onscreen, others wander at the surface and on the edges as offscreen."[35] Ambient sounds (which are the majority of sounds in Beavers's work) "are often the product of multiple specific and local sources (a brook, bird songs) [and] what is important is the space inhabited and defined by the sound, more than its multi-source origin...The more reverberant the sound, the more it tends to express the space that contains it."[36] Beavers works painstakingly on the sound in his films in order to achieve an expression not of the sound source itself but of the space it exists within.

Sound is essential to *Listening to the Space in My Room*. The film depicts four people inhabiting a single house (upstairs, Dieter and Cécile Staehelin, and downstairs, Beavers and his partner, the filmmaker Ute Aurand) in part by the sounds they make: Dieter tunes his cello and practices scales, Cécile reads a German text, Beavers speaks and his projector whirs. The film sets up an equivalence between the resonance of bowed strings in the interior space of a cello and the same sound resonating within the volume of the house's interior. This is similar to the analogy between the interior space of the camera and the interior space of a room (*camera* in Italian) that Beavers explored in *From the Notebook of…* But *Listening* uses sound to describe the space of the interior in far more detail. Beavers deliberated on the title of the film while he was finishing the editing, by turns calling it *Sieben Fenster* (*Seven Windows*), *Tobelhus* (the neighborhood in which the film was made) or *Thresh Hold*.[37] The earlier titles hint at a defining quality of the film in which the threshold of a window delineates the space of four different people but also holds and separates their sounds. The juxtaposition of non-diegetic sounds that "wander" at the surface and on the edges of the frame with the image *within* the frame provides for the incredible immediacy of the space.

The similarities of certain sounds in *Listening* (the lawn mower and the projector, or the cello and recorded music from the soundtrack of Beavers's film *The Suppliant*) further complicate our ability to place them and prolong the time in which they can wander in space without a source. This ambiguity of sound correlates to the movement between spaces in the film and the mimetic movements of the camera: "I could say metaphorically, that a pendulum swings between my sense of self and of these other human beings; it also swings between my rooms on the ground floor and the floors above me and the space outside, and this pendulum (my editing) is suggestive of music."[38] Beavers's use of sound counteracts the flatness of the image by a complex connection of the view seen to the space in which it exists. In this way, Beavers gives the viewer a very clear location within an overall spatial system. Like space,

sound is not necessarily visibly present; its spatial qualities are communicated through our senses in ways that are outside of language.

SPACE: SPACE AS TANGIBLE VOID

In looking at an object we reach out for it. With an invisible finger we move through the space around us, go out to the distant places where things are found, touch them, catch them, scan their surfaces, trace their borders, explore their texture. Perceiving shapes is an eminently active occupation. (Rudolf Arnheim)[39]

When he proposed a systematic study of architectural space in *Strutture e Sequenze di Spazi*, Moretti was sensible of the invisibility of space but was also aware of how conventional architectural representation (plans, sections and elevations) tended to make it flat. Instead he subjected the space of Roman, Renaissance and Baroque architecture to a diagrammatic process whereby all the negative space of the interior was abstracted and rendered in solid plaster. Particularly in the Baroque example of Guarino Guarini's Santa Maria della Divina

37 "A new film [I am making] is in the house in Switzerland. There is color in the film and sound qualities. It is filmed on three floors, so how to suggest vertical structure? The word and concept of 'thresh hold,' spelled with two h's. In this sense there is a relation to *Pitcher of Colored Light*." Robert Beavers interview with the author, May 19, 2011.

38 Robert Beavers quoted in Mónica Savirón, "The Art of Effective Dreaming," *Lumière*, November 2013. www.elumiere.net/exclusivo_web/nyff13/nyff13_14.php

39 Rudolf Arnheim, *Art and Visual Perception: A Psychology of the Creative Eye*, Berkeley: University of California Press, 1974, p. 43.

Provvidenza (a church very similar in form to San Carlo), the resulting object is something wholly unexpected: the fluid transition from one volume to the next belies the linear geometries of the plan (Fig. 22). Beavers's film *The Stoas* (1991–97) contains a similar ambition of making space visible, but with startlingly different means. It begins by simply portraying the inside of industrial arcades in Athens, moving from one end to the other in static shots that discover a continuity of space in the alleys as a box shape. The orthogonal form of these arcades makes the shots resonate with square shapes and projections of squares in space. In one shot, the foreground contains a projection of bright sunlight from a square lightwell (Fig. 23), while the square opening onto the street radiates in the distance. In another shot, a square pallet in the foreground barring entry to the arcade appears to be related to the lightwell of the same arcade because they are the same size in perspective (Fig. 24).

Interspersed with these images of the empty arcades are shots of two hands appearing to hold space between them. In a conversation with Aurand about *The Stoas*, Beavers describes the hands as something similar to Moretti's plaster models. He had initially wanted to "film

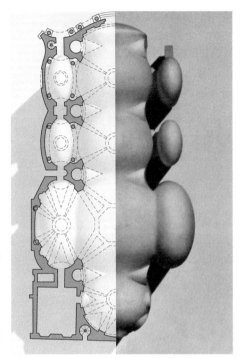

Fig. 22

vases and the space inside the vase that is not seen…the starting point was more the form of the vase than decoration…" But this conception transformed: "[The hands were] all that remained of my initial intention to suggest the space inside the vase that is not seen, the hands remained to suggest this space."[40] Two hands, outstretched towards the camera, the fingers extended but slightly bent as if cupping the air. They are not still, but alive and moving, not holding a tool or touching an object like so many of the other hands in Beavers's films, but simply feeling the emptiness between them (Fig. 25). The image conveys something beyond the visual: the felt sense of holding space between one's hands.[41] Reconciling or uniting the

40 "Conversation about *The Stoas*: Ute Aurand and Robert Beavers," *To the Winged Distance: Films by Robert Beavers*, London: Tate Modern, 2007. See also p. 143 in this volume.

41 Similarly, in *Amor*, the hand feeling the bespoke garment relates to the panning shots of architecture: "There is an urge to unite the eye and hand in touching, and to sense contours by grasping, etc." Robert Beavers correspondence with the author, November 2, 2015.

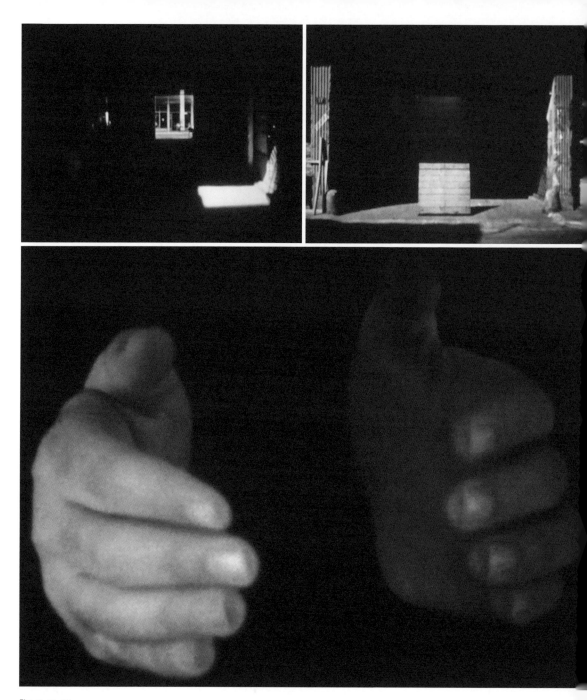

Fig. 23, 24, 25

hand and eye in this manner connects them through the ineffable conduits of the body's perceptual system. Space remains as invisible as air or a void but is also felt. Beavers refers to the pursuit of space with hand and eye in connection with the title for his 18-film cycle, *My Hand Outstretched to the Winged Distance and Sightless Measure*: "The rightness of the contour of space, or an object, is related to the hand. There is a sense of space even as something I would touch with my hand, that there would be a pleasure in proportion and space."[42]

CONCLUSION: TECTONICS AND SPACE
Broadly speaking, Beavers's feeling for tectonics is centered on the connection between handcraft and form. The button and the base of the column, the suit and the faux stone of a rusticated façade – these analogies restore a tangible haptic dimension to architectural details which are often relegated to the status of visual ornament. Like Bötticher, Semper and Ruskin, Beavers reveals that these forms are dynamic and contain life forces inside them and on their surfaces, but are also always related to our sense of having objects in our hands. Conversely, space or the apprehension of space is addressed to the eye and the ear. Anamorphosis creates two-dimensional images from spatial compositions by virtue of the optics of the eye and camera. These images still hold their spatial information, but it has been rendered equivocal. Sound is often allowed the same ambiguity

as image, ultimately emphasizing the space of the shot.

If we treat Beavers's films as architectural treatises, it is fascinating that they eschew the conceptual separation between space and tectonics largely due to the parity of hand and eye. In all of Beavers's work, the camera and the editing table become the locus for a reconciliation of the hand and the eye. Indeed, his camera is an intimately handled thing. From his custom mattes and filters, to the manipulation of the lens turret and his use of the mirror to show his hands working the camera, the eye in the camera is often seeing at the behest of a hand's maneuvering of the field of view. Sometimes, even sounds are synced to the visible gestures of hands, like the sync marks used in sound editing.

In the quotation at the beginning of this essay, Ponge likens the peripetal Greek temple to a stringed instrument. The image operates on the similarities of the two objects: the columns and the strings, the walls of both. It also complicates the analogy by an obvious shift in scale and the fact that while the columns and strings appear similar, one is held in place by compressive forces while another is pulled taut in tension. These correspondences and contradictions are so similar to those in Beavers's work that it is no wonder that Ponge should be one of his favorite poets. A deeper kinship lies in the fact that the instrument was made by hand and, moreover, that the instrument's form invites the hand to play the strings and cause its hidden space to resonate.

42 Robert Beavers interview with the author, October 20, 2016.

Kristin M. Jones

Drowning in Light: *Sotiros*

At once lucid and mysterious, rigorous and rich with emotion, Robert Beavers's *Sotiros* (1976–78/1996) contains no shortage of strikingly beautiful images, whether of a goat surrounded by foliage, a water glass and coffee cup reflecting light and casting shadows on the radiant surface of a white marble table, or a tree's shimmering leaves. The word "Sotiros" means healer or savior in Greek, and the film opens with a serene landscape in the Peloponnese, near the temple at Bassae dedicated to Apollo Epicurius. In an early shot, a shepherd is seen moving on a hillside as if from a god's-eye-view, but the divine soon draws closer to the earthly, manifesting in light and shadow in a Swiss hotel room, and becoming uncannily entwined in a real-life trauma and the creation of the film itself.

The first work in the third part of Beavers's film cycle, *Sotiros* is the only work in which he has incorporated intertitles, and the last in which he has used mattes. The intertitles, which signal that groups of images stand in for speech from a mysterious source, play an extraordinary role. Appearing in white type on a black background, on the left and right sides of the frame, they read "He said," or "he said." – as if preceding and following portions of dialogue. In an interview with Tony Pipolo, Beavers says,

"The 'he' is left unidentified. It is the voice of Sotiros without Sotiros being shown in the film. In one way 'he' is the film."[1]

The titles are followed by pans, some vertical but most to the left or right; often the camera pans inside the hotel room before a cut to a static landscape shot, creating a powerful sense of slipping from one world, or from one mental or emotional state, to another. With a flexible, hypnotic rhythm, the camera movement and editing respond to the passage of light around the walls of the hotel room. The movements throughout are also intricately connected to ambient sounds including the noise of dripping and flowing water, a scratching pen, and rattling coat hangers.

Sotiros originates in three films that Beavers re-edited together, and its creation is inextricably tied to a traumatic event that occurred between the making of the first and the second. As he recounts to Pipolo, after Beavers completed *Sotiros Responds* (1975–76, shot in both Switzerland and Greece and using the dialogic intertitles), he and Gregory Markopoulos traveled to Rome to listen to a recording of music from Alban Berg's *Wozzeck* conducted

1 Tony Pipolo, "An Interview with Robert Beavers," *Millennium Film Journal*, No. 32/33, Fall 1998, p. 19.

He said,

he said.

Sotiros
(1976–78/1996)

by Dimitri Mitropoulos. After leaving the Roman archive where he heard the tape, Beavers saw a dead bird, which he viewed as an omen. Soon afterward, they were struck by a bus outside Athens, and Beavers spent an extended period in the hospital for injuries to his hip and eye. After he was released, and while he was still recovering, he made *Sotiros (Alone)* (1976–77), into which he incorporated a number of brief fragments from *Wozzeck* as well as newly shot footage in the Swiss hotel. The third film, *Sotiros in the Elements* (1978), was the shortest of the three and included experiments with moving mattes.[2] The trilogy, then, combined the first film's concern with healing with material that followed the filmmaker's accident and recovery. In 1996, Beavers turned the 50 minute trilogy into the 25 minute integrated *Sotiros* that exists today.

Throughout *Sotiros* flows the movement of sunlight around the austere hotel room in Switzerland, which contains twin beds, two chairs, a pair of sinks beneath oval mirrors, a desk, and a wall mostly taken up by large windows. Like the titles, the paired furniture and sinks suggest a dialogue as well as an uncanny doubling. The eye-like oval mirrors also rhyme with bodies of water that appear in the film; water glasses appear by the sinks and in a café. Through recurring images and sound, water becomes almost as important as sunlight in *Sotiros*, promising restoration as well as a possible descent into oblivion.

Two human figures in *Sotiros* hold special significance. One is a blind beggar first observed from a distance midway through the film, walking down a city street. After more titles and images of landscapes, streetscapes, and the luminous hotel room, he reappears in medium shot, standing by a wall and wiping his forehead with a handkerchief. Beavers cuts to a panning shot of a glittering sea before returning to the blind man, whose left palm is outstretched. The hand begins to tremble. With a graceful gesture – recalling the use of bodily movements in other films in this cycle – he exchanges the fatigued left hand with his right one, echoing the movement between left and right in the titles and mirrored pans. Later, he is seen again several times, his face partially obscured by a shadow in the center of the frame.

The other is a man filmed in Leonidio, actually named Sotiros, whom Beavers has said "moved about like a village fool."[3] Like the blind beggar, this figure inhabits a world apart from that of passersby, although his antic gestures contrast with the other figure's contained dignity. Shots framing the second man's legs and the shadow he casts on asphalt as he paces about are intercut with images of olive trees; moments in which the frame is filled with red (the result of a colored filter) seem to telegraph unease. Mattes appear on the left and right sides of the frame (not unlike those in *From the Notebook of...* [1971/1998]), and shots of buses moving down city streets take on a faintly ominous, dreamlike quality.

Both figures might be viewed as portending images seen later in *Sotiros* of Markopoulos's

2 Ibid., p. 18.
3 Ibid., p. 19.

Sotiros

eye (shown in close-up and recalling the injury to Beavers's own eye) and Beavers's scarred leg. The beggar evokes blind seers in classical myth, such as the soothsayer Tiresias, as well as biblical stories involving blindness, while the figure of the fool has also been connected to prophecy. In some mysterious way, the blind man and the fool both seem to participate in the generation of the film.

In the last third of *Sotiros,* shots of Beavers's camera on a tripod in the hotel room, and his hands manipulating it, begin to appear, structurally replacing the intertitles. When the hands turn the camera on the tripod, a pan in the opposite direction usually follows. Numerous times the panning shot depicts scenes including doors and shuttered windows along a grey-blue, cobblestoned street in Graz, often partially obscured by mattes, followed by static images – landscapes, eye, glass of water – as if the tripod itself is summoning ambiguous visions.

As in many of Beavers's films, architecture plays an essential role in *Sotiros,* with windows and doors appearing throughout. A shot of the dark interior of a chapel with closed green shutters around which a greenish glow spills in is followed by a view of the building's muted whitewashed exterior. Images of a burned smokehouse in an Austrian forest late in the film contrast with shots of workers building or restoring a structure in Greece in the sunshine near the beginning.

The scar on Beavers's leg, still in the process of healing, appears and reappears in the psychically charged last third of the film, as do shots of

his ear, and Markopoulos's mouth and eye. In multiple images, two fingers seem to touch before they meet; in others a chair is pulled along the floor. Beavers's ear appears in close-up as the first musical fragment from *Wozzeck* is heard on the soundtrack.

Given the multilayered allusions to Apollo, the tripod in part calls to mind a bronze altar, underlining the oracular quality of the voice or voices that speak through the film. Its sudden visibility in the midst of a hypnotic progression of images also intensifies the film's engagement with the spectator. In his text "La Terra Nuova," Beavers writes of achieving "a congruence between 'interior sense' and sense organ." He continues, "This is the means with which a filmmaker creates the individual perspective of his film – a perspective not limited to the analogy of a window but establishing the form in which the spectator will have the unique place of being a living participant."[4]

This sense of being a living participant in *Sotiros* also recalls the Asclepian aspect of the Temenos, whose site in Lyssaraia is near the pastoral landscapes that open the film, and Markopoulos's concept of the filmmaker as "a physician of images," with the act of filmmaking and its results precipitating a restoration in the artist and the spectator.[5] Markopoulos appears later in *Sotiros,* in a startlingly beautiful

4 Robert Beavers, "La Terra Nuova," *Millennium Film Journal,* No. 32/33, p. 41. For a later version of this text, see p. 193 in this volume.
5 Gregory J. Markopoulos, "The Filmmaker as Physician of the Future," *Film as Film: The Collected Writings of Gregory J. Markopoulos,* ed. Mark Webber, London: Visible Press, 2014, p. 231.

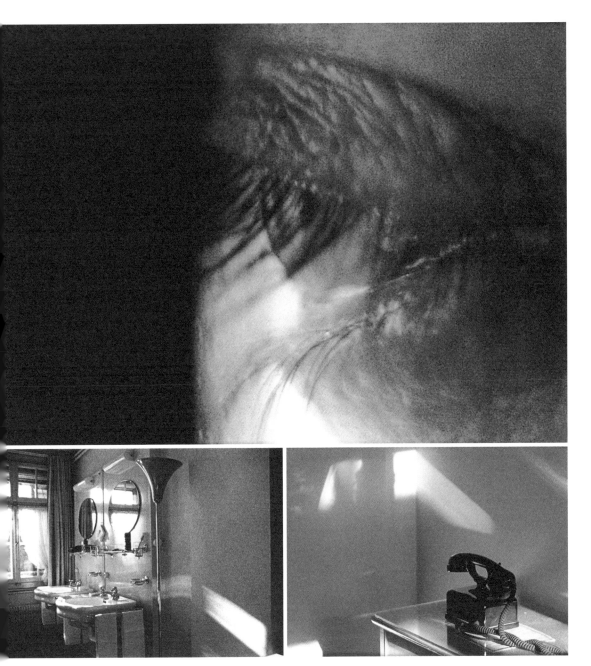

Sotiros

shot, sitting motionless with light glowing on his face; Beavers and Markopoulos are the primary figures in the final section of the film.

Words are out of reach not only in the fragmentary intertitles, but in the writing we see Markopoulos doing in the hotel room without being able to read what it says. Later, he rips up a sheet of paper, presumably the one on which we have seen him writing. The tearing recalls moments in Beavers's *The Painting* (1972/1999), which includes *The Martyrdom of Saint Hippolytus*, a 15th-century painting by an unknown Flemish painter showing the saint, tied to four horses, on the verge of being rent asunder, as well as a torn photograph of Beavers. In discussing *The Painting,* Beavers remarks, "It introduces the theme of tearing as an emblem of intense emotion – the unity of destruction and creation."[6]

The mirrored pans and other doublings, as well as the mirrors in the room, also evoke the death and creative restoration that follow the passage through mirrors in Jean Cocteau's *Le Sang d'un poète* (1930) and *Orphée* (1950).[7] The hotel room in *Sotiros* bears affinities to the protagonist's chamber in *Le Sang d'un poète,* with its mirror, washbasin, easel, and modest furnishings. Cocteau's poet already has a scar on his shoulder when the film begins. His hand is then "wounded" when the mouth of a statue-muse is transferred to the hand; after deriving erotic gratification from it, he drowns the mouth in the washbasin. And yet drowning is a darker theme in *Sotiros*. It is both implicit in the film's traumatic ethos and an explicit element of the *Wozzeck* opera narrative.

Indeed, the emotional, mental, and physical anguish reaches a peak in the sun-spangled hotel room as the several musical fragments from *Wozzeck* punctuating the ambient sounds distill a sense of darkness and unease, especially during rising orchestral music originally composed to accompany the opera protagonist's drowning at the scene where he murdered his common-law wife, Marie. We see a striking, bluish shot of water in the mist fringed by evergreens. The camera pans from the sky above the pond to the murky waters. After Markopoulos discards the torn paper, there is an exquisite shot of the misty landscape from a different angle. Before *Sotiros* ends, Beavers is seen seated in bed, projecting shadows on the wall with his hand – a playful and infinitely mysterious image – as we hear the orchestral music and imagine Wozzeck's death. Light is reflected on the wall, and a vertical shadow in the center of the image expands to fill the frame.

6 Pipolo, "An Interview with Robert Beavers," p. 10.
7 P. Adams Sitney has discussed the affinities between *Le Sang d'un poète* and Beavers's *Winged Dialogue* (1967/2000) and *Plan of Brussels* (1968/2000). *Eyes Upside Down: Visionary Filmmakers and the Heritage of Emerson,* New York: Oxford University Press, 2008, p. 132.

Erik Ulman

Notes on Robert Beavers

Robert Beavers has written that a filmmaker "must protect what he does in the serenity of a thought without words."[1] Perhaps, then, I should not be surprised to find his films hard to write about; when attempting to analyze them, I've found that categories no sooner suggest themselves as utilities than they become impediments, too static to register the dance of the films through their subtle balances and correspondences.

Robert's films may be intricate indeed. What *From the Notebook of...* (1971/1998), for example, leaves in the memory is its disorienting complexity of construction – not only in its editing, built in taut thrust and counter-thrust, but also in the composition of its images, filtered, matted, variously divided, and all this at exhilarating speed, with written notations that disappear before one can finish reading them, much less digest their implications: a work racing just before the grasp of eye and mind. In this early and virtuoso work, Robert investigates, exults in something that will remain at the heart of all his endeavors: the technical properties of film, camera, sound recorder themselves. However, if he never abandons an intense consciousness

of his means, nonetheless his focus after *From the Notebook of...* comes to shift and widen, becoming less narrowly self-reflexive and ever more open to and inquisitive about the external world. What becomes key is sensitive attunement – the judgment of how, for example, a movement of the camera may best bring forth the dimensions of a space; or how the composition of the frame, or the quality of sound, may most indelibly capture an object, whether in forthright or in more mysterious declaration. This seems to me one central principle of Robert's art: a fastidious attention, gleaning distinctive phenomena from the world. Anyone who has seen Robert's films will recall the warm light of *The Ground* (1993–2001), the vivid materiality of the blood crepes or the ice block in *Work Done* (1972/1999), the precise selection of details in *The Painting* (1972/1999); and so captivating are these images that we may fail to attend adequately to the beauty and clarity of the soundtracks – e.g., the polyphony of hammers at the construction site in *Amor* (1980).

But in the properties of his medium Robert continues to find more than finely judged representation. In *Amor*, for example, which is the film of Robert's I've most often been able to see (no coincidence that it has become a special favorite), the camera not only captures the forms

1 Robert Beavers, "EM-BLEM," *The Searching Measure*, Berkeley: UC Berkeley Art Museum and Pacific Film Archive, 2004. See also p. 195 in this volume.

Amor

of spaces (such as the Naturtheater in Salzburg or a Roman piazza), objects (a banknote, details of architecture or clothing), and actions (a man clapping his hands, a tailor cutting a suit); it also self-consciously asserts itself as mechanism in frequent transitions effected through the turning of the lens. To Robert's statement that this turning "[creates] a movement like the eye turned upwards or cast downwards,"[2] I want to respond that in my experience this effect presents no simple extension of human physiology; as Richard Suchenski writes, the "image seems to fly up and down simultaneously," a paradox that foregrounds rather than conceals technological mediation.[3] But then, as I write this, I recall that a hand turns that lens, the same hand which appears in the film so often, alternating its orientation upward and downward in analogy with the rising or falling away of the image. And so an estrangement of identification of eye and lens yields, in its curving detour, a rhyme of lens and hand: reminder, even through technological mediation, how body is source for Robert and indispensable measure.[4]

What I come to here is a second and complementary principle in Robert's work: the coordination of the phenomena that he has harvested from contingency into order, an order built from scrupulous, inventive, patiently perceptive analogy. It is analogy that binds the elements, through shape, function, movement, into a web of resonances, into the whole. This seems to me the central meaning of the title *Amor*. One recognizes the implicit and famous palindrome with ROMA; and the formality of the choice of Latin (although there's only one

word here, I can't forget that the young Robert recognized that in Latin words can fit together "like cut stones"[5]) and, at least initially, of majuscules[6] suggests distance from or strict control of personal emotions or confession. (One should, however, note that there is certainly eroticism in Robert's work, most overtly in some early films or *Wingseed* [1985]; and personal love appears with special force, indeed perhaps with all the more authority through its delicacy and chastity, near the end of *The Hedge Theater* [1986–90/2002].) But "Amor" (as word) has here a fundamentally Empedoclean meaning: Love as Strife's cosmic complement, making One of Many, and "stretching in every dimension… a ceaseless round, / sure and unmoving in the style of a circle."[7]

Amor, then, is what brings the disparate into unity. Its manifestations are manifold: perhaps the simplest is when two hands come together to clap, a moment in which image and sound find their sharpest coincidence. But most manifestations are richer, more oblique – resem-

2 Robert Beavers, "La Terra Nuova," *The Searching Measure.* See also p. 193 in this volume.
3 Richard Suchenski, "AMOR," *The Films of Robert Beavers,* Berkeley: University of California, Berkeley Art Museum and Pacific Film Archive, 2009, p. 14.
4 In "La Terra Nuova" Robert writes: "The same hand that operated the camera now places each image within the phrases of edited film."
5 Robert Beavers, "A Few Points," *To the Winged Distance: Films by Robert Beavers*, London: Tate Modern, 2007. See also p. 165 in this volume.
6 Editor's note: Beavers originally used capitals for the title – *AMOR* – but subsequently this became less important for him.
7 Stanley Lombardo, trans., *Parmenides and Empedocles*, San Francisco: Grey Fox Press, 1980, p. 36.

Wingseed (1985)

blances of image, associations of idea or impli-cation, all reverberating through the course of the film. Some matchings of image themselves contain and honor earlier acts of bringing to-gether, which is to say of culture: on an Italian banknote one finds the reproduction of the gridded facing of a building, a detail Robert no-tices and underlines by juxtaposing representa-tion and model. And as ever Robert privileges associations with the craft of filmmaking, as when the shears that cut a suit imply those that edit film, as, less directly, the sound of ham-mering at a construction site stands in for con-struction as such. An especially important locus of conjunction, visual and intellectual, is the "mezzaluna" (half-moon) shape we see early in

the film as a diagram in a book and again in the world (most insistently in the arcs of the splen-did Piazza Sant'Ignazio) and in the darkened arcs, a result of lens turret movements, that ap-pear over a number of images. This mezzaluna must be so prevalent because it, like the lens and the lens-turning, is curvature as such, Empedocles's very form of Love.

This curvature, I feel, stretches over and holds together the film, through and beyond all mere accumulation of rhyming instances: the serenity which in Robert's view should govern the origin of the film also becomes its guiding principle, its ultimate achievement. Elsewhere Robert has stressed the viewer's participation in the arc of a film: that "the spectator builds the narrative like a bridge in the vibrant lightness of his attention."[8] Such building enacts the spec-tator's discovery of "why an image was cho-

8 Robert Beavers, "The Senses," *The Searching Measure.* See also p. 200 in this volume.

113

sen."[9] And if it's true that Robert, as he says, doesn't "[impose] coherence,"[10] it's also true that what coherence we find is not just our projection, but comes of the rhythms of association and variation, of recurrence and the as it were pedagogical introduction of new and developing motifs, in the recognition of which we too enter a curving sense of the whole, as Robert cites Empedocles in his essay "La Terra Nuova": "a 'totally rounded orb, in its rotundity joying.'"[11]

Forms chime in unison, and separate again into polyphony; world crystallizes into pattern and resonates beyond pattern's boundaries. The simple is achieved, comprehending the complex without extinguishing the independence of its elements, even as they influence one another across so many axes as to have become mutually inextricable. And the labor of filmmaking, of which the films are both product and record, pays fraternal tribute to the other labors necessary to make and maintain of earth a world, an order. (We may note Robert's handsome tribute to Ruskin [his 1975/1997 film], suggesting a shared perception of the continuity of aesthetics and ethics.) Cutting a suit, sewing a buttonhole, sweeping the leaves of the Salzburg hedge theater (in *Amor*, just allowed in from the edge of the frame): these hold no less dignity than is concentrated in the grand architectural achievements Robert has examined and celebrated, or in the splendors of the Greek landscape. Robert's films are indeed erudite; they are also humble, loving, toward quotidian reality.

9 Beavers, "EM·BLEM."
10 Beavers, "The Senses."
11 Beavers, "La Terra Nuova."

Don Daniels

A Master Motif

Aesthetic Benefice in Four Films by Robert Beavers

Artists take what they need from the past and inevitably serve the needs of the present and future. If there is one quality that identifies Gregory Markopoulos as a Modern, it is the salvific aim of his work. The Modern artist may find inexactitude and malpractice all about him, and to rectify this state a spiritual rebirth may be necessary. Markopoulos's vision of a Temenos – a site for experiencing his work (and that of Robert Beavers) toward a spiritual incubation and cure – is a prescription following general diagnosis. In that sense, Markopoulos resembles the later Martha Graham, the Jungian arch-priestess at home in the problematic. It is his rhapsodic gift that saves Markopoulos from authorial over-indictment. His often razor-sharp cinematography cuts through any mythopoeic excess. And his pleasure in cinematic form and style is as apparent as are his accusations.

As for the past, Markopoulos's aesthetic can also appear to echo certain ideas of early German philosophical writers such as Friedrich Hölderlin and Friedrich Schlegel. Hölderlin's concept of Being (a version of the Absolute out of Spinoza) resembles Markopoulos's scattered references to "eternity" in his writings on film.[1] Schlegel's *Fragments* established a tradition in Romantic and Modern art that legitimized the use of the fragmentary statement or gesture, an approach that the avant-garde still claims to this day, including filmmakers who see themselves as experimental or advanced. Markopoulos's conception of what he would call "short film phrases" could be seen as an eventual – whether conscious or unconscious – cinematic version of Schlegel's fragment. And Schlegel's view of the true artwork includes an insistence on the uses of memory, intuition, and presentiment to constitute an approximation of reality. I am thinking of one of Markopoulos's statements that "a vision is always the future. The moment we consider the past or the present we are consumed by the constant future."[2]

The salvific aim of Markopoulos's aesthetic can be seen in *Lysis*, the central work of the trilogy *Du sang, de la volupté et de la mort* (1947–48). There is a loosely evolving narrative in *Lysis* which suggests the philosophical inquiry in the Platonic work of the same name, the Socratic dialogue *Lysis*. The dialogue is a discussion of what constitutes the gift of true friendship, the

1 See, for example, Markopoulos's "A Note (for Jean-Paul Vroom)," in *Film as Film: The Collected Writings of Gregory J. Markopoulos*, ed. Mark Webber, London: The Visible Press, 2014, p. 236–7.
2 Gregory Markopoulos, "Towards a Temenos," *Film as Film*, ed. Webber, p. 347.

finding of the "first friend."[3] In the film we see Markopoulos himself in what appears to be such a search, the protagonist as a Romantic wanderer-poet. In an early montage in *Lysis*, the shots of candles, a pillow, and fruit might suggest that an erotic relationship has revelatory and transfiguring potential. Before a window, hand shadows are silhouetted in sunlight. (Such shadow play will find a role in Robert Beavers's works as well.)

The Socratic dialogue *Lysis* argues that the test of true friendship is for each member of a couple to make the gift of wisdom to the other. This free bestowal would represent the highest, finest gift of all. Within each of his scenes, Markopoulos allows himself a baroque assembly of imageries, which are so strong that he is free to create his own filmic orders of reference. The fragmented play of light and visual composition may even overwhelm the thin narrative thread that we follow. We submit to the visual fragmentation within each sequence as though subject to the same confusion as the protagonist. A spiritual rebirth may require time, and something like a chastened graduation, complete with academic setting, could be said to occur in the third film in the trilogy, *Charmides*. Markopoulos's play with time – so plastic in form, so various in effect – is basic to all of his filmmaking, from the short film phrases in *Twice a Man* (1964) to the enormous temporal scale of his magnum opus *Eniaios* (1948–c.1990). When the complete 80-hour *Eniaios* is eventually screened, Markopoulos's reputation may well experience a rebirth of its own.

If Markopoulos's theme is regeneration, Beavers makes birth itself – an act of creative forthcoming, primal aesthetic generation – a central concern. No definitive word can be spoken on this filmmaker's ongoing project while he is still actively involved in producing it. But Beavers's re-editing of 18 of his films to constitute an enormous three-part statement, *My Hand Outstretched to the Winged Distance and Sightless Measure*, allows us to identify some themes and motifs. This essay will concentrate on one such theme: the gift of artistic parturition. Birth and re-birth are obviously related, but the two filmmakers approach them distinctly. While Markopoulos imagines an alternative to the status quo ("What use is a world that does not contain the gift of friendship?"), Beavers is fascinated with what is given ("What *is* a gift?").

It can also be said that Beavers has had an abiding curiosity about what it is that a motion picture can deliver – can offer up uniquely – because his first unmistakable masterpiece, *From the Notebook of...* (1971/1998), makes the bestowal of cinematic content its central fascination. Through its use of associative editing, moving mattes, and color filters, *Notebook* allows the spectator to see its maker invent a modernized praxinoscope or zoetrope, animation devices of the 19th century.

We watch the filmmaker in the process of making the film that we are watching. As a re-

3 Terry Penner and Christopher Rowe, *Plato's "Lysis,"* Cambridge: Cambridge University Press, 2005, p. 275–278.

From the Notebook of…

sult, we must experience the unreeling work as we find ourselves simultaneously educated in the processes of its invention. Beavers luxuriates in his self-assembled technology, and his excuse for its maximum exploitation is an analysis of the motifs from Leonardo da Vinci's notebooks: birds, waves, clouds, plants, cylinders, shadows, horses, a child, male models, the eye, and geometrical lines and forms which connect the motifs across the length of his 48 minute film. (Beavers re-edited the film to its current length in 1998.) The filmmaker was 23 years old when he delivered himself of this wonder. The older Beavers recognized its place in his oeuvre by making it the first work in the second part of *My Hand Outstretched*.

Notebook allows each motif to argue for itself: the film's editing manages to be both fleet and weighted shot by shot. Each evoked element can refer to Leonardo's study of the world's "complete and proper forms" as filtered through an artist's vision.[4] Beavers was also inspired by Paul Valéry's writings on Leonardo, especially the poet's famous long essay "Introduction to the Method of Leonardo da Vinci," written when Valéry was himself 23 years old.

In the 1894 "Introduction," Valéry emphasizes the combination of scientific rigor and imaginative construction in Leonardo's investigations.[5] As Valéry describes it, *"The pattern of this world* belongs to a family of patterns, of which, without knowing it, we possess all the elements of the infinite group. This is the secret of inventors."[6] In his *Notebook*, Beavers may be constructing a kind of cinematic machine which compares and contrasts certain forms

and thus invents a controlled display of its findings. The "Notebook" of the title would thus refer to Leonardo's famous notebooks, to Valéry's commentaries, and to various notebook entries by Beavers himself (composed in the conception and realization of his cinematic project) that appear in close-up throughout the film.

Part of the intellectual wit of the film is its gathering into "families" of the various motifs that Beavers has chosen to review from his desk and through his Florentine window. We watch the motifs congregate, vary in their combination, and return under new guises. The families not only reform cyclically, but their novel regroupings reveal new configurations, whether of provenance, visual shape, aural dynamic, or abstract form. A lens cylinder that throws a triangular shadow anticipates a nude model's muscled arm and then his profiled penis. The cylinder's triangular shadow on the desktop mirrors a pointed shadow on the surface of the Arno. The slippage of these motivic orders from day to night to day, from isolation via mattes to full-screen display, from naturalist to filtered chromatics, gives a sense of direction for the entirety of Beavers's motion picture: as his materials accumulate, the full confession of cinematic device is made.

4 For quotation from and discussion of Leonardo's *Treatise on Painting*, see Kenneth Clark, *Moments of Vision*, London: John Murray, 1981, p. 19.
5 Paul Valéry, *Leonardo Poe Mallarmé*, trans. Malcolm Cowley and James R. Lawler, Princeton: Princeton University Press, 1972, p. 3–109.
6 Ibid., p. 93.

As the disjunctive fragments recompose themselves into families, the effect is something like that of the scientific concept of "emergence," the way a physical state can give birth to new properties from a dynamic but controlled set of conditions. (I am thinking of British mathematician John Conway's "Life," a cellular automaton described in John H. Holland's book-length exposition, *Emergence*.)[7] There is a natural example early in Beavers's film when the camera pans down toward the Arno's rushing stream, divided and then recomposed around a bridge stanchion, so that standing waves emerge from the resonance of the manufactured crosscurrents. It is my idea that an equivalent "glide," with an emergence of novel forms and meanings, takes place across the *My Hand* films, the motif of birthing or coming-forth appearing in subsequent parts of the cycle.

On one level, Beavers's cinematic machine has what Valéry describes as a poem's self-sufficiency, what Kenneth Burke calls "a directionless reticulation of interrelationships."[8] The critic Hugh Kenner calls such a formal possibility a "parallax" aesthetic, whereby the artist circles around a subject as Proust's Marcel uses a church spire for orientation in time and space. On another level, we travel toward a refined sense of cinematic elegance and grace through what Kenneth Clark calls Leonardo's fascina-

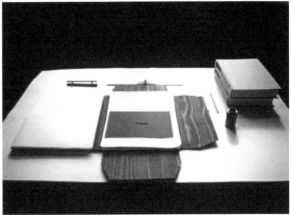

From the Notebook of...

7 John H. Holland, *Emergence: From Chaos to Order*, New York: Basic Books, 1998, p. 138–141.
8 Kenneth Burke, "Towards a Post-Kantian Verbal Music," *Praising It New*, ed. Garrick Davis, Athens: Swallow Press/Ohio University Press, 2008, p. 282.

tion with impulse and continuity, translated here into Beavers's revelation of specific cinematic forms. (Beavers's whirligig produces something more than just rhetorical "elegant variation.") As Valéry eventually suggests, true poetic language may finally be described as magical. In that sense, Beavers has found a poetic language through the magic of *From the Notebook of....*

An "animated" film (and *Notebook* approaches such a form but not quite) can run the risk of over-control, but Beavers avoids this trap through an apparent spontaneity of discovery of the declared family members of his Leonardo motifs. The viewer may participate in sensing the hidden pattern, perhaps discovering in his own response a mood related to the filmmaker's happy finds.

The most dramatic evidence of a generative motif in *Notebook* is aural rather than visual: the explosive sound of the flapping of a bird's wings before any image is seen at the start of the film. Later, we see a bird take off from a man's hand. Later still, we see a hand toss a bird into the air. (Leonardo's dream of human flight hovers over each scene.) The soundtrack captures the powerful avian takeoff and the diminishing flutter of aerial escape. The imagery (both sound and photographic shot) refers to the legend that Leonardo liked to buy a bird in the market on its way to a Florentine table and release it into the urban sky. Beavers's film shows us such captives, their cages, the burst of wing thrust, and the flight of liberation. That sound of impulse and continuity gives *Notebook* its rhythmic germ or kernel. We hear an analogous whirl of machinery under Beavers's moving mattes throughout the film. Perhaps this is one of his agreements with Valéry, who holds in *The Art of Poetry* that a poem begins with a "system of rhythms."[9] Lincoln Kirstein once said that what the master choreographer George Balanchine needed to make a ballet was a fresh rhythmic germ.

In the first film of the *My Hand Outstretched* cycle, *Winged Dialogue* (1967/2000), the sound of birds' wings suggests not only flight but synchronization, an immediate connection between minds tuned to one another through the appreciation and practice of art. That opening heard-but-not-seen wingstress might be taken as annunciatory, a plangent fanfare for the cycle as a whole. Something is being birthed on a large scale.

Beavers's films are often referred to as "classical," and in *Notebook* such an identification seems especially apt. He elevates cinematic technique (and Markopoulos's insistence on "film as film") to the level of released content, the individual component of a motif raised to the role of formal element, and the two combining to distill a rhythm and style unique to each film. Notice the introduction of a sliver of the filmmaker's profile at the edge of many *Notebook* shots, a technique not only emphasizing depth of visual field and the subjectivity of Beavers's vision, but also something like Wayne J. Froman's concept of the "seer" lo-

9 Paul Valéry, "Poetry and Abstract Thought," *The Art of Poetry*, Princeton: Princeton University Press, 1958, p. 61–81.

cated in that field.[10] In Froman's analysis of action painting, the artist's world becomes the enclosed but simultaneously expanded subject of the artwork. No wonder that at the end of *Notebook* the filmmaker has left his room and his studies; we see his profile framing a sunlit newsstand, as if he is eager to buy a newspaper. *Notebook*'s opening aural suggestion of an impulsive birthing of its depicted world eventually produces the benefice of a return *to* the world. An explosion of wings leads to the gift of portraiture, as we see Gregory Markopoulos posed before Beavers's manned camera in the mirrored final shot of the film.

The Painting (1972/1999) returns the filmmaker to artwork, in this case the anonymous Flemish triptych *The Martyrdom of Saint Hippolytus*. Beavers filmed street exteriors in Bern, Switzerland, and the 15th-century triptych at the Museum of Fine Arts in Boston. He cuts between a single long shot of pedestrian and vehicular traffic in the noisy Bern Theaterplatz and details from the altarpiece showing the preparation for the equine-powered dismemberment of the third-century saint: horses have been tied to each of Hippolytus's four limbs, and he is being lifted from the ground by their teamwork. We hear the sound of a whip urging the animals toward their deadly stampede. Each time we hear the sound of the lash, the screen goes blindingly into what appears to be transparent film leader but is actually a shot of

10 Wayne J. Froman, "Action Painting and the World-as-Picture," *The Merleau-Ponty Aesthetics Reader: Philosophy and Painting*, ed. Galen A. Johnson, Evanston: Northwestern University Press, 1993, p. 344.

The Painting (1972/1999)

The Painting

white paper under glass (which can be seen as a line down the middle of the frame).

The viewer can take the interplay between the painting and the urban landscape in several ways. One interpretation might be that the saint's sacrifice is like that of Osiris and Dionysus in that their physical beings were strewn about the ancient world – whereas our modern world distributes energies via technological routing. Subsequent reassembly or re-synthesis may or may not occur. The shot of contemporary cars, motorbikes, and trams catches the quality of our daily life; once, martyrdom itself was ordinary and the victim and his torturers enjoyed just such an objective, indifferent background to life and death. In the juxtaposition of these disparate images, we can see our present world as inheritor of those value systems illustrated in the painting – pagan and early Christian beliefs have helped constitute our modernity – or as a contradiction to such values.

The saint's death served to give birth beyond itself: to the martyr's legend, to the painting the film examines, and to Beavers's film itself. There are two references to such a birthing in Beavers's images. First, the drawing and quartering of Hippolytus is depicted with what appears to be the literal cracking of an optical system. (Here would be another version of Schlegel's fragmentation in modern art.) Several times we see a faint circle produced by a reflection of the camera lens on the glass in the filmmaker's matte box. When the "explosion" of the saint's death occurs in the form of a shot of his tortured body in the painting, it is often followed by a shot of cracked glass; the violent act has broken the glass both literally and metaphorically. The second reference is found in a subsequent sequence of intercut shots featuring a torn photograph of Beavers. We hear the sound of the photo being ripped before we see the evidence of torn portraiture.

As filmic montage, the moment of death for the martyr occurs in a sequence of three images: the spread-eagled body being lifted from the ground, the shattered glass, and the ripped image of the filmmaker. Scattered through the film's juxtapositions are shots of what appear to be dust motes circulating through third- or 20th-century air. (These latter are reminiscent of the particulates utilized by Alain Resnais to frame scenes in his *Love Unto Death* [1984]. They also function like the caught dust particles in the interior paintings of the Danish artist Vilhelm Hammershøi – as emblems of sunlit, daily reality. The motes disperse and resettle.) But the three images (martyr, glass, filmmaker) suggest that the construction of the film we are watching has not only required a destructive gesture but has released its aesthetic burden in a perceptual reknitting.

There is an equivalent attitude toward the function of the film artwork in the writings of the French philosopher-aesthetician Maurice Merleau-Ponty. In his 1948 *Causeries*, he defines filmmaking as follows: "What matters is the selection of episodes to be represented and, in each one, the choice of shots that will be featured in the film, the length of time allotted to these elements, the order in which they are to be presented, the sound of words with which they are or are not to be accompanied. Taken together, all these factors contribute to form a particular overall cinematographical rhythm."[11] Merleau-Ponty is identifying features in what he eventually refers to as the "lining" of an artwork (including a film) and which traditional criticism would call its stylistic and formal elements. He sees such warp and woof as the very substance of the artwork itself, not merely its mechanisms.

For Merleau-Ponty, this unique substance born from the artist's project is sometimes called the "vow" of the work, something like what Paul Ricoeur calls a work's "advent." The release of particular content is accompanied by a "dehiscence" (a bursting forth) or a "deflagration" (an explosion), indicating the force which the insight has pressed upon daily reality in order to free itself.[12] From such a conception of impersonal aesthetic procedures, no wonder the martyr must die; no wonder the lens must crack; no wonder the persona of the filmmaker must be discarded and then redefined in each new work's delivery.

Beavers claims that he read only one volume of Merleau-Ponty when he was young and that he can report no direct influence from the philosopher. Merleau-Ponty had died five years before Beavers began making films. But ideas such as the ones I have been suggesting were not only in the air, like dust motes, during the mid-20th century; Merleau-Ponty's imageries (birth, destruction-creation, phenomenological presence) were elemental enough to take many forms in the parallel thought of widespread artists and aestheticians. It is the philosopher's perceptual aesthetic that generates his categories, perhaps even more than his well-known ontology of flesh, desire, and invisibility; in "Eye and Mind" he says that the "painter's vision is an ongoing birth."[13]

Indeed, there are multiple parallels to be discovered between The Painting and Merleau-Ponty's "Cézanne's Doubt," "Indirect Language and the Voices of Silence," and "Eye and Mind."[14] "Cézanne's Doubt" is partially a critique of Valéry's concept of Leonardo's "method" of artistic investigation, a method that may substitute rigor for life. Merleau-Ponty describes formal ligatures, which he calls "hinges," found in the "lining" of an artwork's reality, hinges which connect with the sound of window shutters being opened and closed in both Notebook and The Painting. Merleau-Ponty sees a work's lining as featuring a kind of "selvage," a self-made hem on the artist's piece of fabric. That border evokes the way Beavers begins and ends The Painting by exploring the perimeters of the depicted action, working his way toward and away from the horrific act at the painting's center. Seen in a philosophical light, the violent benefice of The Painting may be its depiction of a ceremony of perception and sacrifice operative in our modern world under the guise of art-making itself.

Robert Beavers approaches personal, individual trauma through the lens of artworks –

11 Maurice Merleau-Ponty, "Lecture 6: Art and the World of Perception," The World of Perception, trans. Oliver Davis, London: Routledge, 2004, p. 98.
12 Maurice Merleau-Ponty, "Eye and Mind," The Merleau-Ponty Aesthetics Reader, ed. Johnson, p. 121–49.
13 Ibid., p. 129–30.
14 All three essays are included in the Reader.

his own and others'. We see such materials filtered through multiple analogues. Think of the anguish raised to the demoniac intensity of the filmmaker's *Plan of Brussels* (1968/2000). He does something equivalent with biographical data in *Sotiros* (1976–78/1996), which is composed of two parts: first, the interior of a hotel room in Bern, Switzerland, counterpointed with a wide range of images shot in various locations in Greece; and second, the same hotel room during a period when Beavers was recovering from a mid-1970s bus accident in Greece. In the first part of the film, shots of the hotel room are invaded by spots and wedges of lemony sunlight; these interior shots are contrasted with scenes from Athens, Sparta, and Leonidio which have a blue cast, suggesting a different film stock or natural atmospheric filtering. Those lozenges of light on interior walls are harbingers of the promise of exteriority. The words "he said" appear in various shots, perhaps literally indicating that, at some point in time, spoken words in the room related its interior to various Greek sites.

The sense that time is suspended in the work's first part is fascinating. The overarching "present tense" of film places the locales of *Sotiros* outside temporal specificity. We usually assume a cause and effect chronology in the sequencing of a motion picture, but here the scenes in Greece could occur before or after the sojourn in Bern. What could be taken eventually as prescient details are knotted into a skein of specific place and ambiguous sequence thanks to the temporal suspension. Are the urban shots of a blind beggar predictive or

retroactive, given the filmmaker's bus accident? At least once, Beavers has referred to *Sotiros* as "religious" in its subject matter. The questions that form in the viewer's mind may be meant to go unanswered in any conventional sense. Perhaps what is being evoked is something like Jung's "meaningful coincidence" or synchronicity. Beavers's method of editing his films over the course of many years allows him to create juxtapositions that carry out Schlegel's requirement that the artwork contain a combination of memory, intuition, and presentiment.

In the second part of the film, there is a stylistic shift as the editing becomes abrupt; its jagged exits and entrances into therapeutic materials (the recovering filmmaker exercising, resting, and manning his camera tripod) might be described as "magmatic," that is, intense, fragmented, and raw with immediacy. This half ends with a depiction of a piece of paper that is held by two hands, ripped repeatedly by them, the fragments then allowed to fall to the floor accompanied by the sounds of tearing. The image and sound of torn paper may be an echo of the idea of a dehiscence, like that articulated by the torn photograph and the optical explosion in *The Painting*. It is as though the motif appears here as a talisman, guarding the figure of the patient against any recovery that is not transformative – a true parturition, rather than a mere rebirth.

The remarkable soundtrack of *Sotiros* adds to the sense of temporal collapse and expansion. It features traffic sounds from Athens (especially the buses on Harilaou Trikoupi Street) and

Sotiros

Plan of Brussels

eruptive fragments of Alban Berg's score for *Wozzeck*. The scenes in Bern are underscored with traffic noise, which continues under the shots of the Greek countryside. An eventual suggestion of thunder in the city is confirmed later to originate in the Greek hillsides, an example of sound-layering that conflates sources and locales.

My favorite combination of sound and sight occurs in an early sequence: a silver olive grove swaying in strong winds while the sound of street traffic adds to the metallic imagery of tossed leaves. A ticking sound (the cane-tapping beggar?) under a pastoral landscape connects with the dripping of water from the hotel room's leaking faucet. Thus, individual sounds can play a quasi-metonymic role, the isolated sonic detail standing for a general ambience. In the same way that Beavers will include a visual close-up (a cup of coffee) and only later show its location (a Greek café), just so our identification of the origin of certain sound details may occur only retrospectively. In the auditor's memory and imagination, such sonic details, initially heard close up, eventually compose something like an auditory "long shot" achieved over time.

This talent for the slow "reveal" of the nature of the filmed object, sound, or action is everywhere in Beavers's work. One magical example is the discovery in *Efpsychi* (1983/1996) that what appears to be wind-blown grass on a

sandy seaside is actually a close-up of a man's eyebrow. That film's depiction of the old market area in Athens is shot through with the facial features of the filmmaker's young male actor appearing Tchelitchew-like amid façades of the old buildings and street-sign references to the city's famous cultural heroes and legends. Flesh has seldom been made to seem more alive, and building façades suddenly take on an anthropomorphic mystery and pathos. *Efpsychi* is a masterpiece of atmosphere and poetic suggestion. The delayed revelation of the provenance of a visual detail encapsulates the creation-out-of-nothing motif in this artist's cinematic vision: the filmmaker as birthwright.

One last example of the motif of parturition can be found in *The Hedge Theater* (1986–90/2002). The film is, like *Sotiros*, in two parts. The first half finds comparisons between shots in Rome of Borromini's San Carlo alle Quattro Fontane and the waiting birdcages in a *roccolo* in Brescia, Lombardy (followed by shots of Borromini's Sant'Ivo alla Sapienza in Rome and the famous Naturtheater in winter Salzburg). There is a suggestion of book-ending here toward the climax of the third part of *My Hand Outstretched*, since the Naturtheater also figures in Beavers's *Amor* (1980) and the birdcages bring to mind the released birds in *From the Notebook of...* I can't help but think of the "constitutional nets" in the poem *"Reti per uccelli"* by Eugenio Montale.[15] The avians that Montale portrays are captives who know only that they are the creatures of others who decree their captivity; they can only await release. In his 1946 ballet *The Four Temperaments*, George Balanchine

15 Eugenio Montale, *The Collected Poems of Eugenio Montale, 1925–1977*, trans. William Arrowsmith, ed. Rosanna Warren, New York: W.W. Norton and Company, 2012, p. 590–593.

finds comparable imageries of entrapment and release, of homunculi and demiurges, toward an alchemical bestowal of spiritual grace.

Part two of *The Hedge Theater* centers on Il Sassetta's 15th-century panel entitled *Saint Martin and the Beggar,* in the Collezioni Chigi-Saracini in Siena, intercut with more shots of the Naturtheater in full bloom. The panel shows Saint Martin of Tours cutting his cloak in two in order to give half to a beggar. As the camera pans the panel, we hear the rip of the cloak fabric. The film ends with rain washing away winter snow.

The Hedge Theater was 15 years in gestation and was the final film to be completed in the editing of the complete *My Hand Outstretched* cycle. The cutting of the cloak may be another version of the ripping of the photograph in *The Painting.* The return of a sound signaling a birth-gift toward the end of Beavers's cycle is reminiscent of Heidegger's introduction of the "There is / It gives" formulation in the philosopher's later writings ("The Way to Language" and "The Task of Thinking").[16] For Heidegger, saying is a form of "propriation," of ownership; thus, language can bestow upon us some residence in what we own, the very essence of our existence (*Dasein*). The clarity (clearing) that can come with thought suggests what Heidegger calls a "presencing" which could uncover the very subject matter of thought itself. In commenting on Hölderlin's hymn "The Ister," Heidegger refers to such an unbidden bestowal by quoting the concluding lines from that poet's "The Journey":

If someone tries to grasp it by stealth, he holds
A dream in his hand, and him who uses force
To make himself its peer, it punishes.
Yet often it takes by surprise
A man whose mind it has hardly entered.[17]

Nothing in *The Hedge Theater* could be described as "philosophical" in overt terms, but the motif I have been discussing (and which this fourth film adumbrates) may indicate an underlying stratum of "subject matter" in Beavers's poetic thought. His language has developed to the point where a surface metaphor (the gift of the cloak) can allude to a motif (birth) released across a temporally lavish cycle of filmmaking. And the fascination is not only the variety of documented experience drawn upon for the films of that cycle but the variety of ways in which the cinematic revelations are truly surprising in the Heidegger-Hölderlin sense.

The cycle records a continuously aborning aesthetic. We discover that when a gift appears, a kind of unique magic has made itself present. The cycle's emphasis on multifarious inspiration and formal exploration marks Beavers as a true Modernist.

Beavers had made 10 films before *From the Notebook of...* over a period of five years (1966–1970). The formation of an artistic idiom usually takes some time, but Beavers was unusually

16 Martin Heidegger, *Basic Writings*, San Francisco: Harper San Francisco, 1977, p. 415, 449.
17 Friedrich Hölderlin, "The Journey," *Selected Poems and Fragments*, trans. Michael Hamburger, ed. Jeremy Adler, London: Penguin Books, 1998, p. 182–189.

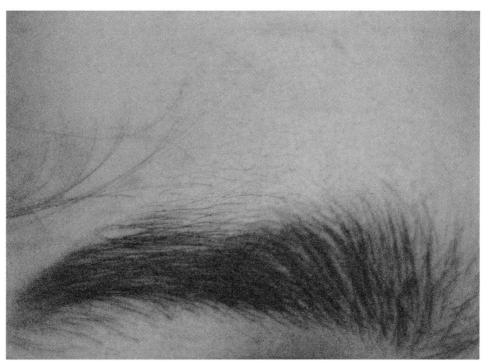

Efpsychi
(1983/1996)

rapid in development: 1970 – an *annus mirabilis* – saw the completion of *Palinode, Diminished Frame*, and *Still Light*. The technical knowledge required to produce *Notebook*'s dazzle is very impressive, but equally so is the poise and lucidity with which it releases the burden of its youthful lived experience. Usually, only musicians and dancers are required to develop so early and so carefully and to hold in readiness such infused and specific strengths in the practice of their skills.

In American culture, we tend to overlook the vital cushion of this preparatory state in the production of art. We say, at most, that the artist has developed "technique" or that he or she has a "gift." (Heidegger tried to specify such held technology by using the term "reserve," as in a holding in reserve.) Beavers's early maturity is another indication that we need new terms for discussing what the young can give so freely, so happily, so fully. An individual stroke in a filmmaker's, a musician's, a dancer's work (image, phrasal element, cadence, gesture) is often underpinned and sponsored by a versed intuition straight from the artist's developing skill, his held "reserve." I am thinking of this filmmaker's later statement that *Amor* has an element of erotic violence, which has turned into something gentler by *The Hedge Theater*.[18] Such a change may seem to appear immediately, upon the release of a film. But its advent may have taken time. It is indeed the high play with large temporal values in Beavers's films that complicates the challenge of a formalist approach for his interpreters.

At the time of this writing, Beavers's latest film, *First Weeks* (2015), takes as its camera subject the newborn son of the filmmaker Luke Fowler. It can be seen as an instant gift to the child's parents. There was just such a precocious emphasis on time in certain titles of Beavers's first films – *Early Monthly Segments*, *The Count of Days* – an emphasis which suggests a presentiment of maturation, the same longing for ripeness that is found in the work of Mallarmé, Proust, and Valéry. Especially in Valéry (as in his poem "Palme") we find a fascination with the patience and endurance required for the eventual benefice of art, whose fruit emerges not only in convulsive parturition but in accumulated growth. It is something like this perception that has allowed a filmmaker's hand to grasp art's amplitude and rule in the offering of his films.

---

18 See program notes by the filmmaker for a March 2013 screening of his films at the Harvard Film Archive ("An Evening with Robert Beavers").

Susan Oxtoby

The Sightless Measure –
Love, Loss, and Eternity

The Hedge Theater (1986–90/2002), *The Stoas*
(1991–97), and *The Ground* (1993–2001), the magnificent concluding trio of works in *My Hand
Outstretched to the Winged Distance and Sightless
Measure,* represent a poetic expression of love,
loss, and mourning. The films resonate with a
world that is enriched by art, architecture, literature, and music, trace an autobiographical
trajectory, and respond to the beauty of the natural world through an attention to landscape
and the seasons.

This essay will address the primary thematic
arc that unites the final three films in the cycle
and speak to the richness and subtlety of their
cinematic expression. My intention is threefold.
First, to offer an appreciation of the poetics (the
themes and leitmotifs as well as formal qualities) of *The Hedge Theater* through an examina-
tion of the film's careful image/sound construction. Next, to consider the exquisite use of
locations and overarching compositional structure in *The Stoas,* a deeply moving work that
uses cinematic space to evoke absence, loss,
passage, and renewal. Lastly, to comment on
how Beavers moves us from a consideration of
the real world to a more abstract sense of the
eternal in *The Ground*, the concluding work in
his cycle that stands as a profound expression of
love and spirituality.

Beavers's aesthetic approach to filmmaking
has long held great appeal and fascination for
me. I find his films to be continually rewarding,
becoming only richer with more study and
thought. Indeed, I marvel at their virtuosic
quality and Beavers's ability to labor single-
handedly as an independent filmmaker (as cin-
ematographer, editor, sound designer and
mixer, and frequently as an on-screen subject)
who works with his materials in a highly sophisticated way. His cinema is a delight not
only for the eyes and ears but for the heart and
mind. Beavers's commitment to the art of filmmaking is philosophical – to a greater understanding of reality, existence, and the self. Yet
his films do not prescribe one line of reading or
analysis, but rather use an open form that offers
each viewer space for interpretation.

~

Like earlier works in *My Hand Outstretched,*
these final films explore themes of self-portraiture and autobiography and can be understood
through the lens of Beavers's partnership with
Gregory Markopoulos, with whom he shared
his life between 1966 and 1992. Earlier in the
cycle, their relationship is referenced in the ecstatic, multiple-exposure superimpositions of
the two men sunbathing nude and swimming

off the Greek island of Hydra in *Winged Dialogue* (1967/2000), and in domestic scenes in *Early Monthly Segments* (1968–70/2002), the Florentine pension in *From the Notebook of...* (1971/1998), and the temporary living quarters of *Sotiros* (1976–78/1996). While each film in the cycle deals with different psychological and emotional states, I find the character and magnitude of expression in the last films especially affecting, perfectly conceived in relationship to one another.

I want to begin by offering a few historical and interpretive notes related to the making of these films that inform my overall analysis. *The Hedge Theater* was made between 1986 and 1990 and filmed mostly in Rome. At the time he began this project, Beavers was 37 years old and had lived with Markopoulos in various European countries for some 20 years. In 2002, he completed the 35mm blow-up from the original 16mm negative and added the stereo soundtrack. This film contains the final on-screen appearance of Markopoulos. *The Stoas* was filmed in Greece (Athens and Arcadia) and completed between 1991 and 1997, a period of time that is marked by the 1992 death of Markopoulos. Even though *The Stoas* was largely shot and edited before Markopoulos's passing, the poetic overtones of this beautiful work seem to carry an indirect relationship to his death. *The Ground* was made between 1993 and 2001, and was filmed on Hydra, the location of Beavers's early *Winged Dialogue*. In essence, *The Ground* can be read as an expression of grief and eternal love.

THEMES AND LEITMOTIFS: *THE HEDGE THEATER*

Beavers uses the syntax of cinema to express ideas and emotions. He foregrounds qualities of the filmed image and articulates spatial relationships between images and between image and sound, just as a poet might use the arrangement of words, assonance, consonance, and rhythm to evoke meaning, or a composer might employ leitmotif, harmony, and compositional structure in musical expression.

An exceptional example of poetic sound/image construction, *The Hedge Theater* utilizes multiple intertwined themes and leitmotifs along with a range of formal strategies. Several themes are established in the opening minutes and then elaborated as the film progresses, allowing for even greater poetic associations. The film takes its name from the Naturtheater or hedge theater in the Mirabell Gardens in Salzburg where Beavers also filmed scenes for *Amor* (1980) and *Wingseed* (1985). Imagery from the Austrian location, filmed in winter and springtime, appears during the last few minutes of the film.

With the opening shot, Beavers sets up the film's first thematic concept, the use and representation of gardens not only in his film cycle but more broadly in the history of literature, Renaissance art, and Baroque landscape architecture (such as the famous garden in Salzburg). The first image is held onscreen for a relatively long time compared with other shots in this work. This stasis allows us a chance to study the establishing scene with its curious, center-frame intersection of a narrow tree trunk with a similarly-sized wooden pole that acts as a bar-

The Hedge Theater
(1986–90/2002)

rier to the pool of water that lies beyond, producing a subtle sense of tension. When Beavers cuts back to garden scenes later on, he presents additional compositions of trees. Two tree trunks growing close together, for instance, evoke the idea of a coupled unity, which is echoed later in the depiction of twinned neoclassical columns or paired lovers – shots of Markopoulos and Beavers themselves.

The theme of self-portraiture is introduced in the second shot of the film: we see Beavers behind the camera filming himself reflected in a mirror. He has his right hand raised in a gesture or signal. Could it be read as an oath or a solemn promise? The gesture is clearly meant to be ambiguous, not fixed in its meaning, but merely suggestive. Throughout the film, we return to imagery of self-portraiture (initially with Beavers alone and later with Markopoulos). There are several images of the filmmaker with sunlight falling on his face, cheek, and neck. Beavers wears a white, long-sleeved shirt that figures prominently, at first worn loosely, unbuttoned. At other times he's seen fastening the collar button or, later, unbuttoning the shirt at the neck. These states of dress or undress conjure up associative meanings, especially in relation to the film's intersecting themes (the brotherhood of the church, his love of Markopoulos, and lessons learned from the story of Saint Martin and the beggar, to which I will return later).

The theme of religious spirituality or, more specifically, Catholicism, enters in the film's third and fourth shots, when we see imagery of a church designed by the Italian architect Francesco Borromini. The grandeur and sublime beauty of the architecture and the inspired way in which Beavers films interior and exterior details (of what are ultimately three different churches and one other building in Rome designed by Borromini) is rich with resonance. The church is a metaphor for space, a state of mind, tradition, faith, devotion, and a sense of grace.

Beavers's montage returns to architectural details, presenting the churches' domes, columns, and carved stone ornamentation such as a cherub and martyr's crown. At one point, Beavers cuts from an image of a stone cross with elaborate extending rays to a shot of a barren tree whose form has a similar radiating shape, and then quickly back to the stone carving – a lovely visual rhyme that is characteristic of the delicate quality of this film. Yet another exquisite moment, both subtle and tactile, occurs when the shadow of a hand passing over fluted church columns is accompanied by the quiet sound of metal being struck gently. The dissociative sound calls attention to the implied sense of touch in the image. Similarly, while the vaulted sound environment of the church – including a Latin mass and organ music – evokes the theme of Christianity, these same sounds are at other times laid under shots of non-church locations (the streets of Rome or landscape imagery), thus functioning as an aural bridge helping to unite disparate poetic elements.

The leitmotif introduced at the one-minute mark of the film, when we see a fleeting image of an empty birdcage, might be read as an

The Hedge Theater

expression of freedom. (The empty birdcage is a recurrent image in this film and one that connects *The Hedge Theater* to the film cycle's overarching metaphor of flight.) Beavers's deft camerawork and exacting montage help tease out and prompt the viewer to question the ways in which the birdcage can be read. And viewers familiar with the *roccolo*, the grove of trees seen in this film, might think of the Italian hunting tradition of setting out cages with decoys, called *richiami,* the song of which attracts other birds. The formal complexity of the barren tree branches in the *roccolo* is wonderfully maze-like – in one shot composition, for instance, it is not obvious which direction is up or down.

Approaching the two-minute mark, we see an extreme close-up of a woman's hands stitching a buttonhole on a white shirt much like the one worn by Beavers. Her skill is noteworthy and in harmony with the theme of craftsmanship that runs throughout the cycle. The image is accompanied by the sound of sewing, representing a somewhat rare instance of diegetic sound, and the motion of sewing is combined with a wonderfully fluid edit that is facilitated by the rapidity of Beavers's hallmark lens turret move. The aperture on the camera closes down at the exact point that links the image of sewing with the following image of church architecture, thereby fusing the two shots almost viscerally.

Beavers often generates double or multiple meanings by establishing relations among distinct objects, spaces, and actions and between disparate images and sounds. The recurring image of sewing, for instance, is a visual metaphor for editing – for Beavers's own work of suturing images, sounds, and thematic elements together. Additionally, the oval shape of the buttonhole rhymes with the church dome and window grates and the eyelet form of one of the pruned trees in the garden.

The first image of Markopoulos in *The Hedge Theater* is introduced around 13 minutes into the film. His presence is powerful despite the fact that his screen time is limited and we never see his face fully. His presence is first anticipated by sounds and images: we hear a passage of organ music and see an ornate church steeple, an interior cupola, a martyr's crown and cherub carved in stone, and then snow falling in the garden. It is within this context that we see a simple, graceful and brief shot of Markopoulos's hand on Beavers's shoulder. The images that follow include a deep blanket of snow that has fallen in the Salzburg garden and, later, a statue of a lion underneath snow. Beavers's hand gently touches Markopoulos's and later, Markopoulos holds Beavers's shoulder firmly and assuredly. Ultimately, in the series of images depicting the men together, Beavers shares control of the filming of their image with Markopoulos. This sharing of the camerawork is symbolic of their intimate relationship.

Beavers also represents their relationship through visual metaphor; in addition to cameraman, lover, and soul mate, Markopoulos is likened to king, lord, and lion. By extension, we can interpret the classical image of the cherub, a winged angel attending to God, as a representation of Beavers. However, another

The Hedge Theater
(top: shot for but not used in film)

reading might see Markopoulos as the combined or integrated lion, king, and angel.

The climax of the film occurs about two minutes from the end, beginning with a black frame and the sound of tearing cloth. The next shot is of a Renaissance painting, *Saint Martin and the Beggar* by Il Sassetta, which depicts the story of the martyr saint who cut his cloak in half to share with a beggar. This Christian narrative of generosity and compassion for the less fortunate rhymes with many of the latent and explicit concerns of the film: the interdependence of self-awareness and relations with others, gratitude for that which is nourishing and essential, the capacity for a felt sense of the wholeness of the world. Beavers cuts between the image of the painting with its red undercoat layer to the complementary green foliage of the hedge theater, depicted during spring rain. The saturated color scheme in the dramatic conclusion contrasts with its earlier muted palette of ivory, white, gold and light grey.

LOCATIONS AND COMPOSITIONAL STRUCTURE:
THE STOAS

It is utterly fitting that Beavers made the aesthetic decision to layer so many rich themes, one after the next, in the structure of *The Hedge Theater*, creating a dynamic counterpoint of rhyming sounds and images that resonates across the film. In the case of *The Stoas*, I am most deeply moved by Beavers's use of location shooting to express the themes of death and passage from this world to an afterlife.

The first seven minutes of *The Stoas* is composed of imagery filmed in Athenian arcades

(*stoa* is the Greek word for a covered walkway or arcade) during the afternoon siesta. The trade stalls are mostly shuttered; where there is usually the bustle of activity, we instead see stillness and hear distant sounds. Beavers's cinematography is exceptional; it captures the atmospheric quality of the arcade and warehouse district. Vintage signage and objects, like an old-fashioned scale with weights, seem almost frozen in time.

Midway through this extended sequence in the arcades, Beavers offers a shot of a stairway seen straight ahead with a shaft of light streaming down from above. There is also a slight fluctuating quality to the lighting in this image (as if an out-of-frame fluorescent is vacillating), and the effect is haunting and mysterious. The multiple shots of the center-framed stairway are an important transitional moment, a metaphor for what lies beyond.

The next large portion of the film is shot in Arcadia, where we encounter a beautiful Peloponnesian landscape with clear blue-green waters (Beavers follows the full length of the Lousios river). Beavers presents shot after shot of landscape imagery, a gorgeous cinematic rendering composed of various perspectives of the river and surrounding trees. As the sequence progresses, a level of drama is achieved as small mountain tributaries join to become the larger flowing river, and the water grows turbulent and dark before ultimately reaching a state of calm. Skillfully filmed and edited, the emblematic river sequence is handled as visual music, at times peaceful and delicate, at times agitated. Beavers gracefully realizes the theme of passage.

The Stoas
(1991–97)

The primary reference to a human presence in the film is a recurring close-up of the filmmaker's hands as they reach out to hold an empty space, something that is both there and *not there*. The gesture has multiple meanings; it is an embodiment of absence but also suggests *all that can be*. The final sequence of *The Stoas* is composed of a series of shots in a vineyard at harvest time. Bountiful mounds of grapes suggest a gift of the gods and a celebration of life – a renewal following loss and grief. The images of the grape harvest and an earlier one – loaves of bread from a bakery in the arcades – evoke Christian iconography.

Measured, patient, lyrical, and intuitive, the underlying design of the film's structure presents a quest for knowledge and greater emotional understanding. For the most part, the soundtrack uses ambient sound, but it also includes a quiet percussive rhythm (mixed beneath the sounds of nature) that originates from a monk's instrument called a *talando*. Beavers's meditative sound design supports the metaphoric journey or passage to an afterlife.

FROM THE REAL WORLD TO THE ETERNAL:
THE GROUND

The Ground is distinguished by its profound expression of the state of mourning. The film is shot on Hydra – sacred ground, where the film cycle begins and ends, a location that binds Beavers and Markopoulos in spirit. *The Ground* is a return to the island's stone ruins and its spectacular views of a small white chapel (both of which we first encounter in *Winged Dialogue*) and beyond to the Myrtoan Sea and distant is-

lands. Beavers presents elements of life on the island that are traditional and timeless: a man chiseling stone, a rooster's crow, a donkey feeding, the sustenance associated with a loaf of baked bread. There are few signs of modernity here. Beavers presents the natural landscape with its lichen-covered stones and the Mediterranean chaparral of low shrubs, grasses, and cypress trees produced by the arid climate. This deliberate representation of life on Hydra, not anchored in any particular era, allows Beavers to set the stage for a far more abstract concept: a poetic expression of the eternal, where his film cycle meets its logical end.

In addition to the images of island life and the stonecutter, there are recurring shots of a man's naked chest; it is clear that the subject is the filmmaker. Beavers cups his empty hand as if to hold something dear and brings it to his chest. As the film progresses, we also see the filmmaker's outstretched hand grasping, as if to hold something that is not there, and then gently releasing. Beavers also pounds his chest in grief and despair, as if to express the idea that *the one who outlives the other must bear the pain*.

There are moments of extraordinary beauty and mystery in *The Ground*. In the delicately poised position of a donkey's hoof or the involuntary spasm of the muscles of its belly, this beast of burden is elevated to a greater level of meaning. The seemingly infinite and ever-changing qualities of light and color are captured in images of the sky and the rich darkness of distant islands as the day grows long. Perhaps most mysterious for me is an image shot from within stone ruins. Light streams

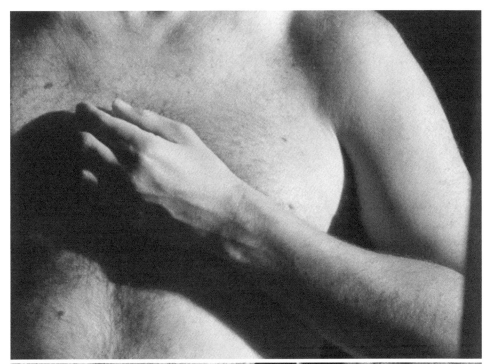

The Ground
(1993–2001)

through a rectangular shape in the old tower, but it is filmed in a way that seems otherworldly.

Across the duration of the film, though not shot in a single day, time seems to progress roughly from morning to dusk. This movement is measured against the protagonist's emotional transition from grief to acceptance.

Yet, there is perhaps another more abstract and profound trajectory in the way Beavers so carefully constructs elements of this final film in the cycle to help move us from the real world to a place that is eternal. The island of Hydra, as represented metaphorically in *The Ground*, is the eternal, the *Sightless Measure*.

Ute Aurand and Robert Beavers

Conversation about *The Stoas*

UTE AURAND: *The first film that I saw of yours was* The Stoas *in 1993, and in the very first minutes there was something that alerted me and touched me deeply. I remember asking myself while watching, 'What is it, where is it coming from?' I couldn't find it in the images. The images seemed quite direct, passageways, stairs, and in between a hand or two. It came from somewhere else and this brings me to the question about your relation to meaning or ideas – even in your title,* The Stoas. *Can you describe from which point you start and how you developed* The Stoas, *from first thought to film?*

ROBERT BEAVERS: I don't know whether the qualities that you responded to were what I started with because I often begin with an intention or an idea that is discarded or transformed before I reach the first image. In *The Stoas* I began with the intention to film vases and the space inside the vase that is not seen. I began with this idea …

… quite abstract or from the Greeks?

RB: I hadn't decided whether the vases would be Greek or Chinese, but the starting point was more the form of the vase than decoration. I was attracted to the beauty of these simple shapes and then to the empty spaces of the arcades in Athens that you see in the film, and the image of my hands holding an empty space is developed from the idea of the vase.

Like holding one?

RB: Yes, that was all that remained of my initial intention to suggest the space inside the vase that is not seen. The hands remained to suggest this space.

So first you wanted to film vases very directly? How did you leave this idea?

RB: I had a sense that it would not work as a film image. The working title was originally *Vases and Stoas*. So the first elements of the film were the spaces of the vases and the arcades, but the vases were soon replaced by the hands holding an empty space, and the lens movements or camera movements also give you a filmic sense of this unseen space inside the vase. The camera angle and the hands suggest my presence, and one could say that I replace the vase with the lens.

Or with you. I think these camera movements open the film beyond its realistic imagery to what I mean by 'beyond meaning'… In the second part of the film, when we are coming to the stream, there I remember thinking that this stream is really filmed beyond realism, these images catch life, in its fundamental beauty and dimension of – I want to say 'love' – when does this third important element, the stream, enter the film?

RB: I had edited the arcades with the images of my hands before I filmed the stream. I felt it was a way to expand both the idea of the arcades and the vase.

In which way?

RB: Because it is liquid, and most vases contain a liquid, and because the arcades, the space inside the arcades, flows just as the river flows between its riverbanks. I used the space of the arcades and the river to reflect on what is ascetic and what is sensuous, and, when I speak about the space inside the vase, I am also suggesting something for the senses to feel. This contrast of the ascetic and sensuous is reflected upon through an intuition. A vase is the essential object or container, and these spaces allow me to reflect, to accept limitation and gain calm.

When you speak about your films, your ideas and even your notes, they are in a way concrete. An idea is expressed in an image. Then you transform it, and it becomes something new, different from its first meaning.

RB: The ideas and notes are steps that I am consciously working with, but when I was filming, I realized that the moment contained an important resolution for me. It is related to a sense of death and to a sense of seeing life from the other side. In this film a crisis was resolved, and the result was acceptance. My visits to the river and to the arcades were the occasion for this experience – this river site gave an awareness, but I didn't film, I waited until the next summer.

And in between the idea was growing?

RB: Yes, and I tried to place a figure in the river and actually filmed someone, then realized that it was impossible. In the mid-1960s, I had read an essay on Chinese landscape painting that drew a parallel between the human form and the vertical landscape of a river.

So the body is the landscape and the river is going through?

RB: The river itself is a body.

This idea helped you to come away from the figure or first to establish it?

RB: It helped me to transfer the idea of the human figure to the river itself.

You are using images or ideas as vehicles to enter other dimensions. You transform the obvious into something subtle and silent, the opposite of meaning, into something personal without being personal. Still, I am asking myself, why are ideas in your films so fundamental as a starting point – in From the Notebook of… *we have the Leonardo notes – why is it necessary?*

RB: I am not comfortable with the directly autobiographical, and this is a way to present the strength and the value of the experience without making a record of my daily life. Even though there are strong autobiographical elements in many of my films, I find that the intention to record should be balanced by sources of active inspiration, the ones that move me to make a film.

Originally published in To the Winged Distance: Films by Robert Beavers, *London: Tate Modern, 2007.*

Haden Guest

Of Place and Portraiture

LOOK HOMEWARD...

For the Massachusetts-born Robert Beavers, *Pitcher of Colored Light* (2007) marked a symbolic homecoming, his first film shot in the United States after 40 years living and working in self-imposed exile in Europe. As if to acknowledge the film's singular place within his oeuvre and career, Beavers partially shaped its delicate portrait of his elderly mother as a lyrical meditation on home and heritage. An idyll of the four seasons filmed sporadically across a three year period in his mother's Cape Cod cottage and garden, *Pitcher of Colored Light* recurs with images of Mrs. Beavers planting flowers, tilling the earth and evoking the genealogical roots and native soil metaphorically explored by the film. Yet, with its symbolic return, *Pitcher of Colored Light* also announced an important departure, a decisive shift in the visionary poetics refined across Beavers's long career that would be confirmed by his two subsequent films, *The Suppliant* (2010) and *Listening to the Space in My Room* (2013). Indeed, these three portraits of friends and loved ones patiently filmed within and refracted through their respective homes reveal Beavers embracing a new intimacy of subject and scale while profoundly revising ideas of place, portraiture and sound long central to his cinema.

The opening of *Pitcher of Colored Light* displays the intricate montage of sound and image used by Beavers to explore the resonant worlds that he discovers within his mother's home. From its first image – the cottage seen from outside and illuminated by dappled sunlight and a lively chorus of unseen birds – the film cuts to a close-up of a vivid red rooster statue inside the house, partially hidden in shadow. Alternating shots of the house and the rooster, now seen from outside looking through a window, are followed by the first image of Beavers's mother, shot in profile and gazing out at her small lush garden, followed soon after by her off-screen voice asking, "Is it the size of a robin?" In this linking of birds heard, but unseen, with the bright rooster and the robin imagined by his mother, Beavers defines the subtle intertwining of real and imaginary that will structure the film. Hitherto largely absent from Beavers's films, the spoken voice signals the more direct register of sound lately embraced by Beavers and, by extension, the restrained mode of poetic documentary adopted by *Pitcher of Colored Light*, *The Suppliant* and *Listening to the Space in My Room*.

The rooster statue is revealing in its difference from the birds that figure prominently in Beavers's previous filmmaking as cinematic metaphors, emblems of the fluttering shutter shared by camera and projector alike and the sweeping vertical flight of image achieved by Beavers through poetic montage and his signature rotation of his Bolex camera lens turret. Notable in this regard is the bird alluded to by the title of Beavers's 18-film magnum opus, *My Hand Outstretched to the Winged Distance and Sightless Measure*. Prominent as well are the flying doves whose release from their cages dramatically opens his groundbreaking film-manifesto *From the Notebook of...* (1971/1998) by invoking the meta-cinematic relationship between nature and moving image embodied by the birds of Étienne-Jules Marey, while also demonstrating Beavers's written proclamation, legible in the eponymous notebook within that same film, that "Film is not an illusion of movement. It is movement." In contrast to the kinds of cinematic and kinesthetic movement boldly refined in *From the Notebook of...*, the red rooster instead embodies a temporal and emotional movement essential to *Pitcher of Colored Light*'s exploration of childhood memory and the creative imagination.

The role of the rooster as point of entry into the gossamer realm of childhood memory is made clear by its association with similarly playful animal figures that appear soon after in the film: first a wide-eyed cat statue and then a stuffed polar bear. Beavers pointedly gives each of the three animals unexpected and gently humorous life, using montage to join the cat statue with the actual felines who hunt, sleep and stalk through cottage and garden alike and accompanying the rooster, in his last appearance near the film's end, with a distant crowing sound. A single dramatic cut, meanwhile, links the stuffed polar bear with the vision of slowly falling snow that marks a quiet mid-point of the film. Igniting objects gathered in the little cottage with a shimmer of private memory, these animistic moments delicately recall a child's magical ability to impart shadow and toy alike with vivid voice and personality. The nuanced exploration of childhood imagination at work within these sequences and across *Pitcher of Colored Light* is softly underscored by passing shots of neighborhood children, glimpsed through the cottage windows, throwing balls and inventing games.

At other key moments *Pitcher of Colored Light* fully adopts the wide-eyed perspective of a child. Take, for example, the openly playful linkage joining two striking close-up shots: the first an off-centered perspective looking down upon Mrs. Beavers's curled grey hair, the second focused on her miniature grey-white dog's curly fur. An almost whimsical mirroring connects the shots, a Eureka!-like montage seemingly inspired by a spontaneous discovery of immediate symmetry, gathering images as if to create a private classificatory system. The film's title, too, is animated by a child-like wonderment with the similar. For while deliberately allowing a possible misreading, or childish misspelling, of "pitcher" for "picture," the title inventively gives equal and simultaneous force to the alternate meanings within the two-words-in-one.

The slippage and spontaneity of meaning in the title is shared by its eponymous referent, a brightly colored glass vessel that first appears as

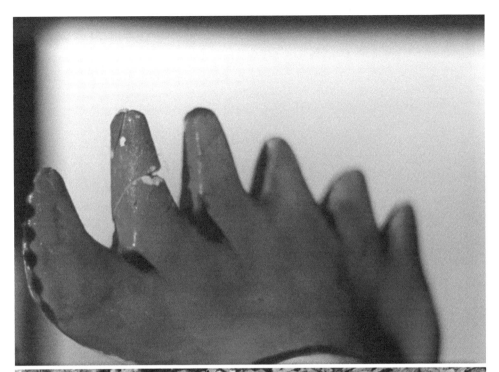

Pitcher
of Colored Light
(2007)

Pitcher of Colored Light

a shimmering shadow illuminating an interior wall of the cottage. An everyday object transformed into an affirmation of pure cinema – a moving "picture" made of light, color, shadow – the glass pitcher emblematizes the pulsing, breathing life given to place and objects throughout Beavers's film. Indeed, a transformative colored light pervades *Pitcher of Colored Light,* uniting, for example, consecutive shots of the woodchip flowerbed in Mrs. Beavers's garden and the thick plush carpet inside her cottage and rendering the two floors similarly alive in a dance of glowing sunlight and wavering shadow. While extending the film's montage of playful symmetry, this lyrical interweaving of vibrant cottage interior and lush garden exterior pays subtle tribute to the meticulously groomed and harmonious worlds patiently created by Mrs. Beavers.

The flowers that recur rhythmically throughout *Pitcher of Colored Light* together form another kind of "picture" given living and unexpected dimensions by Beavers and offered as expressions of his mother's creative imagination. In this way the bright garden blossoms that punctuate the film are echoed by the many bold flower images found within Mrs. Beavers's home: in the floral patterns printed on her bright smocks and dresses, and upon a sofa decorated with twisting vines and blossoms. Especially moving are the flowers that appear as *Pitcher of Colored Light* shifts quietly from fall to winter, in a lyrical passage that includes shots of a sleeping cat and then Mrs. Beavers napping, and her garden blanketed in fresh snow. Interspersed shots of hanging yellow blossoms and

pink flowers seem to be offered here as cherished emblems of that distant, often gentler season, the verdant spring likely dreamt of by Mrs. Beavers and her garden-loving, dozing cat. These flowers beautifully express the subjective shape given overall to objects and to time itself by *Pitcher of Colored Light,* here by poetically re-molding the seasons' cycle by distilling autumn and winter to brisk, heightened transitions while stretching spring and summer to a slower length and languor.

The title, *Pitcher of Colored Light,* with its idea of a fluid object-image poised between reverie and the real, could equally, of course, refer to the hand-drawn colored portrait of a young Robert Beavers that hovers dramatically at key moments during the film. The distinct spark of life given to the framed portrait derives both from its direct gaze at the camera and from the shadowy movement of Beavers's dark reflection upon its glass. He tellingly superimposes his own reflection upon his mother's, carefully adjusting the camera's focus to shift from his doubled image to her reflected figure seated at the kitchen table. Literal form is given here to the mode of refracted portraiture embraced by Beavers's recent films in which objects and interiors give voice to private memories, experiences and desires. At the same time, the drawing-become-mirror suggests the "winged distance" traced by *Pitcher of Colored Light* to be both a literal bridging of the film's present moment and Beavers's childhood past, and a touching expression of the paradoxically simultaneous distance and proximity uniting mother and son.

Pitcher of
Colored Light

The central role of the drawn portrait in *Pitcher of Colored Light* is also defined by its presence as a work of art of a markedly different kind than those historical masterworks of painting and architecture or artisanal handcrafts studied in earlier Beavers films like *The Painting* (1972/1999) and *The Hedge Theater* (1986–90/2002). A work of humble vernacular art, the drawing instead points towards an alternate role of art explored in Beavers's three most recent works, each of which pay tribute to individuals whose creative imaginations shape not painted canvas or marbled column, but lived spaces created gradually over years of dedicated habit and ritual. Mrs. Beavers's imagination is thus revealed through the flowers, garden and colored objects that adorn her world and that impart her Cape Cod house with a certain oneness with nature and, seen through her son's affectionate lens, an almost fairy-tale quality of a little cottage deep in the woods. As if to gently revise Wordsworth's dictum that "the Child is father of the Man," Beavers's superimposition of his and his mother's images lovingly compares the elderly woman's creativity to the visionary and freely inventive mind of a child, suggesting her need for art to be just as open and uninhibited. One of the most poignant moments of the film comes, then, in a quiet confession heard off-screen in which Mrs. Beavers softly sings a hymn that she then promptly mentions, matter-of-factly, to be considering for her own funeral. In a similar manner as the apartments later explored in *The Suppliant* and *Listening to the Space in My Room*, Mrs. Beavers's house is offered as a site for an alternate mode of creation,

not of art per se but of an artistic vision shaped by quiet, life-long dedication to the fleeting beauty of light and nature and the slow passage of time: a more intimate metaphor than previously expressed for the kind of independent art cinema patiently forged by Robert Beavers over the still running course of a life's career.

THE ARDOR OF THINGS

Travel was an important constant of Beavers's filmmaking career which traced a peripatetic voyage through the vast histories of Western European art and architecture, mirroring his 25 years of restless movement across Europe with Gregory Markopoulos. More than simply a return to the United States, *Pitcher of Colored Light* launched a private and less epic pilgrimage, a journey inward towards a realm of personal history and imagination. This new voyage continues in *The Suppliant*, which was also shot in the United States, roughly simultaneously to *Pitcher of Colored Light* but not completed until three years later. Despite its significantly shorter running time of five minutes, *The Suppliant* plunges deeper, yet differently, into Beavers's native soil, dramatically expanding ideas of place, portraiture and the creative imagination explored in the earlier film.

Shot almost entirely within the Brooklyn Heights apartment of Beavers's close friend, the New York art director Jacques Dehornois, *The Suppliant* centers around a small bronze statuette placed prominently within the exquisitely appointed apartment – a young male nude of Greco-Roman style with outstretched arms held high above his head. The statue makes a

The Suppliant
(2010)

striking first appearance – obscured in near dark with only its sinewed contours partially visible, softly traced by Beaver's gliding camera and the glow of reflected sunlight upon its obsidian-like surface. Accompanying a series of close-ups is the rapid, rasping sound of charcoal or graphite worked hard upon paper. The expressive sound and camera suggest an artist sketching, the camera's quick movements evoking busy eyes darting between subject and notebook.

The sketching sound recalls Beavers's film *Work Done* (1972/1999), which succinctly juxtaposes the place and labor of traditional trades – among them, bookbinding, wood chopping and cooking – and their emphatic accompanying sounds: a needle pulling through thick parchment, a chainsaw cutting trees, blood sizzling on a hot griddle. Through repeated close-ups of the works-in-progress, the film carefully assembles these arts of stitching and sundering into a larger metaphor for Beavers's own artisanal work as an editor cutting and binding together 16mm footage.[1] Despite the formal resemblance between the two films, a profoundly different perspective on craft and art is offered in *The Suppliant,* which turns not to patient handcraft but instead to a more mysterious vision of art coming into being. The series of shots tracing the statue through near-darkness thus gives way enigmatically to images of the glowing red embers and flying sparks of a forge – the birthplace, one might surmise, of Dehornois's bronze figure. As the forge vanishes, the statue just as quickly reappears, now fully visible and illuminated for the first time by steady sunlight, a gentler incandescence.

Is this brief image of fire a memory recalled by the statue, as if the figure had been granted a kind of voice or consciousness? Or does the forge spring instead from the imagination of the unseen artist heard sketching the bronze figure? Another equally possible reading could take the statue's Hellenic qualities and primal association with fire as emblems of Gregory Markopoulos and his life-long fascination with the mythology of his ancestral Greece. Accepting the statue as a poetic recollection of Beavers's deceased partner would give further meaning to the intimacy, and even longing, suggested by Beavers's camera as it subtly eroticizes the statue, lingering in a single shot upon the figure's lithe sexual member. Such a reading could extend as well to the melancholy images that follow of an empty, unmade bed with the shape of a human form still impressed across sheets and pillows. While possibly evoking Markopoulos and his death in 1992, the link between statue and empty bed could also be taken as a restrained tribute to Dehornois, the apartment's owner, who died while Beavers was still in the early stages of editing *The Suppliant.*

These subtle evocations of death and longing are ultimately dispelled, however, by the vital bronze body which seems to refuse – and, moreover, to symbolically fill – the absence lingering in the empty bed. Springing to life from the shadows, its arms reaching joyously upward and outward as if sighting a new horizon

1 See James Macgillivray, "Film Grows Unseen: Gregory Markopoulos, Robert Beavers and the Tectonics of Film Editing," *The Journal of Modern Craft*, Vol. 5, Issue 2, July 2012, p. 179–201.

The Suppliant

and future, the statue offers a figure of rebirth that might be taken for Beavers himself and the new path recently followed by his own cinema. As in *Pitcher of Colored Light,* the filmmaker's significant return to a defining place of origin – here New York City – gives way to a profound reflection upon his earlier life. In this way the Lower Manhattan glimpsed from across the East River places at a poetic distance the city where Beavers first met Markopoulos and, in a sense, his life as an artist began. Also distanced, by extension, is the epic 18-film cycle completed by Beavers in close dialogue with Markopoulos's mythopoeic and formally radical cinema.

An expression of time's passage and the long journey made by Beavers from the 1960s heyday of American experimental cinema, the New York City seen from the apartment window is, however, only part of a critical gaze pointedly cast by *The Suppliant* upon the United States. In a brief exit from the apartment, the film takes an unexpected turn to find itself in a chain-linked electrical station parking lot, the kind of concrete and steel no-place cluttered on the peripheries of towns and cities across the U.S. Accompanied by a dull machine hum, the film cuts to a close-up of the fence to compose a crosshatched reinvention of the U.S. flag, with rows of sharp metal stars gleaming behind jagged chain-link stripes. Veering closer to a political statement than arguably seen before in a Beavers film, the alienating cityscape and aggressively metal flag conjure ambivalent emotions about his native land. Unlike Dehornois's or Mrs. Beavers's lovingly decorated interiors and meticulous garden, the post-industrial New World revealed here seems empty and unyielding, utterly void of quietude or sense of home.

With its final image, *The Suppliant* returns to a more open symbolic register, cutting again from the bronze statue to the apartment window, only now to find a falcon perched attentively upon a leafless tree branch. As symphonic choral music surges suddenly onto the soundtrack, Beavers's camera remains fixed upon the statuesque bird. Although immobile, the bird is nevertheless somehow in motion – transformed into a shimmering image by unexplained heat waves floating upward over the frame. Shot in a different season from Beavers's own Berlin apartment, the image of wavering heat recalls for one last time the statue's dream of fire, while the soaring music in turn suggests a new flight and voyage. Like the bronze figure, the bird becomes a polyvalent icon of memory and desire, the guardian of a secret flame and the promise of a place beyond.

CHAMBER MUSIC

Listening to the Space in My Room could be seen as the final and defining part of a major, though unannounced, trilogy formed together with *Pitcher of Colored Light* and *The Suppliant*. Explicitly positioning itself in relation to the previous works, Beavers's latest film pointedly includes images directly quoting *Pitcher of Colored Light* as well as recognizable excerpts from *The Suppliant*. Like the earlier films, *Listening to the Space in My Room* is a lyrically refracted portrait film that defines its subject indirectly, through a

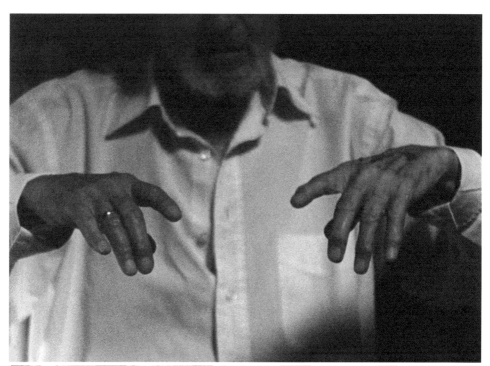

Listening to the
Space in My Room

series of talismanic objects, lived spaces and daily rituals patiently assembled by Beavers. Filmed within the apartment in Zumikon, Switzerland, where he lived for several years, *Listening to the Space in My Room* brings a new dimension to the trilogy by now taking Beavers himself as subject. Beavers, however, carefully avoids any kind of sustained self-portrait by expanding his focus to include the filmmaker Ute Aurand (Beavers's partner) as well as the elderly couple, Dieter and Cécile Staehelin, who were his landlords and upstairs neighbors.

The distinct yet discreet presence Beavers occupies in his latest film is established by the short voice-over he speaks near its opening, carefully reciting the title within a single phrase: "Listening to the space in my room, surrounded by the stillness, each column made of a tree trunk." The relationship defined here between Beavers and the "space of my room" reveals an important attitude toward place orienting his Portrait Trilogy and distinguishing it from the earlier autobiographical films – *Plan of Brussels* (1968/2000) and *Early Monthly Segments* (1968–70/2002), for example – from which it obviously extends. For like *Pitcher of Colored Light* and *The Suppliant*, *Listening to the Space in My Room* is guided by a search within lived spaces for a certain spirit and ineffable presence, a "stillness" and memory that confirm but also point beyond those who dwell, or have dwelled, there. Beavers's recent films bring wholly new meaning to the term "home movies" by giving profound attention to the subtlest textures and tones of domestic life, those fleeting sounds and images invisible to all but those most intimate with the shift of light and season within a particular house or room.

A larger concern for the ineffable is, in fact, shared by the three portrait films. Consider, for example, the sense of transience encapsulated in the sounds and images that close both *Listening to the Space in My Room* – a patch of melting snow revealing green grass – and *Pitcher of Colored Light* – the extended chime of a bell, held over the image of a flower floating in a sunlit glass bowl. Recalling the eponymous vessel and garden that figure prominently in *Pitcher of Colored Light,* the glass bowl and flower at the close of that film could also be read, presciently, as an intertwined figure – a "picture" of colored light – of Dieter and Cécile Staehelin, the elderly couple who exert an indelible presence in *Listening to the Space in My Room*. While the extended chime recalls the music of Dieter Staehelin's cello that opens the film, the flower seems to have been cut from the bountiful garden lovingly tended by his wife. The power of the two films' closing images also lies, however, in the fragility of their forms and their underscoring of the theme of mortality central to Beavers's latest trilogy. Indeed, the floating flower and melting snow offer moving expressions of the grace and dignity given to advanced age by Mrs. Beavers and the Staehelins; the former was in her eighties and the latter in their nineties when Beavers was making his films.

The vivid presence of the seasons within both *Listening to the Space in My Room* and *Pitcher of Colored Light* is an expression not only of the transience uniting so many of Beavers's sounds and images, but also of the cyclicality

*Listening to the
Space in My Room*

and gentle symmetries that interconnect image and meaning across these three post-cycle films. In this way, images from *The Suppliant* appear within *Listening to the Space in My Room*, including a shot of the bronze statue's outstretched arms inserted mid-way, as if to add to the many busy hands dancing across Beavers's film – playing the cello, turning the pages of a book, editing 16mm film, weeding the garden, each a supple expression of the creative imagination at work. A more discreet echo of *The Suppliant* is found in the quiet image of a bed, seen in early morning light, where Beavers's partner Aurand lies asleep. Corresponding, retrospectively and as if in response, to the abandoned bed in *The Suppliant* with its melancholy and almost funereal evocation of the deceased, the image of the tranquilly sleeping Aurand restores life to the empty berth while also pointing toward a nether realm, the world of dreams. In this way, the image of Aurand in slumber visualizes Beavers's second voice-over spoken earlier to recount a dream: "I was awakened by a dream in which I spoke to myself in German. *Ich bin eine andere Person geworden.*" ("I have become another person.")

The dream summarized by Beavers directly relates once more to the impetus expressed across this trilogy, to give active form to ineffable memories, unseen presences and the transitory inventions of the creative imagination. But Beavers's dream of speaking a foreign language and being *"eine andere Person"* also gives expression to the profound humility ultimately shared by the three recent films. The films explicitly describe their subjects – and here

Beavers himself – as being part of a larger world that they create but that also exists beyond them, like the empty apartment that lingers after Jacques Dehornois's death. The red flower that appears suddenly in *Listening to the Space in My Room*, in the midst of a snowy interlude, directly quotes the yellow and pink ones that occur during the winter images in *Pitcher of Colored Light*. And like the images in the earlier film, this brief rapture of new life and transient beauty could be either a vision or a dream. Equally attributable to the dreaming Aurand or to Cécile Staehelin, who appears shortly afterwards reading a book, the red flower also suggests an invisible, associational thread uniting the three women in an unseen garden.

The intimations of the ineffable that repeat throughout *Listening to the Space in My Room* and the rest of the trilogy clearly invite autobiographical and symbolic readings of the films as evocations of mortality, portrait tributes to loved ones from Beavers's life, some since departed. Yet the transience explored across the three films must also be understood as expressions of Beavers's quintessentially cinematic art and his steadfast commitment to discovering and awakening the purest meanings and movements of 16mm filmmaking. While distilling and subtly adjusting the lyrical cinematic portraiture explored by the earlier films, *Listening to the Space in My Room* also carefully reflects upon the unique temporal and sculptural specificity of Beavers's chosen medium. Although the shots of Beavers editing in his Zumikon home have clear precedent in earlier films such as *From the Notebook of...*, they speak differently in today's digital age, reminding us that the exhilarating emotional-vertical leap from image to image also derives from the physical dimensions of the 16mm filmstrip. For the sheer poignancy of Beavers's images and the montage that gives rhythmic life to their fleeting beauty is also an expression of the profound correspondence Beavers draws between the natural, material world that he films and the organic craft and art that is analog, photochemical cinema.

The eponymous room of Beavers's Zumikon apartment subtly affirms the cinema as an organic art. For this is, after all, a "camera" whose wooden beams – "made from a single tree" – are crafted from the same material as Dieter Staehelin's lustrous cello. Within the film's opening sequence, Staehelin's bow dances across the screen, with Beavers's camera capturing the song of wood and string slicing through the air, camera and cello united as instruments uniquely attuned to the music of the world. A series of linked images in *Listening to the Space in My Room* go further still by connecting, through subtle symmetry, the 16mm film unwound on Beavers's rewind bench to the gossamer line of sunlight reflected upon a spider's thread stretched across the garden, to the taut strings of Dieter Staehelin's cello. For Beavers, the purity of cinema and the music of its images come from the material world. The textured music of a tea cup lifted and returned to its saucer, the rustle of a page being turned, offer simple affirmations of cinema as a visionary craft dedicated to and effaced by the world before it.

Listening to the Space in My Room

Robert Beavers editing
Pitcher of Colored Light

Robert Beavers

A Few Points

As a filmmaker who has developed a number of themes and filmic forms,
I draw upon sources of inspiration that are planted long before they become
actual starting points for filming. These sources come from what I see, from
my reading or from any number of impulses in daily life.

The entire cycle of *My Hand Outstretched to the Winged Distance and Sightless
Measure* can be understood in one way as autobiographical, as growing out of
my relation to Gregory Markopoulos, protected by solitude and the spirit that
came from our dedication to filmmaking.

My way of work is a tentative searching, made possible because I hold the
actual filmmaking in my hands as cameraman, film editor, sound technician*
and sound editor. Beginning with a few notes that I continue to write while
the filming progresses, I see my notebook as a place in which to be patient and
to sustain the continuity of the work, to consider future steps and remain open
to unforeseen additions or deletions.

In the filming I hold to the discipline of composing the individual image and
communicate directly through the creation of a particular space. I respond to
a location or figure by choosing the camera angle and distance. I move the
camera less often than I create a movement by turning the lens at the beginning or end of the shot. My interest is to simplify the image and balance
movement with stillness. The transitions are made through the turn of the
lens or a fade. But none of this should be exaggerated.

I think of filmmaking like architecture, the entire process is nourished
through many stages of development, and the vision of each part leads to the
next. The work does not exclude spontaneity. The filming reaches forward

---

* I record and edit my own sound just as I film and edit the image, but in each case there is
someone who contributes to the final result. Christian Beusch at Tonstudio Beusch assists me
in the final sound mix and makes the transfer to 35mm magnetic. Mike Kolvek at Cinema Arts
has color-timed most of my films for printing the projection copies, with the exception of the
ones by Simon Lund at Cineric.

and extends a central impulse. It has a chronology. Observation draws out an interior richness.

The editing is composed through a vision that grows from the beginning to the end. I start by removing two frames from every shot and attach these frames to a piece of white paper and write lists. I edit a film with a minimum of equipment, looking at these pages of film frames, then selecting a film shot and holding it to the light, and looking at the lists, which help to give me an overview of the entire film material. Because I am not usually viewing and reviewing the moving image on my editing table, I have the freedom to create the film in my mind's eye, using my memory of the actual filming and the rhythm that already exists in it. I build the phrases of images by looking at these pages of small 16mm film frames. It is a process of active memorizing and then making sudden leaps. Searching for how the images communicate with each other is only one part of it. I am also judging the length as much by the physical measure of the film strip as by its duration in time.

Sometimes I am interested in creating a close-knit or solid structure in the final film. I liken this to the experience that I had when briefly studying Latin as a boy. I noted how the words in the sentences that I was translating fitted together like cut stones, this was very different from English. I created poly-phonic rhythm imposed by the editing in my early films; in my later films I have sought to balance camera movements and the movement within the frame with moments of stillness so that the rhythm is not solely marked at the film cut.

Reaching the truth in an instant; returning to the instance and in the image reaching the truth: It is a wonder that comes out of the unseen; the projected image shows this.

This text was composed for the 2007 Tate Modern
retrospective and published in the accompanying brochure
To the Winged Distance: Films by Robert Beavers.

Robert Beavers

Acnode

Every sense organ has two directions within it. One is utilitarian and connected to appetite; the other possesses a surplus that becomes articulate in
the body, in the emotions and spirit.

———————— I ————————

What is valuable as preparation before filmmaking?
Attention and fullness.
Humility in and beyond emotion: This stillness allows me to observe the
movements of the senses, to see the concrete elements of time beyond their
appearance and to build the film with these elements.

Abstinence and silence: To move within the unknown and place the making
there. An interior solitude exists to balance the exterior impure loneliness felt
in everyday life.

The spiritual growth of the filmmaker is not of direct interest to the audience.

———————— II ————————

What are the specific energies of Film? The closed-and-open shutter, black
then white, is our tool. It suggests depth, suggests what is behind (or after) an
image: its negative, the afterimage.

Golden energy exists between one shot and the next, in the filming and in the
editing. It is different for each work.

The use of each concrete element of filmmaking has a value in itself as
the means to reach a vital quality in the image and sound and not as a self-
reflective gesture.

III

Movement in stillness, stillness in movement; psychic value of movement and stillness in nature: mineral, plant, and animal.

A movement that appears to be still: water in a bath, the continuous, barely noticeable flow, back and forth.

The stillness of a tree rotating upon its trunk: Does this movement come from one's own profile and eye movement, and the tree reflects this, or is it related to the movement of the sun and Seasons? The impression is of the tree moving within itself while remaining still.

A glass. The empty object contains the idea of its fullness.

The soul projects movements in the body, and other movements are projected from the body into the soul.

Weight as movement; heat and sunlight as movement.

A highlight (the strongest point of reflected light) moves more quickly within a camera movement ... and in the same direction as the movement?

The highlight passes from one edited frame into the same part of the next image; the highlight moves like a projection.
Projection is not only through the frame to the screen, there is also the 'suspended projection' from one image into the next on the screen.
The projection to the screen is obviously in Space; the second, adds Time.
'Projection' is extension in space and time.

IV

The Senses create Space and Time.

Sight and psychic depth are the same or opposites.

The many qualities of Time and their underlying unity: The use of these different qualities within the continuous unity of film. Each moment contains

multiple perceptions within it. Technique can sustain these seemingly opposed
tenses in the same frame.

The question of precision is central to a work's value and is also present as
an illusion when it concerns detail and finish. Harmony beyond the weakness
of unnecessary detail is the goal. The form of a film should not be realized
beyond its content: In some of my early films the finish of the work is not
accompanied by an equal fullness.

The final precision within a film is the making of actual space.
The image which creates a place for the viewer; the image projects a
completion of itself into a solid form. There is a great strength when the
composition forms a spectator's active seeing:
La Sacra Famiglia (Michelangelo),
L'Ultima Cena (Leonardo),
Frescoes by Pontormo in the villa at Poggio a Caiano or the Camera dei
Misteri in Pompeii.

chora: limit of the interval in ancient Greek
music: the same word is still used to mean 'place.'

v

Precision in the making … what use for the inequality of units?
Measure is based upon the perception of the interval; sound and image mark
the interval.
Each shares it in particular ways. Their importance is as much in the harmony
of the interval as in the image and sound itself.
Two units of measure – image and sound – the strength and weakness of each:
Two different senses of space and time. Does inequality within the image
balanced by a different inequality in the sound allow a third quality to arise
as measure?

Composition of the film frame may dictate the length of the image.

The sound also measures the interval while being carried forward in the
life of the image, through the faster or slower rhythms of each. Could one

color and its particular afterimage create a certain subjective quality that can be quickened or retarded by the sound?

One quality in the editing is like rhyme and another like meter. The meter-like quality is *not necessarily* the shot length; it can go beyond the shot and be strong enough to pass through the entire film. The rhyme-like quality and its free associations are not to be exaggerated and should be controlled and strengthened by the metric.

Rhythm-movement-interval: three words to describe one central quality.

VI

To develop more than one voice in the film and sustain them ... neither interior voices nor human voices:
Sound contained in certain materials and brought out of these materials by *light?*
Can the eye read the sound in an object?

A tone appears from touching an object that is natural to the object yet *slightly more.*
A finger moves lightly across a piece of metal and the low sound of a horn is suggested.

The life of a sound should inhabit the film frame.
Can the pitch of sound be a unit of measure in the film?

VII

A color placed beside other shades of the same color changes or clarifies that of the first. It will also show what sympathies to other colors it contains.

Green is said to derive from yellow and blue as a pigment color, but, in the past few days while looking at green trees, I had an impression that it was like looking at *no color,* as the tone became brighter and stronger so did the impression of colorlessness.
Is this because the green in Nature is closer to qualities of translucent

color or is it from the light passing so strongly through the leaves or is it my state of mind resulting from the length of viewing? "The flying away of color."

A single color cannot be seen by itself. The eye begins to forget it as color and sees it only as lightness or darkness.

Color's qualities of space:
When one object is placed upon another object of the same color – a red shoe on top of a red book – does each object lose part of its color quality? What is lost is the complementary color that surrounds each physical color, and it is this quality that gives it vibrancy.

It is a great delight to see one color under another in the points at which the under-color comes to the surface. Under-color: pure and deep; second color: a light pastel one; the two together suggest a certain space. I am thinking of certain Sienese painters.

Color as the direction of light?
The matte in front of the camera is one means of showing direction, ex. the matted images in *Sotiros (Alone)* and the images in which light penetrates the flesh.
Color as the direction of light upon the frame as well as in the image.

Luminosity is not reflection of light but a bright clarity that can be seen into.

VIII

The eye is superior to the other senses because it moves.

The hands also move; there are similarities between the two eyes and the two hands – a perspective in each pair. This is the active part of each sense; there is also stillness in each sense as a counter-balance.

What is the force within observation where the observer gains a power over the object; and the more patient the observation within its stillness, the greater is the force that accumulates towards a later action…?

This could be described as abnegation, as the mental distance that the mind obtains in refraining from an immediate reaction and then carries towards a more stable and far-reaching purpose.

Beauty: Accept the *nature* of the observer to discover the form of the observation.
On seeing the blind man whom I had filmed, I thought of how I look through the lens and doubted that I had realized the best use of the camera or reached its life-meaning.

What is technique? One thing at a time and that one thing thoroughly?

To develop the use of a film-element unto itself and to give it space in which to articulate its meaning is not a formalism if the filmmaker develops his own purpose and the technique becomes a discipline that unlocks one mystery after another.

How can the film be more 'of a voice' while neither distorting nor manipulating the image?

IX

Each camera movement opens a form in space; it is the unit of the camera's abstract pattern within a particular space.

Camera movements easily dissipate into repetitive gestures. Unless a distinct quality is achieved, the camera movement will interfere with the composition, the editing or the movement within the frame. How can it become a significant force in harmony with the composition and editing and possess necessity?

Each point of editing causes its own movement. It is a movement-in-place, a *locomotion*. There may be more movement for the spectators' eyes in each point of editing than in following the path of a camera movement.
If there is an object moving, seeing this movement transforms how one sees any still object that is also in view. The movements of the eye are carried over and punctuate how one sees the rest of the composition.
In seeing a moving object one tries to encompass the path of the movement;

in seeing a still object, to hold its contours. These are two different states, yet they can alternate and interweave.

The order of the eyes' different expressions and movements: the eyes look at something then move away from this particular object then return to it, yet with each return they gain a different expression.
Or the movements of the eyes from one fixed point to another can reflect a particular emotion in which each new look gains another level. Imagine the complexity of two persons in conversation and their interwoven eye movements and facial expressions.

At one moment a thought may come into being through the eyes' movements from one object to another, and in other moments the eyes may move according to an existing thought (?).
A change from one emotion to another is not necessarily followed by a change in our facial expression or related to what we see; but can there be a total change of thought without any physical sign of change in the face?

These notes were written mostly during the mid-1970s while Beavers was preparing his Sotiros films; he edited them for publication at the time of his 2010 retrospective at the Austrian Film Museum, in the brochure Robert Beavers: Die ausgestreckte Hand.

Of the title, Beavers says: "I used this mathematical term simply to suggest 'scattered thoughts' that are related indirectly to each other. 'An acnode is an isolated point not on a curve, but whose coordinates satisfy the equation of the curve. The terms isolated point *or* hermit point *are equivalent terms.' (Encyclopedia of Mathematics)."*

Robert Beavers

Selected Notes Filmed in *From the Notebook of...*

15.9.70 Film convention is time flowing forward in the mind of the viewer.

12.12.70 While at the Hallenbad sitting at one end of the pool and gazing in front of myself after some moments the place became an image, the same but perfect – the image suspended in a great space

18.9.70 Projector (to project) = Platonic idea of the eyes being the light source illuminating the object.

[...] 22.7.69 The shutter in the camera is like the wings of an insect; both create movement one in space the other in the eye.
Film is not an illusion of movement it is movement.

[...] 12.6.70 Edit the length of a shot in relation to the distance of image or matte from camera.

15.3.71 Close the window shutters to a crack; film my reflection in the mirror as my head moves in front of the narrow light.

Color as a description of light

It will be first on one side then the other, an outline of light instead of shade.

[...] 27.3.69 Sound in relation to the distance of camera to subject; in relation to the light and shade of the frame.

3.1.70 With an object and its shadow; as the object moves closer to the surface of the shadow, it becomes more clearly defined. When the shadow moves back towards the light it is less in focus.

A series of shots which begin with soft shadow not showing the object; then the object moves toward the shadow hardening it and into the frame.
The light should be behind and to one side of the object.

[...]   The screen becomes a side of a projected object

[...]   8.7.69 Gaumont – color process / Messter – optically compensated projector / Reynaud – mirror theatre / Lauste / Tykociner } optical sound

        Make the composition equal the editing

      31.8.70 Film in which each shot is 24frs.; each object is seen from 36 angles. Lighting from above.

[...] 23.10.70 A film of mistakes to show the process of creating by factual mistake

[...] 12.6.70 Projection of the image onto glass or a mirror with a second focus change to return to the original.

      9.9.70 The sound should start at a very high or low speed and graduate to normal 1 cut / second sound

      9.7.69 Note the first frame of a shot sometimes receives more exposure

[...] 31.3.70 Ordered Kodak filters nos. 29, 22, 12, 61, 48, 36

7.4.70 The above are too dark

29.9.69 use a white matte against a black background. Will the movement of the matte stop the light? Use filter in slot.

[...] 25.2.69 Each personal detail evolves or counters the matte

[...] 24.2.69 Association of filters with sounds, change of exposure with change in volume

19.10.68 Change focus with filter, superimpose object

[...] 19.11.68 A film in which the audience watches both the screen and the projector.

25.3.71 Projection – perspective

"All objects transmit their image to the eye in pyramids, and the nearer to the eye these pyramids are intersected the smaller will…"

8.7.69 Editing the last section, will superimpose the filter colors causing various shadings of grey; by superimposing same shot but one with emulsion up, the other with base up.

9.10.68 Color and black moving across the frame / ← color | black → [horizontal] / ← color | black → [vertical]

[...] 30.3.70 Cut the filters and place them on glass composing each take to the live views.

1.6.70 Film of an image appearing in the base of filters.

7.4.70 One color should be added to another as the film progresses from the live image to still.

[...] 28.10.70 When filming the density filters there should be a white space at one end and black at the other

26.10.70 Various grey from white through grey to black – a horizontal movement increasing or not the image.

[...] 21.12.69 As the camera records past and future, the projector may also.

22.2.71 The filters must change the natural colors of each frame, not just relate to each other.

21.2.71 Matte – geometry in time

27.2.71 Past-depth of the screen / Present surface of the screen / Future span before the screen

14.1.71 Film at close range to remove the color from its object

11.11.70 Use a b/w stock with color filters for the 'live view' and a color stock with (just) the same filters.

11.7.70 When filming the filters the color should alternate from center to the sides

[...] 18.11.70 Raising the limbs in a phallic oath

4.2.70 Castilian theory of correspondence sound and color.

25.1.69 Colors moving on moving screen

15.12.69 Fifty or a hundred day-faces and the same number in the evening

26.5.69 To film all my actions having nothing to do with making films.

This text is a selection of notes from Beavers's film From the Notebook of... *(1971/1998). The notes are arranged in the order of appearance in the film.*

Robert Beavers

From the Notebook of...

When I filmed *From the Notebook of...* in 1971, I had already developed the use of mattes with colored filters as a structural and expressive means. My earliest films, made between 1967 and 1970, presented various erotic and spiritual themes in the context of the places where I had been living. I began to see the film frame as a many-faceted whole that could unite a quantity of diverse visual elements in the same composition. I superimposed images, editing on several bands of film, each with its own rhythm, and brought these layers together in printing the film. I also tried to edit directly the optical sound track, using the same measures as in the image. The result was a dominance of the image's rhythm and a grotesquely aggressive sound accompaniment, but I nonetheless developed the patterning and positioning of image fragments within the film frame that led to *From the Notebook of...*

In all of my early films, it was as if I were creating the film in the small compendium that held the filters and mattes in front of the lens. I moved the focus between the extreme nearness of the colored filters and the scene in front of the camera, and as I changed the exposure, the mattes-shapes appeared and disappeared. Through these manipulations both inside and in front of the camera, the image began to breathe, and this eventually suggested a more appropriate use of sound.

At the center of my earlier films, I had often placed an isolated male figure, juxtaposed against a prismatic abstraction of colors to suggest particular states. Later, I decided to replace these figures by filming myself as filmmaker and to balance the view of a city or landscape with that of myself, filming. The first film of this type was *Diminished Frame* (1970) with its black & white images of West Berlin and views of my hand(s) placing colored filters inside the camera.

The starting point for *From the Notebook of...* was more complex. I began to prepare a film inspired by Leonardo da Vinci's notebooks and by my reading of Paul Valéry's essays on Leonardo's creative method. Through Gregory Markopoulos's commitment and the generosity of the painter-filmmaker Silvio

Loffredo, I was able to live in Florence for several months. My reading of Vasari's Leonardo biography led me to my first location and the scene of doves being set free from a shop next to the Bargello. The flight of doves is carried forward in the turning pages and juxtaposed to my opening of a window onto the Florentine rooftops. Starting with the bird's wings and my turning pages, the sound develops through a variety of image/sound metaphors.

I am an observer in these various locations, quickly gathering image and sound in darting movements then returning to my room and reflecting on the details, placing them with my notes. There is a graphic development of the film frame as page. I used the mattes to superimpose diverse elements of color, text, sound and image in one composition. The matte in front of the camera plays between the horizontal notebook and the vertical window, turning like a page or window shutter.

One of the central points of inspiration for me was Leonardo's observation of shadows. I used the surface of my notebook and desk to translate some of his observations into film and also discovered the shadow as a place for sound. Both the matte and shadow are vehicles that join together diverse details of image and sound.

I realized later that my written notes place the spectator in the position of a reader while seeing the film. There is a constant movement between the different ways of seeing images and reading a text. The film is also a hybrid between silent and sound film because, when we read, we are creating our own subjective sound in reading, and each of my written notes in the film may become an occasion for the spectator to reflect with his or her own voice.

Towards the middle of the film, I placed a Bolex camera on my table, and its aperture becomes another threshold for sound. The whirring camera shutter joins the rushing water of the Arno, or the click of the single frame mechanism becomes the tapping of a hammer, and because Leonardo was also a musician, I added a few notes of the viola.

As the film progresses we pass from the apparent stillness of reading to seeing movement through the rhythm of editing; the counterpoints and juxtapositions within the page establish the film's rhythm.

At the end, I close the notebook and the window and the last note reads, "Film all of my actions that have nothing to do with filmmaking."

These program notes for From the Notebook of… *have undergone various edits since Beavers first composed them in the 1990s. This version was edited for inclusion in* Cinéma exposé / Exhibited Cinema: Exhibiting artists' films, video art and moving image, *Ed. François Bovier and Adeena Mey, Lausanne: ECAL / Les presses du réel, 2015.*

Robert Beavers

Sotiros

A Sequence of Notes*

Each film is a step towards a more solid and clear time element.

The path of light that enters the room and moves along three walls appears only during a few winter weeks, on the infrequently clear days between noon and one o'clock. This movement of sunlight underlies each of the three films and is progressively condensed; twenty-five minutes, ten minutes, slightly more than six and a half minutes. (This is accentuated by the nearly equal number of images in the second and third films.)

The camera tends to follow or counter the movement of light. Where the highlight has ended on the wall above the beds in the first two films, it begins in the third. It is not a contradiction; rather, the sun's angle has changed slightly; when the light enters the room towards the sinks, the mirror reflects it to the wall opposite. From this point, the light completes its circle, and the reflection continues as 'the words' in the camera's counter-movements.

The energy released by the moving camera changes the meaning of the film cut. It changes both the function of the spectator's sight and the projected light.

A pattern of camera movements away from fixed points becomes a measure of the interval. The pattern *rests* upon the screen as the film is projected. If the camera movement is into the film cut, an opening is made into darkness or light; it negates, in part, the closure of the film cut or at least carries it differently.

* This sequence of notes is Beavers's own textual rendering of and response to his *Sotiros* trilogy of films: *Sotiros Responds* (1975–76), *Sotiros (Alone)* (1976–77), and *Sotiros in the Elements* (1978). The marginal column contains the shot numbers for each of the three films. The text was composed in 1978 and originally published in Rome under the Temenos imprint in 1980. It corresponds to the *Sotiros* trilogy as it existed in 1980 with a total duration of 43 minutes. Beavers integrated the three films into a single 25 minute *Sotiros* in 1996.

Sotiros *Responds* (1–3)	Near Vassae and the temple of Apollo Sotiros, the highlight moves along the horns of a goat as it turns: an almost circular camera movement within the room. There is the sound of a key turning in a door.

(9–24)   A shadow passes over the white highlight of the street; the river, Evrotas, can be heard above the sound of its surface. A shepherd climbs the hill, the pillow, *He said*; view towards the bottom of the hill with a surface sound of the pillow turned at an angle. Footsteps. Movement to the window, sound of the river; the shepherd is sitting against a rock at the bottom of the hill, a movement from the bed to the window. The camera: light is moving in the room. The total sound is limited neither by an object or person in the image, yet the basic acoustic is taken from the room, and the volume of individual sounds increases or decreases in a movement parallel to the image. Walls both limit and carry sounds; like the relation 'inside-outside,' there is no absolute barrier between the outdoor sounds and the interior.

The voice, *He said*, is silent and set in the context of the room until the end of the first film; out of the same dialogue is drawn the melodrama of the second film and the reflected voice of the third.

The silent statement does not express but presents an image or series of images. Expression is closer to meter and sound; stillness and silence are closer to the object.

(14–17)   The first silent statement is held in grey: *waves, blind man against the wall, highlight on an asphalt street*: horizontal camera movement, static, movement in the frame.

(25–28)   The second statement is similar: *tree, red, street scene*: vertical camera movement, static, short horizontal movement towards the end of the image. The monochrome frame of saturated red has 'replaced' the blindman.

(30–33)   Respiration: the breath's diastole-systole is parallel to the outside-inside, open-close, light-shadow of the image. The curve of the grey wall in front of which the blindman stands fills the entire frame. The silent roundness is there even when its outlines are not shown, like the unconscious pleasure of full breath.

Another grey wall appears in *Sotiros* (*Alone*) translated into a different language far from the blindman's dignity.

(40–54)   While something is being made, boundaries and viewpoints are in flux; possibility includes the presence of opposites. The human quality and its psychology arise out of the image afterwards. The worker bends over a space that will become both floor and ceiling. *He said*, contains this place: *the wall of rushes, a village square crossed by a truck, a movement across the marble table-top and coffee cup, shadows of automobiles crossing the highlighted street, a space of blue, the head turning near.*

(66–67)   Perspective: the opposites of near and far negate each other's mystery like the negation of green by red in projected light and leave the Present transparent as a drop of water.

(69–85)   From different directions along Harilaou Trikoupi Street, one sees an arrow sign (… ropolis 29), the Priamos windows and neo-classical façade, buildings opposite these windows, the grey wall, etc. In this setting the blindman remains in harmony with the silent statement; his sense (its physical absence) is near to thought.

Surface sounds of writing and of the chair moving against the floor. Six images held in green between the darkness of the chair's shadows and the luminous full frame of the window shutter.

(87–92)   *He said, "A cloud in the shape of…,"* the light concentrated on the door, writing; *"… a worker moves out of frame, Evrotas." he said.*

The titles draw the dialogue towards the image and the film's limits, this voice in which each figure shares.

(94–98)   The next statement seems to contradict the earlier ones; its person and tense are different from the others, containing an image recalled from the first Vassae location and a figure within the room. His face is touched by the same light as the door, and his stillness creates more silence than if the room were empty. This word appears again in the second and third films.

The shifting pattern of camera movements becomes a pendulum turning in the solidness of projection. The pattern, its curve, passes through the image.

(99–110)   The movement of clouds is reflected alternately as light and shadow on the pine trees and in the room. The sound of automobiles is heard inside, upwards to the ceiling, and as an uninterrupted procession of vehicles in the street.

(111–113)   He said, "Waves until the highlight: A blue sky into which rises the emblematic white corner." (Ambiguously first seen as the corner moving upwards, – hesitation – then recognized as a camera movement downwards.)

(119–123)   If the image evokes a statement, it also allows a way of listening to sounds that are usually ignored like an unknown language. The sense of each sound, – its direction, volume, echo – speaks of its own space and is reflected in the image and its movement.

The room becomes a silent conductor through which a multitude of particulars move into relation.

The dialogue of the image continues to develop. He said, "The full frame of red is closed by the shutter" (the red which is in the camera) "... the movement of one hand extends gently and holds one coin (the image of it) for another." he said.

(124–141)   The surface hiss of water is heard through the wall with the distant sound of bells chiming; the camera moves from the sinks to the window. He said, "A worker bending over; the Evrotas reflecting a cloud and surrounded by trees; the empty sink." The doors open near the blindman: echoes of the water draining.

One understands that Film is not the image-sound but what is reached in (and through) the image-sound. Awareness becomes silently transparent; a separate life is projected: χώρα means 'the place' and in ancient music, the limit of each interval; ὥρα καὶ χώρα the final precision in time is Space.

(134–137)   He said, "A doorway with green reflected in the shadow, the sheep eating leaves from a fig tree, the blindman."

The atmospheric clarity, the nearness of distant objects seen in Greece, shares the same quality for its sound.

(138–139)   The ringing sound of a glass echoes in the camera movement from the sink to the opposite wall of the room.

(140–145)   The Kafenion: a coffee and glass of water rest on the table; the silhouette of a fan is projected above a conversation in which the middle figure shows the size of an object with his hands. Part of the conversation rises upwards then descends along the door; the shadows of a handshake turn and part. The pleasure of afternoon light rests in its luminous vacancy.

(147–151)   Enter the waiter and greetings of old men. *He said, "A knoll with sheep, automobile shadows traveling across the street, the Priamos façade."*

The voice of the film, the dialogue of its images, speaks more directly than performance. Its simplicity merely appears elliptical.

(152–175)   The context of the statements fluctuates towards the exterior; the Evrotas is first seen in the distance and is reflected in the camera movement upwards to the ceiling of the room. The sounds of an action, – the rubbing of cloth, footsteps, the opening of a closet and vibrating wire hangers – are heard between the silent image statements and the extended presence of the river.

(183–199)   Then the titles lose their connection to the preceding statements; the sound of conversation enters from the unseen hallway adjacent to the room and is alternately heard between the tearing of paper. "Gastarbeiter" are talking in an Italian dialect about money or some other complaint. "Wir arme Leute." The voices are heard indistinctly and are dominated by the nearer sound of the paper: *He said*, becomes one side; the other, *he said*. – a conversation juxtaposed to a corner of the room.

If one looks at a particular incident, its phrases may vary while its outline remains the same as numerous others. This unspoken form can be observed with a calm and unifying sympathy; an equivalent pattern of little fates within the film's image and sound grows until it becomes the unexpected and fully

185

natural result, – not in the sense of Memory's subjective chronologies, but towards its invisible presence.

(200–205)   The value of projection begins with a movement of light to the screen; yet there is a second level, counter to the first, of shadows in the image, – the movement of darkness in light – and even a third level, of light and complementary color in the shadow. The turning footsteps of Sotiros, a fool gesturing to himself, are projected down upon the reflected brightness of the street. The bed turns at an angle, recalling the opening images of the hill and shepherd.

(207–222)   He turns in the square to the sounds in the unseen hallway; a parallel movement in the room from the windows to the door. The camera tilts again: the sound of birds. *"His footsteps..."* interrupted by the chirping birds and the counter-movement from the door to the windows, *he said.* The sound of footsteps in the distance. *He said, "The trunk of the olive tree turning, waves..."* Light from the dark blue sky reflects brightly on the white frieze and pilaster *"... the shadows of footsteps crossing the street, the same quantity of shadow as the glass of water and cup of coffee." he said.*

A projected image contains the camera angle and the angle of projected light to the screen.

(224–230)   The sunlight rests diagonally on the wall above the beds; the footsteps are heard approaching. Seen from above and in the distance, a figure stands near the threshed wheat. The faint sound of his call follows and echoes. *He said, "The green shutter, surrounded by white outside, by black inside. Red."*

He said, The silence of the titles differs in itself from the silence of any other image, the one leads into the other and prepares the space for the voice of the image.

(233–240)   A movement on both sides of the shutter, between the dark interior which suggests sound, and the white exterior close to silence; the final statement, the final location. A movement across the green chair, its shadow and sound, to the exterior and sound of the birds.

(Alone) = not alone.

The new relation of image and sound in the Self is the measure.

Sotiros
(Alone)
(1–10)

A first image of shaving is followed by others: the leg, the faucet, the chin, etc. My hand turns the tripod handle from left to right, the eye turns from right to left; the two parts are one movement in the Self.

The tripod holds the center as a pivot of the plot; it turns between what is said and is heard. The context moves from the Greek to the German, yet like the tripod itself, a point of balance is formed from these different directions.

From the background of *Sotiros Responds*, the sounds now have an active part in suggesting the psychic placement of each scene-fragment. The clockwise movement of light gathers the new actions, with which the six quotes from Alban Berg's *Wozzeck* become a single Voiced highlight moving in the room.

(10–25)

The "dark" images of shaving, of cut branches, etc. are contrasted to green-white highlights around the sink, faucet and glass. The sounds of water reflect light, even the sound of a single drop…

$$\text{ἥ τε τοῦ ἔτους ὥρα καὶ χώρα καὶ φύσις}$$
$$\text{τοῦ θεραπευομένου σώματος}$$

and the music heightens this intense physical atmosphere from which the film generates its fullness in the body.

All of the exterior views – the field, the street scenes, an alley, and later, the forest and pond – complement the *Wozzeck* quotes.

"… langsam–! Eins nach dem Andern!"

The Self is not a self-portrait.

(26–44)

Parallel to the tripod and its horizontal movements are the images of a foot extended into the light, then of a leg wound, a finger touching the edge of the frame, and finally the leg standing. These images of the leg are like the small

Greek votive offerings which show the part of the body that has been healed, – usually an ear, a leg, genitals or eyes. In ancient times, they were made of marble, now they are metal foil, but the shape and size have remained nearly unchanged for more than a millennium.

The eye moves from its inner corner to its outer corner beyond the edge of the frame. The figure at the table is writing…

(46–47)   "Er kriegt noch mehr Zulage! Tut Er noch Alles wie sonst?: Rasiert seinen Hauptmann? Fängt fleissig Molche? Isst seine Bohnen?" The grey walls and the street with tram tracks are filled by the matte till the entire frame is black; the spectator listens to the above quote in this darkness.

The vertical black matte is a passage from the interior binocular fold of the spectator towards the screen and equals the (negative?) force within Sight which unifies the image.

(48–59)   The Self is balanced between an image of an ear listening within the frame and the listening of the spectator to the image-sound; as between an eye turning in the frame and the depth within the spectator's sight.

The sound of rubbing begins in the folds of a finger and is placed on the highlight of the leg. The sound of the film is not what would be heard if the same sound were heard by itself on a magnetic tape; only when a quality in the image animates the listening does it become the Sound.

(59–80)   The finger-tips are seen from the inside of the hand, an image of tact; yet, as they move towards the center of the frame the focus is interrupted by a jaggedness, when the eyes must adjust to the single point where the hands will touch.

On close observation the dialogue of any two figures is like a meeting of finger-tips; the reflection extends and intermingles before the hands actually touch. The dialogue exists in this immaterial balance between left – right, movement – counter movement, speaker – listener.

The psychomachia of dark images and light: a shadow of the head turning, figures crossing an alleyway, the hand upon the knee, etc. are opposed to the translucent colors of flesh, which are held close to the surface of the frame by the matte.

The luminous yellow of certain images comes from the sunlight as it enters the matte and skin; there is a continuity of light, matte and skin – a quality of growth and destruction.

Light has become one color.

(81–82)   "Ich rieche Blut!" Berg's phrase is heard with an image of ashes, – the ruin of an old smokehouse at Wallfahrtskirche Strassengel.

(86–88)   Because the matte is part of the frame yet not of the Image, it creates a space through which the sound is projected in the Self, e.g. the sound of a closet door is heard with a matted image of the leg; a silent shadow of the leg follows, then the door is opened into the matte as the sound of metal clothes-hangers vibrates.

(90–93)   "Heiland! Ich möchte Dir die Füsse salben –" The fingers touch; the sound of the hangers vibrates through the matted image of the grey house-front. A hand comes into frame and rests upon the knee; it is like the hand on the tripod.

The space which is nearest to the senses contains a psychic character, a kind of second face in front of the actual one. It is this character which projects itself during intense emotion and not the senses.

(101–103)   The reflected light and shadow is held on a piece of paper as a second screen within the frame; when torn and thrown aside, the "projection" moves to the wall; the dark forest path carries this action to the matted image of the torso, over which the sound of the paper is heard.

(106–107)   "Ich wasche mich mit Blut! – das Wasser ist Blut... Blut..." The camera pans down from the pines to their reflection in the pond, and the sound continues downwards into a drowning.

(112–115)
      The action resolves in the final quaver rhythm of Berg's opera. Listening
to this sound carries one back to the beginning; the elements which have

(116–120)
      been united depart like the ripples on water: the hand leaves the tripod
and reappears as a triple shadow, the final turn towards stillness, towards
disappearance.

Space = voice and echo.

Sotiros in   Unlike the preceding films, the third begins with a sound before the first
the Elements   image; it is the same acoustic repeated in its clearest order.
(1–5)

(6–8)   The eye-glass lens concentrates the light within its shadow; it turns upon the
white wall of the final location of *Sotiros Responds*. The sound of a key is heard
in the clockwise panning of the room, followed by the blindman with the
matte over his eyes and again the eye-glass shadow as a projection of sight.
He said, When… the sound of the Evrotas in the frame of the white wall…
ⁿɘʜW reflected in the reverse panning, right to left, of the room.

Words are attracted to the space of the image; in reaching the film they
separate into a pattern.

(9–19)   The closely heard sound of rustling sheets extends through the next eleven images: the grey wall, a tree trunk and its shadow, the eye turning, the wall and
inside, the ederdown, *return …* ᴎɿυɈɘɿ. It permits the series to include an unexpected image of the olive tree… *there… he said*. In the light of the room… ɘɿɘʜɈ.

The titles now do not create a silence; they are part of seeing-into-reading.
Beyond the first film's closed space or the second film's dialogue is the transformed image – sound (and word-sound), the brightness of which is felt in
the rhythm of the film's total Voice.

Each use of the matte reveals a different sense: one suggests an eye-movement
or is related to the binocular fold, another is towards sound or touch. (e.g. The
(23–24)   shadow against the white wall is edited to the figure in the curve of the grey
wall behind the blindman.)

The film draws closer to the ear; what is heard is the relation of sound to the
suggested movement. The *elements* from the earlier films, animated by the
combined matte and title or the matte and sound, are transposed into new
(25–26)   phrases; the hand appears in the turning from one side of the frame to the
other, – touching the sound and surface.

The meaning of each word is defined by its placement in the film.

(40–45)   At the angle in the room between the window and sink, the full pressure of the sound is heard as the water rushes from the faucet into the drain; then a single drop, like the window tassel, is both heard and seen, – lachryma in the hollow of the tree, *still* in the faucet, … ⵏⵉⵜⵣ in the light of the room.

(47–49)   The drop continues to lengthen in the faucet, while the sound echoes – *red*. The window cord and tassel are like the path of each drop … ⵀⵓⵜ, reflected in the mirror, recalling the saturated color of the first film's statements and the blood motif of the second.

Each phrase contains images of Greece and of the room, yet the sounds place the balance towards a particular Tense. The sound of each drop of water in the above film-phrase suggests the interior and the Past, just as the outdoor sounds and images of Leonidion dominate the next moments, – exterior and Present.

(58–60)   The image is no longer measured by a simple turn of the matte from left to right or right to left. Now the matte turns to the center of the frame, where it nearly disappears, then into the next image in which the matte continues turning. The 'blindness,' which is part of the binocular fold, sustains the movement as it joins the image of leg, tree and key.

Counter to the turning of the matte at the middle of the frame is the path of the automobiles, the donkey and Sotiros. Each one crosses the square diagonally and equals the diagonal of light and shadow in the room.

(72–75)   Even the chair and table, animated by a sound, become part of the exterior: the sound of sheep turns upon the table leg, the root-like tree trunk and in the ear.

(102)   The camera moves across an object; in projection this becomes a turning of the object towards the spectator.

The key = each word, forwards and backwards.

Robert Beavers

The Searching Measure

LA TERRA NUOVA

The act of filming should be a source of thought and discovery. I am opposed to the film director's conception of theatrical mise-en-scène *in front of the camera* and to the cameraman being asked to create a *style* for the image. By dividing the act of filming between director and cameraman, the image is reduced to illustrating a preconception; whereas, in the hands of a filmmaker, the camera functions to create an image that is newly seen, one that projects into the past and future.

Like the roots of a plant reaching down into the ground, filming remains hidden within a complex act, neither to be observed by the spectator nor even completely seen by the filmmaker. It is an act that begins in the filmmaker's eyes and is formed by his gestures in relation to the camera. In a sense he *surrounds* the camera with the direction of his intuition and feeling. The result retains certain physical qualities of the decisive moment of filmmaking – the quality of light and space – but it is equally surprising how a filmmaker draws what he searches for towards the lens.

The basic intentions for a particular work are balanced against the opportunities and obstacles that appear during the actual filming. A branching out of intention continues to develop as the filming progresses. The original impulse may suddenly encounter an obstacle that sends the filmmaker in a different direction towards a stronger image. The result is recognized without hesitation because it is measured against an interior sense of balance. The filming is *a search for correct contours,* and it is activated by a physical sense that is similar to trying to find a location that has been seen only once. Memory searches for the right direction.

Drawing together details and hints, this sense is nearest to touch in its awareness of proportion. It is this quality in the filming that I compare to the roots
of a plant.

This same search leads to the film's individual perspective, which the spectator
will later enter as the single living participant. Taking an example from
Michelangelo's *Sacra Famiglia*, I would suggest that the circular form of the
painting is completed by the curved wall and figures in the background that
draw the viewer into a "totally rounded orb." Imagine how a film can extend
such a perspective in time, bringing it closer to the subjective sense of how we
see. It was with such an impulse that I used the full circle of the camera lens in
Amor, turning it in front of the aperture to create a movement like the eye
turned upwards or cast downwards. I allowed the lens to suggest a rounded
field of vision amplified in the form of the film: a "totally rounded orb, in its
rotundity joying" (Empedocles).

A continuity develops for the filmmaker between the physical structure of the
medium and each action involved in the filming, whether simple or complex,
and this bodily sense is extended in other ways during the editing. The same
hand that operated the camera now places each image within the phrases of
edited film. Even the simple unwinding and rewinding of film rolls is part of
this process and can help to release an insight leading to the film's distinct
form.

From one side:

Each film should contain its own invention. A filmmaker maintains a continuity in his work; he reaches in one direction and returns in another with something new in hand.

The film does not follow in the footsteps of a thought; it is released from the thought without abandoning it. I am aware of the way in which "observing" becomes "directing," aware of the power that exists in Seeing. The making of a film allows one to move back and forth, observing-directing.

The value of the actual filming is seen in the action of a moment. It is hidden until one makes the choice that reveals it and can neither be achieved by correction nor fully explained.

Excellence – Enchantment: this has a clear source in *disegno*. Harshness, vulgarity, and the continuous opposition of profit may appear to overwhelm, yet a sense within the eye and hand maintains its own strength, its own point of origin, and becomes a protection against deceptive choices.

As a way to concentrate, a filmmaker may remove him- or herself from any expectation of acceptance by the public. There is no fear of isolation while the filming continues; its development should be response enough. Instances of understanding also arise that are more a direct agreement in life than appreciation of aesthetic qualities in the work.

" ... *sine avaritia, quod est maximum; nullum enim opus vere sine fide et castitate fieri potest.*" ("... without greed, that is most important; no real work can be done without faith and clean hands.") – Vitruvius

From the other side:

Seeing the projected image contains a search, then the sense of having found what was sought and of this carrying one further.

The spectator must discover why an image was chosen, and the silence of such a discovery is a moment of release. A filmmaker's work is to make the film and to protect what he does in the serenity of a thought without words.

Projection is the means. Memory creates the actual seeing. One of the realities of Film is the delay with which certain images reveal their worth. It will not happen during a first viewing, and it may not happen until a much later one, that an image discloses its *emblematic meaning* equal to the entire film.

The image is central. The order is based on the way the image *holds in projection*. It is as different from a natural view as a musical note is from noise.

A balance of opposites exists between the film and the spectator, whose sight is heightened and enlivened by the projection. An editing movement or camera movement causes the spectator to be still to observe it. He is transported in his stillness, in the lightness that is natural to sight, weightless and open.

"Actor" and filmmaker face each other in a relation that is the source for how a figure is presented in the film. It is the recourse of one to the other rather than the actor himself who appears in the film. Each gesture of self-assertion or denial is transformed and becomes part of the vital space of the film frame.

Rather than beginning with a character or presenting a predetermined psychology, the filmmaker finds the reality of form in the physical expression of the features of a particular face, in the harmony of light resting upon and within this face. In certain movements lasting less than a second, each feature of the actor's face projects beyond its boundaries.

To recognize the outline of a person's nature – *his image* – is not a common experience. It happens at that moment when habits of seeing open toward a sudden self-awareness, when the filmmaker registers the other's face opposite him. Imagine the complex pattern that is made by the eyes' movements, how they move away from and directly or indirectly back to the point of attention, then consider how the movements between the eyes of the actor and filmmaker establish a stillness at certain moments. These are the moments in which the figure of the actor gains its distinctness in the images of *one* film. Unlike casting, the search is for a reality within the actor's individual physiognomy, for a generosity that will not fade, all of which is suggested by the phrase "the outline of a chosen person's nature." The face carries a double sense, first as a direct element within the film frame and second as a performance. Only when both are present will the face be like a voice containing its own lyric within the film as a whole.

Because of this symmetry the face is both meaning and mask. One looks upon the actor's face as much as into it. Between profile and frontal or upper and lower halves of the face, each angle of the features suggests a particular sense. A face sometimes takes on the ambiguity of a pattern, or at other moments possesses a subjectivity that turns back upon itself to *see* its own outline. Each close-up allows the features to equal the entire figure. Details that might be considered too insignificant to carry expression can for that very reason hold a key to the later editing of image and sound.

Robert Beavers

EDITING AND THE UNSEEN

The living quality of the film image: it is enough in itself to discover a means to achieve this. The many hours of patient editing, this listening to the image and waiting for it to speak and reveal its pattern. Often unexpected, it is recognized in its rightness.

There is the choice of what to discard and the direction of what is included. The discipline comprises never *editing out* as a means of correcting the image. The scale of the film, its dimensions, is a result of how the editing is sustained without interruption. A filmmaker must guard against moments of lost concentration when the moment of growth, narrative growth, might be lost.

I place the pieces of film that are of no further use in one corner of the table. When these have accumulated, I must clear them from the table; their presence alone is an obstacle. They must be out of view to make a space for the next choice in the editing.

I memorize the image and movement while holding the film original in hand; the memorizing gains a weight and becomes a source for the editing. To view the film on an editing table would only distract me from this process and create the illusion that editing is done in the viewing.

The editing responds to holding the image in hand and to the weighting of memory and is protected from an overdetermined intention. There should be almost no need to view the film projected until the editing is completed.

Sustained by the awakening of emotion united to strength, I reach beyond the life-likeness of the actor and the shadow of his performance to his figure gathering the life that is in the light of the image.

Where is the strength found to gather the images in a pattern that instills life in the editing? *From within a solitude of being where the filmmaker endures and accepts moments when a single color is the only sign of feeling in an environment where all else is opposition.* The great reality of color: *I respond to it directly in the editing, when one image is set after another in a phrase unified by the variations of one tone.*

The choice of length is a judgment of worth enlarged beyond the filmed image into the clarity of the edited film phrase. *I approach the image through the unseen order of the phrase.* Like the repeated walking to the filming site, this is created by a pattern of returning and adding to the film as it develops in the editing.

The total and true direction of the work is seen finally as each film continues to grow by the decisions made even after the film's completion.

Robert Beavers

THE SENSES

Anticipation is a fateful quality that exists outside the simple line of time. A spectator's senses are alive within their own past, drawn together into a unity. The weight of this moment before seeing or hearing is balanced between the gathered physical sum of the senses and the self reaching forward into awareness.

Attention creates a different tense. We are alive through anticipation in the present moment, colored by this reaching forward into the future. The movement of the eyes is a question answered by "It is here." The image nourishes how we see. It enlivens all our senses by concentration and praises the instant.

What may appear as mere elements of image and sound in projection can speak to us in the shape of the interval as the pattern of the film rests upon the screen. The spectator builds the narrative like a bridge in the vibrant lightness of his attention. The coherence is not imposed nor does it exist as literature to be discarded by a discursive understanding.

To hold the image more than to be held by it. The quiet of this corresponds to the strength in restraint from which the fullness of anticipation and recognition arises. Anything seen or heard truly cannot be submerged by later circumstance. It lives within one's own being even when not visible.

The necessity that is woven into the film by the filmmaker and the psychic direction of the spectator create at certain moments a congruence fed by eros, history, and temperament ... and by the always changing physical world. It is at this distance that the pattern of the film can be seen and heard.

The scale of the film is not separate from its length but entails more – it entails the choice that gives each measure and detail its eloquence. This is what lasts after a projection and remains with the spectator as an attunement, adding to how he or she sees the world.

These essays appeared in substantially different versions in the annual Temenos film programs presented in Greece in the 1980s and in later program notes and publications including Millennium Film Journal, *No. 32/33, Fall 1998. Beavers edited and gathered the texts under a single title,* The Searching Measure, *in conjunction with 2004 screenings at the Pacific Film Archive, Berkeley.*

Appendix

Filmography

Robert Beavers is responsible for concept and realization (including camera, sound recording, editing) for all the following films. All works were originally shot on 16mm film. Since the mid-1980s, all of Beavers's films have been printed at Cinema Arts with the exception of *Amor, Ruskin,* and *Efpsychi,* which were printed at Cineric Inc. Christian Beusch, of Tonstudio Beusch, has created the final sound mix for all films.

All camera originals or negatives, internegatives, interpositives, magnetic sound tracks, optical sound tracks and projection copies of the works are preserved in the Temenos Archive. A star (*) marks those early works which Robert Beavers no longer shows publicly.

The filmography builds on the version created by Mark Webber in 2007 for Tate Modern, London. It has been revised and expanded by Alexander Horwath in 2010 and by Rebekah Rutkoff in 2016.

~

Spiracle *

1966, 16mm, color, sound, 12 minutes
CAST Tom Chomont
FILMED IN USA (New York City)
PREMIERE EXPRMNTL 4, Casino Knokke-le-Zoute, December 1967

On the Everyday Use of the Eyes of Death *

1966, 16mm, color, silent, 9 minutes
FILMED IN Italy (Rome)
NOTE The camera original was destroyed by the filmmaker.

Winged Dialogue

1967/2000, 16mm, color, sound, 3 minutes
CAST Robert Beavers, Gregory Markopoulos
FILMED IN Greece (Hydra)

and

Plan of Brussels

1968/2000, 16mm, color, sound, 18 minutes
CAST Robert Beavers, Gisèle Frumkin, René Micha, Jacques Ledoux, Pierre Apraxine, Dimitri Balachoff and others
TEXT *Duvelor* by Michel de Ghelderode
FILMED IN Belgium (Brussels)
NOTE The final edit combines both films on a single reel.
PREMIERE Austrian Film Museum, Vienna, May 21, 1996
ORIGINAL VERSIONS *Winged Dialogue*, 1967, 16mm, color, sound, 18 minutes. Premiere: International Short Film Week, National Film Theatre, London, August 25, 1968. *Plan of Brussels,* 1968, 16mm, color, sound, 29 minutes. Premiere: Filmklub Zurich, Kunstgewerbemuseum, Zurich, March 13, 1969
— *Winged Dialogue* details with growing clarity the desperate beauty and sexuality of the body animated by its soul, essence blindly reaching out, touching, in brilliant patterns through and beyond those of the vanishing images, expressed vividly in the after-image on the mind, on the soul's eye. (Tom Chomont)

Shedding all traces of narrative in *Plan of Brussels*, Beavers filmed himself in a hotel room, both at his work desk and lying naked on the bed, while in rapid rhythmic cutting, and sometimes in superimposition, the phantasmagoria of people he met in Brussels and images from the streets flood his mind. (P. Adams Sitney, *Film Comment*)

Early Monthly Segments

1968–70/2002, 35mm, color, silent, 33 minutes
CAST Robert Beavers, Gregory Markopoulos, Tom Chomont
FILMED IN Switzerland, Germany (Berlin), Greece
NOTE The *Early Monthly Segments* appear twice in the context of the full *My Hands Outstretched* cycle, the second time with minimal soundtracks.
PREMIERE Toronto International Film Festival, September 2003
— *Early Monthly Segments*, filmed when Beavers was 18 and 19 years old, now forms the opening to his film cycle, *My Hand Outstretched to the Winged Distance and Sightless Measure*. It is a highly stylized work of self-portraiture, depicting the filmmaker and his companion Gregory Markopoulos. The film functions as a diary, capturing aspects of home life with precise attention to detail, documenting the familiar with great love and transforming objects and ordinary personal effects into a highly charged work of homoeroticism. (Susan Oxtoby, Toronto International Film Festival)

The Count of Days

1969/2001, 16mm, color, sound, 21 minutes
CAST Stefan Sadkowski and others
TEXT Fragments from "Petermann verliess den Hinterhof" by Stefan Sadkowski
FILMED IN Switzerland (Zurich)
NOTE The final edit includes part of *Early Monthly Segments* on the same reel.
PREMIERE Austrian Film Museum, Vienna, May 21, 1996
ORIGINAL VERSION *The Count of Days*, 1969, 16mm, color, sound, 43 minutes. Premiere: 18th International Film Festival Mannheim, October 1969.
— The film is seen as though upon and through the structure of its spiritual partitions. One might say that there are three elements or levels to the images: narrative, descriptive or analytic, and abstract. *The Count of Days* is not an account so much as an accounting of the essence of the days in which three separate persons are related at points … a penetration through the masks and habits of these days to reveal the nature of the charade and the arena in which it is enacted. (Tom Chomont, *Film Culture*)

View *

1969, 16mm, color, sound, 8 minutes
FILMED IN Switzerland (Zurich)
NOTE The camera original was destroyed by the filmmaker.

Palinode

1970/2001, 16mm, color, sound, 21 minutes
CAST Derrick Olsen and others
MUSIC *Wagadus Untergang durch die Eitelkeit* by Wladimir Vogel
FILMED IN Switzerland (Zurich)
NOTE The final edit includes part of *Early Monthly Segments* on the same reel.
PREMIERE Austrian Film Museum, Vienna, May 21, 1996
ORIGINAL VERSION *Palinode*, 1969, 16mm, sound, 34 minutes. Premiere: Club Nuovo Teatro, Milan, April 1970
— In *Palinode* a disk-shaped matte continually shifting in and out of focus alternately blocks part of the image or contains it. Its respiratory rhythm matches operatic fragments of Wladimir Vogel's *Wagadu*, as the camera studies a middle-aged male singer in Zurich, singing, eating, window shopping, meeting a young girl. The filmmaker told himself, "Don't let yourself know what that film is about while you are making it." (P. Adams Sitney, *Film Comment*)

Diminished Frame

1970/2001, 16mm, b/w and color, sound,
24 minutes
CAST Robert Beavers and others
FILMED IN Germany (West Berlin)
NOTE The final edit includes part of *Early Monthly
Segments* on the same reel.
PREMIERE Austrian Film Museum, Vienna,
May 22, 1996
ORIGINAL VERSION *Diminished Frame,* 1970,
16mm, b/w and color, sound, 30 minutes.
Premiere: Filmstudio 70, Rome, April 1971
— There is a balance between a sense of the
past seen in the views of West Berlin, filmed
in black & white, and a sense of the present
in which I filmed myself showing how the
color is created by placing filters in the camera's
aperture. I searched for signs of war's aftermath
and a few moments of daily life. (Robert Beavers)

In training a traveler's gaze on a largely unfamiliar place, the themes of *Diminished Frame*
also resonate with Walter Benjamin's influential
concept of the *flaneur*. Benjamin considered the
flaneur's roaming gaze a condition of modernity
that forecast the technology of the movie camera
– Beavers's film renders the idea concrete and,
at the same time, complicates it since the link
between the spectator's gaze and the camera's
perceptual mode is interrupted by the geometric
shapes of the mattes. (Henriette Huldisch,
My Hand Outstretched: Films by Robert Beavers,
Whitney Museum)

Still Light

1970/2001, 16mm, color, sound, 25 minutes
CAST Ronald Krueck, Nigel Gosling
FILMED IN Greece (Hydra) and England (London)
PREMIERE Austrian Film Museum, Vienna,
May 22, 1996
ORIGINAL VERSION *Still Light,* 1970, 16mm, color,

sound, 60 minutes. Premiere: Goethe House,
New York, December 13, 1971 (unconfirmed)
— The first half of the film explores delicate
nuances of lighting, color and depth as Beavers
shoots the face of a young man in various locales
on the Greek island of Hydra, using a variety of
customized masks and filters. The man's face
remains constant throughout, surrounded by
iconic elements in the landscape, like a pulsating
Renaissance portrait. *Still Light*'s second half was
shot in the London flat of art critic Nigel Gosling.
The two halves of *Still Light* bring to mind any
number of structuralist binarisms: youth and
age, creation and criticism, action and reflection,
living landscape and mummified text. (Ed Halter,
New York Press)

From the Notebook of…

1971/1998, 35mm, color, sound, 48 minutes
CAST Robert Beavers, Gregory Markopoulos
and others
FILMED IN Italy (Florence)
PREMIERE New York Film Festival – Views from
the Avant-Garde, October 9, 1999
ORIGINAL VERSION *From the Notebook of…,*
1971, 16mm, color, sound, 60 minutes. Premiere:
Centro Culturale San Fedele, Milan, February 11,
1972
— *From the Notebook of…* was shot in Florence
and takes as its point of departure Leonardo da
Vinci's notebooks and Paul Valéry's essay on da
Vinci's process. These two elements suggest an
implicit comparison between the treatment of
space in Renaissance art and the moving image.
The film marks a critical development in the
artist's work in that he repeatedly employs a
series of rapid pans and upward tilts along the
city's buildings or façades, often integrating
glimpses of his own face. As Beavers notes in his
writing on the film, the camera movements are

tied to the filmmaker's presence and suggest his investigative gaze. (Henriette Huldisch, *My Hand Outstretched: Films by Robert Beavers*, Whitney Museum)

The Painting

1972/1999, 16mm, color, sound, 13 minutes
CAST Robert Beavers, Gregory Markopoulos
FILMED IN Switzerland (Bern), USA (Boston)
PREMIERE Kunsthalle Basel, January 19, 1999
ORIGINAL VERSION *The Painting*, 1972, 16mm, color, sound, 20 minutes. Premiere: Cinematografischer Salon, Innsbruck, October 14–15, 1972
— *The Painting* intercuts shots of traffic navigating the old-world remnants of downtown Bern, Switzerland, with details from a 15th-century altarpiece, *The Martyrdom of Saint Hippolytus.* The painting shows the calm, near-naked saint in a peaceful landscape, a frozen moment before four horses tear his body to pieces while an audience of soigné nobles look on; in the movie's revised version, Beavers gives it a comparably rarefied psychodramatic jolt, juxtaposing shots of Gregory Markopoulos, bisected by shafts of light, with a torn photo of himself and the recurring image of a shattered windowpane. (J. Hoberman, *The Village Voice*)

Work Done

1972/1999, 35mm, color, sound, 22 minutes
FILMED IN Italy (Florence) and Switzerland (Grisons)
PREMIERE New York Film Festival – Views from the Avant-Garde, October 9, 1999
ORIGINAL VERSION *Work Done*, 1972, 16mm, color, sound, 34 minutes. Premiere: Festival of Independent Avant-Garde Film, National Film Theatre, London, September 14, 1973
— Bracing in its simplicity, *Work Done* was shot in Florence and the Alps, and celebrates an archaic

Europe. Contemplating a stone vault cooled by blocks of ice or the hand stitching of a massive tome or the frying of a local delicacy, Beavers considers human activities without dwelling on human protagonists. Like many of Beavers's films, *Work Done* is based on a series of textural or transformative equivalences: the workshop and the field, the book and the forest, the mound of cobblestones and a distant mountain. (J. Hoberman, *The Village Voice*)

Ruskin

1975/1997, 35mm, b/w and color, sound, 45 minutes
FILMED IN Italy (Venice), Switzerland (Grisons) and England (London)
PREMIERE Auditorium du Louvre, Paris, May 5, 1998
ORIGINAL VERSIONS
First version: *Ruskin*, 1974, 16mm, b/w and color, sound, 60 minutes. Premiere: Festival Internazionale del Film sull'Arte e di Biografie d'Artisti, Asolo, May 30, 1974
Second version: *Ruskin*, 1975, 16mm, b/w and color, sound, 65 minutes. Premiere: unknown
— *Ruskin* visits the sites of John Ruskin's work: London, the Alps and, above all, Venice, where the camera's attention to masonry and the interaction of architecture and water mimics the author's descriptive analysis of the "stones" of the city. The sound of pages turning and the image of a book, Ruskin's *Unto This Last*, forcibly remind us that a poet's perceptions, and in this case his political economy, are preserved and reawakened through acts of reading and writing. (P. Adams Sitney, *Film Comment*)

Sotiros

1976–78/1996, 35mm, color, sound,
25 minutes
CAST Robert Beavers, Gregory Markopoulos
MUSIC *Wozzeck* by Alban Berg
FILMED IN Greece (Athens, Sparta, Leonidio),
Austria (Graz, Rein) and Switzerland (Bern)
NOTE Three films are now combined within
a single work.
PREMIERE International Film Festival Rotterdam,
February 5, 2000
ORIGINAL VERSIONS
Sotiros Responds, 1975–76, 16mm, color, sound,
25 minutes
Sotiros (Alone), 1976–77, 16mm, color, sound,
12 minutes
Sotiros in the Elements, 1978, 16mm, color,
sound, 6 minutes
Premiere: Movie 1, Zurich, May 12–13, 1978
— In *Sotiros*, there is an unspoken dialogue and
a seen dialogue. The first is held between the
intertitles and the images; the second is moved
by the tripod and by the emotions of the filmmaker. Both dialogues are interwoven with the
sunlight's movement as it circles the room,
touching each wall and corner, detached and
intimate. (Robert Beavers)

The film's title suggests there is a "protagonist." "Sotiros," meaning healer, redeemer, is one
of many designations of Apollo. He is immediately evoked in the landscape shots of Bassae,
the site of a temple devoted to Apollo Epicurius.
Celebrating one of the god's primary attributes,
the film is suffused with the presence and mobility of light, which the crosscutting between the
hotel room and landscapes, cityscapes, and
worksites delineates. No secondary player to
human action, the god of light is center stage,
reveling in his manifold manifestations: time-
teller, space-marker, shape-changer – adjutant

of the eye as well as its deceiver. (Tony Pipolo,
The Films of Robert Beavers, Berkeley Art Museum
and Pacific Film Archive)

Amor

1980, 35mm film, color, sound, 15 minutes
CAST Robert Beavers
FILMED IN Italy (Rome, Verona) and Austria
(Salzburg)
PREMIERE Austrian Film Museum, Vienna,
March 4, 1980
— *Amor* is an exquisite lyric, shot in Rome and
at the natural theater of Salzburg. The recurring
sounds of cutting cloth, hands clapping, hammer-
ing, and tapping underline the associations of
the montage of short camera movements, which
bring together the making of a suit, the restoration of a building, and details of a figure, presumably Beavers himself, standing in the natural
theater in a new suit, making a series of hand
movements and gestures. A handsomely designed Italian banknote suggests the aesthetic
economy of the film: the tailoring, trimming,
and chiselling point to the editing of the film
itself. (P. Adams Sitney, *Film Comment*)

EYΨYXI (Efpsychi)

1983/1996, 35mm, color, sound, 20 minutes
CAST Vassili Tsindoukidis
FILMED IN Greece (Athens)
PREMIERE New York Film Festival – Views from
the Avant-Garde, October 1997
ORIGINAL VERSION *Efpsychi*, 1983, 16mm, color,
sound, 35 minutes. Premiere: Austrian Film
Museum, Vienna, January 25, 1983
— The details of the young actor's face – his eyes,
eyebrows, earlobe, chin, etc. – are set opposite
the old buildings in the market quarter of Athens,
where every street is named after a classic ancient Greek playwright. In this setting of intense

stillness, sometimes interrupted by sudden sounds and movements in the streets, he speaks a single word, *teleftea*, meaning "the last (one)," and as he repeats this word, it moves differently each time across his face and gains another sense from one scene to the next, suggesting the uncanny proximity of eroticism, the sacred and chance. (Robert Beavers)

Wingseed

1985, 35mm, color, sound, 15 minutes
CAST Arno Gutleb
FILMED IN Greece (Anavvysos, Lyssaraia)
PREMIERE Temenos, Lyssaraia, September 7, 1985
— A seed that floats in the air, a whirligig, a love charm. This magnificent landscape, both hot and dry, is far from sterile; rather, the heat and dryness produce a distinct type of life, seen in the perfect forms of the wild grass and seed pods, the herds of goats as well as in the naked figure. The torso, in itself, and more, the image which it creates in this light. The sounds of the shepherd's signals and the flute's phrase are heard. And the goats' bells. Imagine the bell's clapper moving from side to side with the goat's movements like the quick side-to-side camera movements, which increase in pace and reach a vibrant ostinato. (Robert Beavers)

The Hedge Theater

1986–90/2002, 35mm, color, sound, 19 minutes
CAST Robert Beavers, Gregory Markopoulos
FILMED IN Italy (Rome, Brescia) and Austria (Salzburg)
PREMIERE London Film Festival, National Film Theatre, November 17, 2002
— Beavers shot *The Hedge Theater* in Rome in the 1980s. It is an intimate film inspired by the Baroque architecture and stone carvings of Francesco Borromini and *Saint Martin and the*

Beggar, a painting by the Sienese painter Il Sassetta. Beavers's montage contrasts the sensuous softness of winter light with the lush green growth brought by spring rains. Each shot and each source of sound is steeped in meaning and placed within the film's structure with exacting skill to build a poetic relationship between image and sound. (Susan Oxtoby, Toronto International Film Festival)

The Stoas

1991–97, 35mm, color, sound, 22 minutes
CAST Robert Beavers
FILMED IN Greece (Athens, Gortynia)
PREMIERE International Film Festival Rotterdam, February 5, 1999
— The title refers to the colonnades that led to the shady groves of the ancient Lyceum, here remembered in shots of industrial arcades, bathed in golden morning light, as quietly empty of human figures as Atget's survey photos. The rest of the film presents luscious shots of a wooded stream and hazy glen, portrayed with the careful composition of 19th-century landscape painting. An ineffable, unnameable immanence flows through the images of *The Stoas*, a kind of presence of the human soul expressed through the sympathetic absence of the human figure. (Ed Halter, *New York Press*)

The Ground

1993–2001, 35mm, color, sound, 20 minutes
CAST Robert Beavers
FILMED IN Greece (Hydra)
PREMIERE International Film Festival Rotterdam, January 30, 2001
— What lives in the space between the stones, in the space cupped between my hand and my chest? Filmmaker/stonemason. A tower or ruin of remembrance. With each swing of the ham-

mer I cut into the image and the sound rises from the chisel. A rhythm, marked by repetition, and animated by variation; strokes of hammer and fist, resounding in dialogue. In this space which the film creates, emptiness gains a contour strong enough for the spectator to see more than the image – a space permitting vision in addition to sight. (Robert Beavers)

Pitcher of Colored Light

2007, 35mm, color, sound, 23 minutes
FILMED IN USA (Falmouth, Massachusetts)
PREMIERE documenta 12, Gloria-Kino, Kassel, September 14, 2007
— The shadows play an essential part in the mixture of loneliness and peace that exists here. The seasons move from the garden into the house, projecting rich diagonals in the early morning or late afternoon. Each shadow is a subtle balance of stillness and movement; it shows the vital instability of space. Its special quality opens a passage to the subjective; a voice within the film speaks to memory. The walls are screens through which I pass to the inhabited privacy. We experience a place through the perspective of where we come from and hear another's voice through our own acoustic. The sense of place is never separate from the moment. (Robert Beavers)

The Suppliant

2010, 35mm, color, sound, 5 minutes
FILMED IN USA (Brooklyn, New York)
PREMIERE New York Film Festival – Views from the Avant-Garde, October 3, 2010
— My filming for *The Suppliant* was done in February 2003, while a guest in the Brooklyn Heights apartment of Jacques Dehornois. When I recollect the impulse for this filming, I remember my desire to show a spiritual quality united to the sensual in my view of this small Greek statue.

I chose to reveal the figure solely through its blue early morning highlights and in the orange sunlight of late afternoon. After filming the statue, I walked down to the East River and continued to film near the Manhattan Bridge and the electrical works; then I returned to the apartment and filmed a few other details. I set this film material aside, while continuing to film and edit *Pitcher of Colored Light*; later I took it up twice to edit but could not find my way. Most of the editing was finally done in 2009; then I waited to see whether it was finished and found that it was not. In May 2010, I made several editing changes and created the sound track with thoughts of this friend's recent death. (Robert Beavers)

Listening to the Space in My Room

2013, 35mm, color, sound, 19 minutes
FILMED IN Switzerland (Zumikon)
CAST Robert Beavers, Ute Aurand, Dieter Staehelin, Cécile Staehelin
PREMIERE Toronto International Film Festival – Wavelengths, September 9, 2013
— Robert Beavers films his room in Zurich, and its immediate surroundings, during the editing of his previous film *The Suppliant*. The seasons go by, and he observes, with great warmth, his neighbors and hosts, an elderly couple. While he, a musician, plays the cello, she tends to the garden. All three characters share a space, though never at the same time, and a dedication to their respective activities: music, gardening, filmmaking. A celebration of light and color and an intimate ode to existence. (Courtisane Festival)

First Weeks

2015, 16mm, color, silent, 3 minutes
CAST Fowler-Sworn family
FILMED IN Scotland (Glasgow)
PREMIERE National Gallery of Art, Washington,
D.C., October 10, 2015

Shared Table

2016, 16mm, color, silent, 4 minutes
CAST James Edmonds, Sílvia das Fadas,
Alexandre Favre, Yulia Mukha, Nina Zabicka
FILMED IN Germany (Berlin)
PREMIERE Courtisane Film Festival, Ghent,
March 25, 2016

Both entries at the end of the filmography,
First Weeks and *Shared Table,* are considered by
Robert Beavers as "incidental" or "semi-private"
works. At the time of publication, he had not
yet decided about their status in his filmography.
First Weeks is the result of a visit to Luke Fowler
and Corin Sworn in 2013: a portrait of their
newborn child, Liath. *Shared Table* was filmed
in his Berlin studio in August 2015 and shows
a group of young filmmakers who are helping
to restore the splices in Gregory Markopoulos's
Eniaios IX–XI.

~

The preservation of *Sotiros* by the Whitney
Museum of American Art was made possible
by a grant from the National Film Preservation
Foundation. A grant from The Guild of St George
and in-kind support from Cineric Inc. enabled
the preservation of *Ruskin*. The restoration of
From the Notebook of… was made possible by
the Austrian Film Museum, which is also a
partner in joint restoration efforts with the
Temenos Archive. Funding from the G. & B.
Schwyzer-Winiker Foundation in Zurich sup-
ported the production of *Pitcher of Colored
Light, Listening to the Space in My Room,* and
The Suppliant.

Selected Bibliography

PUBLICATIONS AND ESSAYS BY ROBERT BEAVERS

Still Light: Film Notes & Plates. With an Introduction by Jonas Mekas, Florence: Il Torchio, 1971

Hauptprobe for a Spectator, Milan: Pettinaroli, 1978

Sotiros: A Sequence of Notes, Rome: Pioda, 1980

"Lyssaraia – Filme in mythologischer Landschaft," *Neue Zürcher Zeitung* (Zurich), December 19, 1980

"Markopoulos in Passing" (Letter to the Editor), *Film Comment* (New York), November-December 1993

"Writings," *Millennium Film Journal* (New York), No. 32–33, Fall 1998

"Independent Shadows and Double Figures," *Film direkt* (Zurich), November 2000

The Searching Measure: Writings by Robert Beavers, Berkeley: UC Berkeley Art Museum and Pacific Film Archive, 2004

"Efpsychi," in: *My Hand Outstretched: Films by Robert Beavers*, New York: Whitney Museum, 2005

"A Few Points," in: *To the Winged Distance: Films by Robert Beavers*, London: Tate Modern, 2007

"Acnode," in: *Robert Beavers: Die ausgestreckte Hand*, Vienna: Austrian Film Museum, 2010

"The Red Ottoman: Memories of a Fraught yet Productive Relationship," in: *Das sichtbare Kino. Fünfzig Jahre Filmmuseum: Texte, Bilder, Dokumente*, ed. Alexander Horwath, Vienna: FilmmuseumSynemaPublikationen, 2014

"Taking It Into Our Own Hands," in: *60. Internationale Kurzfilmtage Oberhausen / Short Film Festival Oberhausen* (catalogue), Oberhausen: Karl Maria Laufen, 2014

"From the Notebook of…," in: *Cinéma exposé / Exhibited Cinema: Exhibiting artists' films, video art and moving image*, eds. François Bovier and Adeena Mey, Lausanne: ECAL/Les presses du réel, 2015

Editor's Note: Between 1980 and 1986, Robert Beavers and Gregory J. Markopoulos also jointly published several program texts for the Temenos film screenings in Greece. Beavers's writings in these publications have been revised over time and published elsewhere (see above) as well as in the present volume.

ABOUT ROBERT BEAVERS:
BOOKS AND BROCHURES

Gregory J. Markopoulos, *Film as Film: The Collected Writings of Gregory J. Markopoulos* [1950–1992], ed. Mark Webber, London: The Visible Press, 2014

P. Adams Sitney, *Visionary Film: The American Avant-Garde, 1943–2000*, New York: Oxford University Press, 1979 [2nd edition], 2002 [3rd edition]

Beavers / Markopoulos = dedicated issue of *Millennium Film Journal* (New York), No. 32–33, Fall 1998 [See individual essays under "Periodicals"]

My Hand Outstretched: Films by Robert Beavers, with an essay by Henriette Huldisch and notes by Robert Beavers, New York: Whitney Museum, 2005

To the Winged Distance: Films by Robert Beavers, with essays by Robert Beavers and Mark Webber and a conversation between Ute Aurand and Robert Beavers, London: Tate Modern, 2007

P. Adams Sitney, *Eyes Upside Down: Visionary Filmmakers and the Heritage of Emerson*, New York: Oxford University Press, 2008

The Films of Robert Beavers, with essays by Tony Pipolo, Rebekah Rutkoff, P. Adams Sitney, Richard Suchenski, and Gregory J. Markopoulos [1967], Berkeley: University of California, Berkeley Art Museum and Pacific Film Archive, 2009

Harry Tomicek, "Programm 46: *Work Done, Ruskin, Amor*," in: *Was ist Film. Peter Kubelkas Zyklisches Programm im Österreichischen Filmmuseum*, eds. Stefan Grissemann, Alexander Horwath, and Regina Schlagnitweit, Vienna: FilmmuseumSynemaPublikationen, 2010

Robert Beavers: Die ausgestreckte Hand, ed. Alexander Horwath, with essays by Robert Beavers, Rebekah Rutkoff (in English), Harry Tomicek, Georg Wasner, Mark Webber, and a conversation between Renate Sami and Robert Beavers (in German), Vienna: Austrian Film Museum, 2010

Richard Suchenski, *Projections of Memory: Romanticism, Modernism, and the Aesthetics of Film*, New York: Oxford University Press, 2016

Rebekah Rutkoff, "Film," in: *Liquid Antiquity*, eds. Brooke Holmes and Karen Marta, Athens: DESTE Foundation for Contemporary Art, 2017

ABOUT ROBERT BEAVERS:
PERIODICALS, NEWSPAPERS, PROGRAMS

Gregorio Napoli, "Terza Giornata della Settimana Internazionale di Palermo – Il Destino dell'Uomo in Stile d'Avanguardia," *Giornale di Sicilia* (Palermo), December 30, 1968

Pierre Lachat, "Pläne und Kalender. Filme von Robert Beavers," *Tages-Anzeiger* (Zurich), October 31, 1969

Tom Chomont, "A Note on *The Count of Days*," *Film Culture* (New York), No. 48–49, Winter-Spring 1970

Jonas Mekas, "Movie Journal," *The Village Voice* (New York), September 10, 1970

Frank Zaagsma, "Naar film-kijken op een nieuw manier: Experimenten van Robert Beavers," *de Volkskrant* (Amsterdam), October 5, 1971

Pierre Lachat, "'Die Sprache der Diamanten' – über die Filme von Robert Beavers," *Tages-Anzeiger Magazin* (Zurich), No. 39, October 30, 1971

Alfred Fröhlich, "Meine Richtlinie ist meine Persönlichkeit: Ein Gespräch mit dem amerikanischen Filmmacher Robert Beavers," *Arbeiter-Zeitung* (Zurich), October 20, 1971

Robert Setlik, "A Particular Type of Film, a Particular Film Maker," *The Patriot Ledger* (Quincy, MA), December 2, 1971

Jonas Mekas, "Movie Journal," *The Village Voice* (New York), December 16, 1971

Jerven Ober, "Markopoulos introduceert Robert Beavers," *Skrien Filmschrift* (Amsterdam), No. 28, January 1972

Ermanno Comuzio, "Robert Beavers, Cineasta Americano, e la funzione dell'Avanguardia, oggi," *Cineforum* (Bergamo), No. 118, October-December 1972

Guglielmo Volonterio, "Quando inizio un film il messaggio è ancora incerto," *Corriere del Ticino* (Lugano), February 27, 1973

René Micha, "Robert Beavers ou le cinéma absolu," *Art International* (Paris), Vol. 17, No. 6, Summer 1973

Renzo Beltrame, "Due Film," *D'Ars, anno XIV* (Milan), No. 66–67, 1973

Scott Hammen, "Notes on Three Films by Robert Beavers," *Afterimage* (Rochester), Vol. 2, No. 3, June 1974

Harry Tomicek, "Zu den Filmen von Gregory J. Markopoulos und Robert Beavers," *Neue Zürcher Zeitung* (Zurich), August 5, 1977

Harry Tomicek, "The Analysis of Beauty. Anmerkungen zu Filmen von Robert Beavers," *Neue Zürcher Zeitung* (Zurich), March 28, 1980

André Gerely, "Filmemacher auf Durchreise. Sebastian Schadhausers 'Arno Schmidt' und

Robert Beavers 'Work done,'" *Film & Ton-Magazin* (Munich) Vol. 26, September 1, 1980

Harry Tomicek, "Filme von Robert Beavers" (program essay), Vienna: Austrian Film Museum, March 5–27, 1993

Harry Tomicek, "Unbekannte Frühwerke von Robert Beavers" (program essay), Vienna: Austrian Film Museum, May 21–22, 1996

David Sterritt, "Recognizing the Poetic Value of Film," *The Christian Science Monitor* (Boston), October 2, 1996

Paul Arthur, "Avant-Garde Retreat," *Film Comment* (New York), November-December 1996

Tony Pipolo, "An Interview with Robert Beavers," *Millennium Film Journal* (New York), No. 32–33, Fall 1998

P. Adams Sitney, "Robert Beavers: Observing and Directing *Wingseed*," *Millennium Film Journal* (New York), No. 32–33, Fall 1998

Paul Arthur, "Between the Place and the Act: *Efpsychi*," *Millennium Film Journal* (New York), No. 32–33, Fall 1998

Tony Pipolo, "*Ruskin*: A film by Robert Beavers," *Millennium Film Journal* (New York), No. 32–33, Fall 1998

P. Adams Sitney, "Majestic Images," *Film Comment* (New York), March-April 2001

Ed Halter, "Robert Beavers," *New York Press*, May 2, 2001

J. Hoberman, "Renaissance Man," *The Village Voice* (New York), March 12, 2002

George Baker, "Film Rebuff," *Artforum* (New York), May 2002

Holland Cotter, "Spiritual America, From Ecstatic to Transcendent," *The New York Times*, March 8, 2002

Henriette Huldisch and Chrissie Iles, "Frames of Mind: The Films of Robert Beavers," *Artforum* (New York), September 2005

Roberta Smith, "Avant-Garde Films 'Repatriated' at Last," *The New York Times*, October 21, 2005

Don Daniels, "Tour Guides: Naruse, Beavers, Quanz," *Ballet Review* (New York), Vol. 34, No. 4, Winter 2006

Ian White, "Robert Beavers," *Art Review* (London), February 2007

Andrew Bonacina, "Robert Beavers," *Frieze* (London), June-August 2007

P. Adams Sitney, "Look Homeward," *Artforum* (New York), September 2007

Mark Webber, "Robert Beavers," *Aurora 2008: The Infinite Measure* (catalogue), ed. Adam Pugh, Norwich: Aurora, 2008

P. Adams Sitney, "Winged Distance / Sightless Measure: Program One – A Conversation between Robert Beavers and P. Adams Sitney," *The Evening Class* (October 14, 2009): http://theeveningclass.blogspot.co.at/2009/10/winged-distance-sightless-measure.html

Michael Guillén, "Winged Distance / Sightless Measure: A Conversation With Robert Beavers," *The Evening Class*, Part One (October 14, 2009): http://theeveningclass.blogspot.co.at/2009/10/winged-distance-sightless-measure_5054.html, Part Two (October 25, 2009): http://theeveningclass.blogspot.co.at/2009/10/winged-distance-sightless-measure_3062.html

Michael Guillén, "Winged Distance / Sightless Measure: Robert Beavers On…," *The Evening Class* (October 25, 2009): http://theevening-class.blogspot.co.at/2009/10/winged-distance-sightless-measure_25.html

Stefan Grissemann, "Die ausgestreckte Hand des einsamen Uhrmachers," *Frankfurter Allgemeine Zeitung* (Frankfurt), November 25, 2010

Rebekah Rutkoff, "Hands Outstretched: On Robert Beavers's cinema of transcendence,"

Moving Image Source (December 2010): www.movingimagesource.us/articles/hands-outstretched-20101217

Volker Pantenburg, "Colored Light. Über die Retrospektive der Filme von Robert Beavers im Österreichischen Filmmuseum, Wien," *Texte zur Kunst* (Berlin), No. 81, March 2011

James Macgillivray, "Film Grows Unseen: Gregory Markopoulos, Robert Beavers and the Tectonics of Film Editing," *The Journal of Modern Craft* (London), Vol. 5, No. 2, July 2012

Rebekah Rutkoff, "Small Books about God: The American Artistry of Jonathan Edwards and Robert Beavers," *Framework: The Journal of Cinema and Media* (Detroit), Vol. 53, No. 2, Fall 2012

Michael Sicinski, "Image Control," *Nashville Scene* (Nashville), March 21–27, 2013

Mónica Savirón, "The Art of Effective Dreaming," *Lumière* (November 2013): www.elumiere.net/exclusivo_web/nyff13/nyff13_14.php

Rebekah Rutkoff, "Swiss Air," *Artforum* (New York), January 2014

Aliza Ma, "A Hand in the Eye Reaching Out into Space: Robert Beavers on *Listening to the Space in My Room*," *Cinema Scope* (Toronto), No. 57, Winter 2014

David Phelps, "Sound Images," *Lumière* (September 2014): www.elumiere.net/especiales/beaversmark/web/01_listening_eng.php

Manohla Dargis, "One of the New York Film Festival's Best Movies Isn't at the Main Event," *The New York Times*, October 6, 2016

Contributors

UTE AURAND is a filmmaker who lives and works in Berlin (www.uteaurand.de). She studied at the Deutsche Film- und Fernsehakademie Berlin and her films have been shown at festivals and venues including the Toronto, Berlin, Rotterdam, Oberhausen, DocLisboa and MediaCity film festivals, Austrian Film Museum, CCCB Barcelona, Tate Modern, National Gallery of Art (Washington D.C.), Harvard Film Archive, Pacific Film Archive, and the Robert Flaherty Film Seminar. In Berlin, she curated *Filmarbeiterinnen-Abend* (Women Filmmakers Evenings, 1990–95) and *Sie zum Beispiel* (She, for Example, 1995–96). She co-founded the group FilmSamstag (www.filmsamstag.de).

DON DANIELS is a New York writer who has published on film and dance since the 1960s. He is the Senior Editor of *Ballet Review*. Daniels's ballet scenarios have been realized by the choreographer Peter Anastos in two works: *Forgotten Memories* and *Domino*. He assisted Francis Mason in editing the book *I Remember Balanchine*.

LUKE FOWLER is a British artist, filmmaker and musician. He has developed a practice that is simultaneously singular and collaborative, poetic and political, structural and documentary, archival and deeply human. With an emphasis on communities of people, outward thinkers and the history of the left, his 16mm films tell the stories of alternative movements in Britain, from psychiatry to photography to music to education. While some of his early films deal with music and musicians as subjects, in later works sound itself becomes a key concern. Fowler lives and works in Glasgow.

HADEN GUEST is Director of the Harvard Film Archive (HFA) and Senior Lecturer in Harvard's Department of Visual and Environmental Studies where he teaches courses in film history and curatorship. As curator of the HFA cinematheque he has organized many avant-garde film programs and introduced American audiences to the work of such directors as João César Monteiro and Ha Gil-Jong. He is writing a critical history of post-Carnation Revolution Portuguese cinema. Guest was a producer of Soon-Mi Yoo's *Songs from the North*, winner of a Golden Leopard in the 2014 Locarno International Film Festival.

KRISTIN M. JONES is a writer and editor based in New York. She has written about film, contemporary art, and culture for publications including *Artforum*, *Millennium Film Journal*, *Frieze*, *Film Comment*, and the *Wall Street Journal*.

JAMES MACGILLIVRAY is a principal and founder of Lee and Macgillivray Architecture Studio (www.LAMAS.us), an international office based in Toronto that experiments on architectural precedent, representation, and form. He has published widely on the relationship between film and architecture, but also more generally on architectural aesthetics. He teaches architecture at the University of Toronto and has taught at the University of Michigan where he was the Muschenheim Fellow in 2011. Prior to founding LAMAS he worked as a designer at Steven Holl Architects and as a project manager at Peter Gluck and Partners Architects.

RICARDO MATOS CABO is an independent film programmer and researcher. He edited the book *Cem Mil Cigarros – Os filmes de Pedro Costa* (2009). Recently he has written about the early films of Jean Grémillon and the work of French filmmaker and writer Raymonde Carasco.

SUSAN OXTOBY is the Senior Film Curator at the University of California, Berkeley Art Museum and Pacific Film Archive (BAMPFA), a position she has held since 2005. She worked for 12 years at Cinematheque Ontario, where she was the Director of Programming from 1997 to 2005, and launched the Wavelengths program at the Toronto International Film Festival, which she curated for its first five editions. Currently, she serves on the National Film Preservation Board, an advisory group to the Library of Congress. She programmed a spotlight of Robert Beavers's films at the Toronto International Film Festival (2000) and organized a US tour of his films in 2009, timed with a presentation of *My Hand Out-stretched to the Winged Distance and Sightless Measure* at BAMPFA.

REBEKAH RUTKOFF is a New York-based writer. She is the author of *The Irresponsible Magician: Essays and Fictions* (2015) and her essays on the films of Robert Beavers and Gregory Marko-poulos have appeared in a variety of magazines and journals. She is the recipient of grants and fellowships from the Institute for Advanced Study, Princeton, the Creative Capital | Andy Warhol Foundation Arts Writers Grant Program, the Onassis Foundation, and Princeton University.

NOAM SCHEINDLIN is an Associate Professor at LaGuardia Community College, City University of New York. He is working on a book exploring the relationship between meaning, emptiness and narrative in the works of Georges Perec and Marcel Proust. His articles on these and other topics have appeared in various scholarly journals.

P. ADAMS SITNEY is Professor Emeritus of Visual Arts, Princeton University. He wrote *Visionary Film*, *Modernist Montage*, *Vital Crises in Italian Film*, *Eyes Upside Down* (in which there are three chapters devoted to Robert Beavers's films) and *The Cinema of Poetry*. He writes on cinema for *Artforum*. He was an editor of *Film Culture,* one of the founders of Anthology Film Archives and the director of several international expositions of American avant-garde films.

ERIK ULMAN is a Lecturer in Music at Stanford University. He studied composition at UCSD with Brian Ferneyhough, and with Helmut Lachenmann at the Stuttgart Musikhochschule; he has taught at UCSD and at the University of Illinois at Urbana-Champaign. His music has been performed around the world; among his distinc-tions are a commission from Harvard's Fromm Foundation and a portrait concert at the Fun-dación Jumex in Mexico City, in conjunction with its Cy Twombly retrospective; he is currently the featured composer in the wasteLAnd concert series in Los Angeles (2016–17). Ulman is also a writer and a violinist, and he co-directs, with Marcia Scott, the arts organization Poto (potoweb.org).

Illustrations

ILLUSTRATIONS IN JAMES MACGILLIVRAY'S "TECTONICS AND SPACE"
Fig. 1: Drawing of wooden roof and column building system as origin of Greek orders by Spini. Gherardo Spini, *I Tre Primi Libri di Gherardo Spini sopra l'Instituzioni de Greci et Latini Architettori. Intorno agl'ornamenti che convengono a' tutte le fabbriche che l'Architettura compone*, Venice, 1568/69.
Fig. 2: "The Primitive Hut" frontispiece by Charles-Dominique-Joseph Eisen. Marc-Antoine Laugier, *Essai sur l'architecture*, Paris: Chez Duchesne, 1753.
Fig. 10: Plan of the Piazza Sant'Ignazio by Filippo Raguzzini. Redrawn by the author from Robert Harbison, *Reflections on Baroque*, London: Reaktion, 2000, p. 62.
Fig. 12: "Abstract Lines" in John Ruskin, *The Stones of Venice*, 4th Edition, Vol. 4, London: J. M. Dent & Sons, 1935, p. 216.
Fig. 13: "Leafage of the Vine Angle" in John Ruskin, *The Stones of Venice*, 4th Edition, Vol. 2, London: J. M. Dent & Sons, 1935, p. 308.
Fig. 14: Daguerreotype detail, Noah's Vine, the Ducal Palace South-East Angle, by John Ruskin and John Hobbs, c.1849–1852. *Carrying Off the Palaces: John Ruskin's Lost Daguerreotypes* by Ken Jacobson and Jenny Jacobson, London: Bernard Quaritch Ltd, 2015.
Fig. 15: Diagram showing the derivation of San Carlo's plan from that of St Peter's. Redrawn by author from Paolo Portoghesi, *Storia di San Carlino alle Quattro Fontane*, Rome: Newton & Compton, 2001, p. 73.
Fig. 22: Composite plan of Guarino Guarini's Santa *Maria della Divina Provvidenza* with plaster model of interior volumes by Luigi Moretti. Redrawn by the author from Luigi Moretti, "Structures and Sequences of Spaces," *Oppositions: A Forum for Ideas and Criticism in Architecture*, Vol. 4, trans. Thomas Stevens, New York: Wittenborn Art, 1974, p. 135.

FilmmuseumSynemaPublications
Available English Language Titles

Volume 28
ALAIN BERGALA
THE CINEMA HYPOTHESIS.
TEACHING CINEMA IN THE
CLASSROOM AND BEYOND
Translated from the French
by Madeline Whittle
Vienna 2016, 136 pages
ISBN 978-3-901644-67-2

Alain Bergala's *The Cinema Hypothesis* is a seminal
text on the potentials, possibilities, and problems
of bringing film to schools and other educational
settings. It is also the passionate confirmation of
a love for cinema and an attempt to think of art-
education differently. The book stages a dialogue
between larger concepts of cinema and a hands-
on approach to teaching film. Its detailed insights
derive from the author's own experiences as a
teacher, critic, filmmaker and advisor to the
French Minister of Education. Bergala, who also
served as chief editor of *Cahiers du cinéma,* pro-
motes an understanding of film as an au-
tonomous art form that has to be taught accord-
ingly. Confronting young people with cinema can
create friction with established norms and serve
as a productive rupture for both institution and
pupil: perhaps more than any other art form, the
cinema enables a lived, intimate experience of
otherness. *"The Cinema Hypothesis is actually an*
erudite and absorbing deliberation on cinema's
receding cultural status, and a passionate appeal
for its rescue ...". (Fandor) – *"The Cinema Hypo-*
thesis must be of considerable interest to those
involved in teaching cinema on any level. ... "
(Sight & Sound)

Volume 26
JEAN-MARIE STRAUB &
DANIÈLE HUILLET
Edited by Ted Fendt
Vienna 2016, 256 pages
ISBN 978-3-901644-64-1

Jean-Marie Straub and
Danièle Huillet have dis-
tinguished themselves as
two of Europe's most inventive, generous and
uncompromising filmmakers. In classics such as
Not Reconciled, Chronicle of Anna Magdalena
Bach, Moses and Aaron, Class Relations, Antigone,
and *Sicilia!,* they developed unique approaches
to film adaptation, performance, sound recording, cinematography, and translation, working
throughout Germany, Italy and France since the
early 1960s. This book is the first English-language
"primer" on Straub and Huillet and has been
published on the occasion of an extensive touring
retrospective of their work in North America
and Europe. It features original essays by Claudia
Pummer, John Gianvito, Harun Farocki, Jean-
Pierre Gorin, Ted Fendt, and Barbara Ulrich, as
well as François Albera's career-spanning interview with the two filmmakers. Tracing the history
of their films, their aesthetics, and their working
methods, the book places special emphasis
on the presence of Straub and Huillet in the
English-language world and includes a rich array
of previously unpublished documents and
illustrations. *"A must for anyone with an interest*
for intellectual and experimental art film."
(epd film) – *"An immensely useful tool for framing*
and enhancing the duo's films." (Cinema Scope)

Volume 24
BE SAND, NOT OIL
THE LIFE AND WORK OF
AMOS VOGEL
Edited by Paul Cronin
Vienna 2014, 272 pages
ISBN 978-3-901644-59-7
An émigré from Austria
who arrived in New York
just before the Second World War, Amos Vogel
was one of America's most innovative film histo-
rians and curators. In 1947 he created *Cinema 16*,
a pioneering film club aimed at audiences thirsty
for work "that cannot be seen elsewhere," and
in 1963 was instrumental in establishing the
New York Film Festival. In 1974 he published the
culmination of his thoughts, the book *Film as a
Subversive Art*. In the words of Martin Scorsese:
"The man was a giant." This is the first book
about Vogel. *"An indispensable study. If the book
is invaluable for gathering together numerous
never-before-collected or previously unpublished
pieces by Vogel himself, the newly commissioned
essays by various scholars are every bit as wel-
come."* (Film Comment)

Volume 23
HOU HSIAO-HSIEN
*Edited by Richard I.
Suchenski*
Vienna 2014, 272 pages
ISBN 978-3-901644-55-0
Hou Hsiao-hsien is the
most important figure in
Taiwanese cinema, and his
sensuous, richly nuanced films reflect everything
that is vigorous and genuine in contemporary
film culture. Through its stylistic originality and
historical gravity, Hou's body of work opens up
new possibilities for the medium. This volume
includes contributions by Olivier Assayas, Peggy
Chiao, Jean-Michel Frodon, Shigehiko Hasumi,
Jia Zhang-ke, James Quandt, and many others as
well as conversations with Hou Hsiao-hsien and
some of his most important collaborators over
the decades. *"Delicious is a good word for this
book, an absolute necessity for every serious
cinephile."* (David Bordwell)

Volume 19
JOE DANTE
*Edited by Nil Baskar
and Gabe Klinger*
Vienna 2013, 256 pages
ISBN 978-3-901644-52-8
In the often dreary land-
scape of Hollywood's
blockbuster era, the
cinema of Joe Dante has always stood out as
a rare beacon of fearless originality. Blending
humor with terror and trenchant political satire
with sincere tributes to "B" movies, the "Dante
touch" is best described as a mischievous free-
for-all of American pop culture and film history.
This first English language book on Dante includes a career-encompassing interview, a
treasure trove of never-before-seen documents
and illustrations, and new essays by Michael
Almereyda, J. Hoberman, Bill Krohn, John Sayles,
and Mark Cotta Vaz, among many others.
*"The closest we currently have to a full-blown
autobiography, the book does an admirable job
as a single-volume overview."* (Sight & Sound)

Volume 17
A POST-MAY ADOLESCENCE.
LETTER TO ALICE DEBORD
By Olivier Assayas
Vienna 2012, 104 pages
ISBN 978-3-901644-44-3
Olivier Assayas is best
known as a filmmaker, but
cinema makes only a late
appearance in his book. This reflective memoir
takes us from the massive cultural upheaval that
was May 1968 in France to the mid-1990s when

Assayas made his first film about his teenage years. The book also includes two essays on the aesthetic and political legacy of Guy Debord, who played a decisive role in shaping the author's understanding of the world. "*Assayas' voice is clear, urgent, and persuasive. For him the matter at hand, the subject that keeps slipping away, is the story of how he came to know the work of Guy Debord. This is nothing less than the story of his life.*" (Film Quarterly)

Volume 16
OLIVIER ASSAYAS
Edited by Kent Jones
Vienna 2012, 256 pages
ISBN 978-3-901644-43-6
Over the past few decades, French filmmaker Olivier Assayas has become a powerful force in contemporary cinema. Between such major works as *Irma Vep, Les Destinées, Summer Hours, Carlos* and *Clouds of Sils Maria*, he has charted an exciting path, strongly embracing narrative and character and simultaneously dealing with the 'fragmentary reality' of life in a global economy. This richly-illustrated monograph includes a major essay by Kent Jones, contributions from Assayas and his most important collaborators, as well as 16 individual essays on each of the filmmaker's works.

Volume 15
SCREEN DYNAMICS
MAPPING THE BORDERS
OF CINEMA
Edited by Gertrud Koch,
Volker Pantenburg,
and Simon Rothöhler
Vienna 2012, 184 pages
ISBN 978-3-901644-39-9
This volume attempts to reconsider the limits and specifics of film and the traditional movie theater.

It analyzes notions of spectatorship, the relationship between cinema and the "uncinematic", the contested place of installation art in the history of experimental cinema, and the characteristics of the high definition image. Contributors include Raymond Bellour, Victor Burgin, Vinzenz Hediger, Tom Gunning, Ute Holl, Ekkehard Knörer, Thomas Morsch, Jonathan Rosenbaum and the editors.

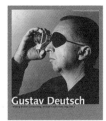

Volume 11
GUSTAV DEUTSCH
Edited by Wilbirg Brainin-Donnenberg and Michael Loebenstein
Vienna 2009, 252 pages
ISBN 978-3-901644-30-6
According to Viennese filmmaker Gustav Deutsch, "film is more than film." His own career proves that point. In addition to being an internationally acclaimed creator of found footage films, he is also a visual artist, an architect, a researcher, an educator, an archaeologist, and a traveler. This volume traces the way in which the cinema of Gustav Deutsch transcends our common notion of film. Essays by Nico de Klerk, Stefan Grissemann, Tom Gunning, Beate Hofstadler, Alexander Horwath, Wolfgang Kos, Scott MacDonald, Burkhard Stangl, and the editors.

Volume 9
FILM CURATORSHIP
ARCHIVES, MUSEUMS, AND
THE DIGITAL MARKETPLACE
By Paolo Cherchi Usai,
David Francis,
Alexander Horwath,
and Michael Loebenstein
Vienna 2008, 240 pages
ISBN 978-3-901644-24-5
This volume deals with the rarely-discussed discipline of film curatorship and with the major

issues and challenges that film museums and cinémathèques are bound to face in the Digital Age. *Film Curatorship* is an experiment: a collective text, a montage of dialogues, conversations, and exchanges among four professionals representing three generations of film archivists and curators.

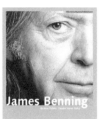

Volume 6
JAMES BENNING
Edited by Barbara Pichler and Claudia Slanar
Vienna 2007, 264 pages
ISBN 978-3-901644-23-8
James Benning's films are among the most fascinating works in American cinema. He explores the relationship between image, text and sound while paying expansive attention to the "vernacular landscapes" of American life. This volume traces Benning's artistic career as well as his biographical journey through the United States. With contributions by James Benning, Sharon Lockhart, Allan Sekula, Dick Hebdige, Scott MacDonald, Volker Pantenburg, Nils Plath, Michael Pisaro, Amanda Yates, Sadie Benning, Julie Ault, Claudia Slanar and Barbara Pichler.

Volume 5
JOSEF VON STERNBERG
THE CASE OF LENA SMITH
Edited by Alexander Horwath and Michael Omasta
Vienna 2007, 304 pages
ISBN 978-3-901644-22-1
The Case of Lena Smith, directed by Josef von Sternberg, is one of the legendary lost masterpieces of the American cinema. Assembling 150 original stills and set designs, numerous script and production documents as well as essays by eminent film histori-

ans, the book reconstructs Sternberg's dramatic film about a young woman fighting the oppressive class system of Imperial Vienna. The book includes essays by Janet Bergstrom, Gero Gandert, Franz Grafl, Alexander Horwath, Hiroshi Komatsu and Michael Omasta, a preface by Meri von Sternberg, as well as contemporary reviews and excerpts from Viennese literature of the era.

Volume 4
DZIGA VERTOV
DIE VERTOV-SAMMLUNG
IM ÖSTERREICHISCHEN
FILMMUSEUM
THE VERTOV COLLECTION
AT THE AUSTRIAN FILM
MUSEUM
Edited by the Austrian Film Museum, Thomas Tode, and Barbara Wurm
Vienna 2006, 288 pages ISBN 3-901644-19-9
For the Russian filmmaker and film theorist Dziga Vertov KINO was both a bold aesthetic experiment and a document of contemporary life. This book presents the Austrian Film Museum's comprehensive Vertov Collection, including many unpublished documents and writings such as his extensive autobiographical "Calling Card" from 1947.

....

All FilmmuseumSynemaPublications are distributed internationally by Columbia University Press (**cup.columbia.edu**). In the German-language area please also see **www.filmmuseum.at**.